EISENHOWER AND
LATIN AMERICA

STEPHEN G. RABE

EISENHOWER AND LATIN AMERICA

THE FOREIGN POLICY OF ANTICOMMUNISM

THE UNIVERSITY OF NORTH CAROLINA PRESS
CHAPEL HILL AND LONDON

The paper in this book meets the guidelines for
permanence and durability of the Committee on
Production Guidelines for Book Longevity
of the Council on Library Resources.

98 97 96 95 94   7 6 5 4 3

Library of Congress Cataloging-in-Publication Data

Rabe, Stephen G.
  Eisenhower and Latin America.

  Bibliography: p.
  Includes index.
  1. Eisenhower, Dwight D. (Dwight David), 1890–1969.
2. Latin America—Foreign relations—United States.
3. United States—Foreign relations—Latin America.
4. United States—Foreign relations—1953–1961.
I. Title.
FI418.R23   1988   327.7308   87-12493
ISBN 0-8078-1761-9 (alk. paper)
ISBN 0-8078-4204-4 (pbk.: alk. paper)

Designed by Anne Keyl

THIS BOOK WAS DIGITALLY MANUFACTURED.

FOR GENICE

CONTENTS

ACKNOWLEDGMENTS

In investigating and writing this book, I incurred many scholarly debts. I should like to thank the staffs of the National Archives in Washington, D.C., and the Federal Archives Center in Laguna Niguel, California. I invariably found the archivists at the Hoover, Roosevelt, Truman, Eisenhower, and Johnson presidential libraries to be both efficient and helpful. In particular, I am indebted to the gracious and knowledgeable staff at the Dwight D. Eisenhower Library in Abilene, Kansas. I am also grateful for the assistance I received from staffs who guided me through manuscript collections at the following schools: University of Arkansas, Columbia University, Princeton University, University of Oregon, and Yale University. Without financial aid, it would have been impossible to visit these institutions. The Lyndon Baines Johnson Foundation, the Albert J. Beveridge Foundation of the American Historical Association, and the Travel to Collections Program of the National Endowment for the Humanities all generously supported my research. I was able to devote a full year to writing with a National Endowment for the Humanities Fellowship for Independent Study and Research. Portions of this work first appeared in *Peace and Change* 11, no. 1 (Spring 1985), and *Conflict Quarterly* 6, no. 1 (Winter 1986). Both journals kindly granted me permission to use this material. Finally, I want to thank Professor Robert A. Divine of the University of Texas, Professor Burton I. Kaufman of Kansas State University, and Professor Thomas G. Paterson of the University of Connecticut for their support.

Stephen G. Rabe
Dallas, Texas
1 January 1987

INTRODUCTION

A remarkable interpretation of the leadership and foreign policies of President Dwight D. Eisenhower has recently emerged. Traditionally, Eisenhower has been portrayed as an ineffectual leader who left the conduct of foreign policy to his militantly anti-Communist secretary of state, John Foster Dulles. The results of Dulles's diplomacy were a distorted perception of the Soviet Union, a nuclear arms race, and, as in Vietnam, ominous commitments around the world.[1] But scholars are now challenging the notion of a passive president overwhelmed by the formidable Dulles. Instead, they write about a president who ended the Korean War, took a balanced approach toward the Arab-Israeli conflict, and worked for a nuclear test ban treaty. President Eisenhower, they say, curbed military spending, scorned belligerent military officers, and warned of the "military-industrial complex."[2] Indeed, many scholars now affirm Eisenhower's boast that "the United States never lost a soldier or a foot of ground in my administration. We kept the peace. People ask how it happened—by God, it didn't just happen, I'll tell you that."[3]

This new interpretation stresses not only that Eisenhower was a strong and effective leader, but also that he knew how a president should act in a thermonuclear age. As historian Robert Divine has opined, "the essence of Eisenhower's strength" was "in his admirable self-restraint": he avoided hasty military action and refrained from extensive involvement in the internal affairs of other nations. His successors, however, ignored the Eisenhower legacy of moderation and prudence. Presidents John Kennedy and Lyndon Johnson accelerated the arms race with the Soviet Union and plunged the nation into debacles such as the Bay of Pigs invasion and the Vietnam War. Richard Nixon recklessly widened the war in Indochina. Historians now seem to agree with Divine that Eisenhower served as "an enduring model of presidential restraint." Eisenhower, who once ranked a lowly twenty-second in presidential performance polls, approached the "near great" category with his eleventh-place standing in a recent poll of historians—and his reputation will continue to rise, predicts Stephen Ambrose, his preeminent biographer. Eisenhower gave the nation eight years of peace and prosperity, and "no other president in the twentieth century could make that claim."[4]

For those who seek a peaceful and secure world, the Eisenhower presidency is appealing. Eisenhower understood the dangers of a nuclear arms race. He also frequently vetoed Pentagon spending plans, for, as he told Secretary of State Dulles, "security through arms is only a means (and sometimes a poor one) to an end. Peace, in a very real sense is an end in itself. . . ."[5] But much about the Eisenhower years remains to be analyzed before Eisenhower can be proclaimed the model chief executive. Scholars have only recently begun to write about U.S. policies in the 1950s in areas such as Africa, Latin America, the Middle East, and Southeast Asia.[6] During Eisenhower's presidency, the Soviet-American confrontation shifted from the battlegrounds of Europe and China to the Third World. This superpower rivalry was complicated by the fervent nationalism and rising aspirations of Third World people. A mature understanding of Eisenhower's leadership qualities, his commitment to peace and change, and his place in history will only come when his policies in the Third World are fully explored.[7]

What follows is an examination of the Latin American policy of the Eisenhower administration, with a focus on the role President Eisenhower played in developing and implementing that policy. Newly available primary sources allow for such a study and a testing of "Eisenhower revisionism." During the past decade, the Eisenhower Library has opened for research the National Security Council (NSC) policies for Latin America, progress reports on NSC policies prepared by the Operations Coordinating Board, and summaries of NSC meetings on Latin America. The library also holds the Ann Whitman File, an extraordinary resource maintained by the president's personal secretary. The Whitman File consists of Eisenhower's personal diary, transcripts of his telephone conversations, personal correspondence, and memorandums of conversations with foreign officials. Moreover, the records of Secretary Dulles and his successor, Christian Herter, are available, and the Department of State has declassified at the National Archives in Washington some of its records on relations with Latin America during the Eisenhower years.[8]

Because primary source material was closed, little has been written heretofore on inter-American relations during the 1950s. In any case, historians, foreign policy analysts, and political pundits have assumed that the records would reveal little of significance. President Eisenhower himself set this tone. In his memoirs, he gave only a cursory and defensive review of inter-American relations during his presidency. In the account of his first term, he confessed that because of problems in areas geographically close to Russia and China—Iran, Korea, Formosa—he perhaps neglected and took for granted U.S. neighbors in the Western Hemisphere. In writing about his second term, however, Eisenhower argued that he recognized the need for socioeconomic reform in Latin America and built the framework for the economic aid program that would be dubbed the Alliance for Progress in the Kennedy administration. As for Cuba, he wrote that he was surprised by the rise to power of Fidel Castro and his turn to communism, and he abjured responsibility for the Bay of Pigs fiasco of April 1961.[9] The president's brother, Milton Eisenhower, supplemented this view in his memoir, *The Wine Is Bitter*: he emphasized that the Alliance for Progress was conceived in the late 1950s, and he urged Americans to support President Kennedy's reform efforts in Latin America.[10]

The Eisenhowers were reacting to the criticism of the Latin American policy of the United States that swelled during the 1950s and became a campaign issue during the 1960 presidential race between Kennedy and Vice-President Richard M. Nixon. Following World War II, Latin Americans bitterly complained that the United States ignored them, that it sent billions of dollars of foreign aid to former enemies and virtually nothing to them, its staunch wartime allies. Latin American leaders called for a "Marshall Plan for Latin America." By the mid-1950s, Latin American democrats such as Rómulo Betancourt of Venezuela, José Figueres of Costa Rica, and Eduardo Santos of Colombia were also claiming that the administration preferred dictatorships to reformist, democratic regimes, because Secretary Dulles's only goals for Latin America were to promote U.S. investments there and, in particular, to eliminate Communist influence.[11] These charges were largely ignored by the U.S. public until 1958, when Latin Americans hounded Vice-President Nixon during his tour of South America and a mob nearly killed him in the streets of Caracas, Venezuela.[12] The Democratic party seized upon the Nixon incident and the troubles in Cuba to underscore their contention that the Republicans had squandered the influence and prestige of the United States and were losing the battle with the Soviet Union for the allegiance of the Third World.[13]

In their histories of the Kennedy administration, Democrats reiterated the charge that Eisenhower and his advisors had left inter-American relations in a shambles, and they claimed ownership of the Alliance concept. President Kennedy publicly accepted full responsibility for the Bay of Pigs. But his advisors implied that Eisenhower had left Kennedy with few options toward Cuba.[14] In essence, this debate was reminiscent of the bickering in the 1930s between members of the Hoover and Roosevelt administrations over who should take credit for the origins of the Good Neighbor policy. The debate also confirmed traditional interpretations of Eisenhower as inept and oblivious to the currents of international affairs.

Although avoiding partisan rancor, scholars who have surveyed postwar inter-American relations have basically adopted the Democrats' view that the Eisenhower administration was neither innovative nor informed in its approach toward Latin America. As had been the case during the Truman years, the Eisenhower administration's only concerns for Latin America were to eradicate Communist influence and to promote U.S. free trade and investment principles. In response to the Cuban Revolution, the United States began to support social development. But, as one historian concluded, "the change produced by the Eisenhower administration was belated and of inadequate dimensions." Indeed, historians of inter-American relations frequently lump the years between 1945 and 1960 together as an unhappy, dull, and insignificant interregnum between the Good Neighbor and the Alliance for Progress.[15]

The one notable exception to scholarly disinterest in inter-American relations for the period 1945–60 has been the case of Guatemala. In his memoirs, Eisenhower proudly recalled that in 1954 he gave "indirect support to a strictly anti-Communist faction" to overthrow President Jacobo Arbenz of Guatemala. Eisenhower and his advisors believed that Arbenz was probably a Communist and that certainly his regime was dominated by Guatemalan Communists who were loyal to the Soviet Union. The president authorized the Central Intelligence Agency (CIA) to give the Guatemalan rebels, who were led by Colonel Carlos Castillo Armas, two P-51 fighter-bombers, because "I knew from experience the important psychological impact of even a small amount of air support." Eisenhower proclaimed the triumph of Colonel Castillo Armas a critical cold-war victory and cited it as a reason why he deserved a second term as president.[16]

Historians have agreed that the United States aided the Guatemalan rebels. But they have also found that Eisenhower was modest about his own and the CIA's role in the overthrow of Arbenz. Using the resources of the Eisenhower Library and other documents obtained through the Freedom of Information Act, they have demonstrated that the CIA developed an elaborate and sophisticated plan to undermine Arbenz, a popularly elected leader—and at the center of the plotting and intrigue was President Eisenhower.[17] These revelations have even caused some to reassess their earlier judgments of the Eisenhower presidency. Blanche Wiesen Cook, for example, contributed to Eisenhower revisionism with her influential *Dwight David Eisenhower: Antimilitarist in the White House*, an essay based on secondary sources. The "declassified Eisenhower" proved to her, however, that, although "Eisenhower's commitment to peace was real, it was limited to nuclear détente and the prevention of large-scale international warfare." And yet, Eisenhower wanted to destabilize communism and promote American values and business abroad. The alternatives to war "involved a range of political-warfare activities that included covert operations and counterinsurgency," actions that often could be measured only "in terms of repression and reaction."[18]

The effect of these studies of the U.S. response to the Guatemalan Revolution has been to suggest that Eisenhower's foreign policy goals and strategies were intricate and complex and that commentators who have enthusiastically praised Eisenhower may have been as simplistic as those who once ridiculed him.[19] An analysis of inter-American relations during the 1950s can transcend the important but narrow debates about which administration founded the Alliance for Progress and bungled the invasion of Cuba and can add to our understanding of both Eisenhower and U.S. foreign policy. The Eisenhower administration faced the same issues—interventionism, economic nationalism, human rights, extracontinental threats—that have dominated inter-American relations in the twentieth century. How Eisenhower and his advisors addressed these challenges, how they altered traditional responses, and how they shaped new ones are the subjects of this study. Few still doubt that Eisenhower was a strong, decisive, and intelligent leader. The task now is to determine what kind of presidency and what kind of foreign policies Eisenhower gave the United States.

CHAPTER 1

LATIN AMERICAN POLICIES

1933–1952

During the presidential campaign of 1952, Dwight Eisenhower deplored the state of inter-American relations. In a speech in New Orleans on 13 October 1952, he charged that Latin Americans had lost confidence in the United States. He recalled that during World War II "we frantically wooed Latin America"—but after the war the Truman administration "proceeded to forget these countries just as fast," and "terrible disillusionment set in throughout Latin America." The United States reneged on promises to cooperate economically with its neighbors. The result was economic distress, "followed by popular unrest, skillfully exploited by Communist agents there." "Through drift and neglect," the Truman administration had turned a good neighbor policy into "a poor neighbor policy." Eisenhower promised change.[1]

In his New Orleans address, Eisenhower expressed sentiments that were popularly held in both the United States and Latin America. Inter-American relations were strong and cordial between 1933 and 1945 because of Franklin Roosevelt's "Good Neighbor Policy." But, since 1945, relations had deteriorated, because President Harry S Truman and his advisors neglected Latin America. In making these charges, Eisenhower did not explain why the Good Neighbor policy worked or why the Truman administration would foolishly abandon such a popular and productive approach. Moreover, Eisenhower did not propose any new policies for Latin America. He implied, however, that he would return to the principles of Roosevelt's Good Neighbor and discard the practices of the Truman administration. Indeed, the course and conduct of inter-American relations during the Roosevelt and Truman administrations would profoundly influence Eisenhower's policies toward Latin America.

When Franklin D. Roosevelt assumed office in March 1933, he found inter-American relations dangerously strained. The most explosive issue was the question of intervention. Under the aegis of the "Roosevelt Corollary" to the Monroe Doctrine, the United States, during the first three decades of the twentieth century, had repeatedly intervened in the internal affairs of Caribbean and Central American nations. As the dominant power in the Western Hemisphere, the United States claimed the right to exercise, in Theodore Roosevelt's words, "international police power" to ensure that Latin Americans paid their international debts and respected foreign lives and property. Military interventions, by forestalling European influence in Latin American affairs, also upheld the Monroe Doctrine and barred any threat to the Panama Canal.

These repeated violations of their sovereignty incensed Latin Americans. At a stormy inter-American conference in Havana in 1928, Latin American delegates led by Argentina, Mexico, and El Salvador resolved that no state had the right to intervene in the internal affairs of another. The United States successfully tabled that resolution, but officials gradually concluded that the United States would have to alter its tactics. Prior to his inauguration, Herbert Hoover made a goodwill tour of South America. His administration also embraced the "Clark Memorandum," an analysis of the Monroe Doctrine prepared in late 1928 by Department of State officer J. Reuben Clark. This memorandum repudiated Theodore Roosevelt's claim that the Monroe Doctrine sanctioned intervention; nevertheless, the Hoover administration declined to disavow firmly and publicly the right to intervene in Latin America.[2]

Whatever goodwill Hoover created in Latin America was undermined by the economic catastrophes that beset his administration. Between 1929 and 1933, the value of inter-American trade declined by 75 percent. The economic depression in the United States probably accounted for most of the decline, but Latin Americans blamed the high duties imposed by the Hawley-Smoot Tariff of 1930 for their woes. The collapse of inter-American trade rocked Latin America. Turmoil and suffering spread throughout the hemisphere, and governments were overthrown. With their economies vitally dependent on trade, Latin Americans could not generate income to service their international debts, and they defaulted on their loans. They also began to question free trade and investment principles.[3]

Franklin D. Roosevelt and his advisors quickly repaired inter-American relations. They withdrew U.S. troops and financial advisors from the Caribbean. The administration also relinquished treaty rights, such as the Platt Amendment of 1903, that the United States had imposed on Cuba (the Platt Amendment, although nominally guaranteeing the independence of Cuba, served as a pretext for intervention). And, beginning with the Seventh International Conference of American States held in Montevideo, Uruguay, in late 1933, the U.S. delegation consistently voted with Latin Americans on resolutions outlawing military intervention. This process culminated in 1948, during the Truman administration, when the United States accepted the charter of the Organization of American States, which prohibited any state from intervening "directly or indirectly, for any reason whatever, in the internal or external affairs of any other state."

The Roosevelt administration also revived inter-American trade. Armed with the Reciprocal Trade Agreements Act of 1934, which gave the president the power to reduce tariffs by up to 50 percent in exchange for equivalent concessions, the administration negotiated, by the end of 1939, trade agreements with eleven Latin American countries. By 1939 the value of U.S.–Latin American trade had nearly doubled from its 1933 low, although it was still significantly below its 1929 peak. In addition, the administration responded to economic nationalism in Latin America. It tacitly conceded that Latin Americans needed to diversify their economies when, in 1940, it granted Brazil a $45 million credit to construct a steel mill. It grudgingly accepted Mexico's expropriation of the holdings of U.S. oil companies, and it helped Venezuela write its oil law of 1943, a bill that required foreign oil companies in Venezuela to share at least 50 percent of their profits with Venezuela.[4]

These Good Neighbor policies not only resolved key differences with Latin America but also helped forge a strong wartime alliance. By February 1942, eighteen of the twenty Latin American nations, in solidarity with the United States, had either declared war or severed relations with the Axis powers. A year later, Chile became the nineteenth nation to break relations, leaving Argentina the only neutral nation in the Western Hemisphere. Of those nineteen nations, sixteen permitted the development in their territory of air and naval bases that were available to U.S. forces. Two nations—Brazil and Mexico—actively participated in the war: Brazil sent an expeditionary force to Italy, and Mexico sent an air squadron to the Pacific.

Latin America's economic contributions to the Allied war effort were even more significant than its military undertakings. Its commodities and raw materials were crucial to the Allied victory. During the war, nonmilitary agencies of the U.S. government bought nearly $2.4 billion worth of commodities from Latin America out of an approximate total of $4.4 billion spent throughout the world. The United States relied on Latin America for such strategically vital raw materials as beryllium, copper, manganese, mica, quartz crystals, tantalum, tin, tungsten, and zinc. Venezuela supplied Great Britain with as much as 80 percent of its oil imports. Even recalcitrant Argentina sold beef and wheat to the Allies. In effect, Latin America served as an arsenal for the United States and the United Nations.[5]

The solid support that Latin America gave the United States during World War II has prompted analysts to lavish praise on the Good Neighbor policy. Scholars have labeled it a "new era," "the golden age of Pan American cooperation," and the "most successful" policy in the history of U.S. foreign relations. They have also observed that, for the first time, it was established that the Department of State was not simply a handmaiden for U.S. capitalists but, rather, "that there was a national interest of the United States in its relations with Latin America, different from and superior to the private interests of any sector of business enterprise or of business enterprise as a whole."[6] Historians have debated the origins of the Good Neighbor policy, perhaps because, as one scholar puckishly noted, "the idea of the United States truly acting as a friend to another nation was so novel as to spur defenders of every administration to place the 'true' beginnings of the policy with their particular man."[7] Dwight Eisenhower understandably wanted to affirm these policies during the 1952 campaign.

Other scholars, however, see more continuity than change in the Good Neighbor policy. Although President Roosevelt no longer ordered marines to Latin America, he did not forfeit the power of the United States in the Western Hemisphere. The United States replaced the Platt Amendment with the Trade Treaty of 1934. By controlling Cuba's access to the U.S. sugar market, the United States retained leverage over Cuban political and economic life; and U.S. soldiers still patrolled the military and naval base at Guantánamo Bay. Haiti and the Dominican Republic were no longer in financial receivership, but the Roosevelt administration required them to deposit their funds in New York banks and insisted that U.S. bankers oversee the repayment of international debts. This arrangement, as one State Department official put it, preserved "the fiction of Dominican sovereignty over the customs service." The administration also pointedly informed Chile in 1943 that it would be deprived of postwar economic aid if it did not declare war against Germany and Japan. Secretary of State Cordell Hull refused between December 1943 and June 1944 to grant diplomatic recognition to the Bolivian government of Gualberto Villarroel because of its alleged Nazi sympathies, and the administration deployed as much diplomatic pressure as it could muster, albeit unsuccessfully, to force Argentina into the Allied camp.[8]

The Roosevelt administration not only flexed U.S. diplomatic muscle but also increased U.S. power and influence in Latin America, especially in South America. The effect of World War II was to devastate Germany and weaken Great Britain, the two major competitors of the United States for trade and investment in South America. The United States eagerly assisted Latin Americans in confiscating German commercial holdings. To ensure hemispheric solidarity and counter any Nazi propaganda, the State Department, led by Nelson Rockefeller and his Office of the Coordinator of Inter-American Affairs, saturated Latin American newspapers, airwaves, and movie theaters with visions of the North American way of life; the State Department would later approvingly conclude that "it was the greatest outpouring of propagandistic material by a state ever." The War Department also expanded U.S. influence by disbursing $400 million for military equipment through the Lend-Lease program. By the end of the war, U.S. military officers had replaced Western Europeans as the principal advisors to South American military units.[9]

Scholars have also questioned whether the Roosevelt administration fashioned new foreign economic policies. The reciprocal trade treaties confirmed traditional patterns of trade, with Latin America supplying raw materials and primary agricultural products and importing manufactures and processed foods. The State Department, under Secretary of State Hull, conceded Mexico's right to expropriate oil holdings, but it refused to countenance nationalized industries, which excluded foreign capital. The department repeatedly refused to grant a loan to Petróleos Mexicanos or PEMEX, the Mexican national oil company, until U.S. oilmen were again allowed to invest in Mexico. In Venezuela, the oil law the department negotiated gave Venezuela additional oil income; but the law also expanded the holdings of U.S. oil companies and gave them long-term contracts in fields that would prove to be rich and immensely profitable.[10]

In sum, the Roosevelt administration pursued traditional sphere-of-influence goals in Latin America: it wanted to exclude foreign influence from Latin America, preserve U.S. leadership in the hemisphere, dominate the Caribbean basin, and maintain political stability. Military intervention had proved costly, unpopular, and counterproductive—it had not produced peace and order, and it had jeopardized the expansion of trade and investment. In any case, the tumultuous Caribbean and Central American nations achieved their own stability in the 1930s under dictators like Fulgencio Batista of Cuba, Anastasio Somoza of Nicaragua, and Rafael Trujillo of the Dominican Republic. These dictators enforced their rule by controlling their countries' national guards, institutions that U.S. forces had organized and trained during the years of occupation. Even as it waged war against dictatorship in Asia and Europe, the Roosevelt administration conducted cordial, often effusive, relations with these Caribbean tyrants, because they bowed to U.S. leadership, professed to be anti-Nazi, and kept their countries quiet. The Good Neighbor policy was, as one historian has observed, "in terms of means not ends, the antithesis of the previous policy of force diplomacy."[11]

In addition to protecting national security, the Roosevelt administration carried on the U.S. mission of shaping and guiding Latin America's development. Prior to 1933, when U.S. marines and soldiers ruled Caribbean nations they tried not only to stabilize them but also to create for Latin Americans what North Americans expected of local governments: an orderly society populated by the law-abiding. In particular, they reorganized public finances, constructed roads, enforced health and sanitary measures, and recruited and trained a national militia. They tried to teach respect for law and order and the sanctity of private property, the "values of Main Street."[12] The Roosevelt administration, in turn, with its reciprocal trade agreements, sugar quotas, oil policies, economic and military aid, and cultural and propaganda offensive, also attempted to build a hemispheric system under the leadership of the United States and cast in its ideological mold. As the perceptive Brazilian foreign minister Oswaldo Aranha saw it, the Good Neighbor was a crusade, "because it had something of the Red Cross, the Salvation Army, Rockefeller Foundation, religious philanthropy, and expansionist Puritanism which is the heart and soul of this country." The Roosevelt administration assumed an affinity of interests in the hemisphere; a reformed capitalist system would protect the liberties and enhance the lives of North and South Americans. It would also keep Latin America open for U.S. traders and investors.[13]

Although the Roosevelt administration may not have radically restructured Latin American policies, it nonetheless inspired many Latin Americans. The New Deal, the Atlantic Charter, and the Four Freedoms motivated progressive groups like the American Popular Revolutionary Alliance or "Aprista" movement of Peru and Acción Democrática of Venezuela to believe that they could break the power of the military and the landed oligarchy and establish popular governments committed to social reform. Latin American democrats like Rómulo Betancourt of Venezuela, José Figueres of Costa Rica, and Eduardo Santos of Colombia deeply admired Franklin Roosevelt and considered him a friend of Latin America. Moreover, the idealistic rhetoric of the war against fascism seemed to undermine the legitimacy of dictators at home. In Central America, for example, in 1944 dictators fell in Guatemala and El Salvador, and Somoza had to relax his hold on Nicaragua.[14] Before the outbreak of the war, the United States had worked closely with its neighbors at regional conferences on hemispheric security and had implied that the Good Neighbor was the "keystone" of U.S. foreign policy. During the war, the United States pledged that, once the enemy was defeated, it would support the economic development and diversification of Latin America. With victory assured, Latin Americans now dreamed of Pan-American cooperation and substantial economic aid.

Latin Americans would have been disappointed with the postwar policies of the United States, even if President Roosevelt had been able to complete his fourth term. The people in the State Department most closely linked with the policy of assigning priority to inter-American relations—Undersecretary Sumner Welles and Laurence Duggan, chief of the Latin American division—had left government.[15] But the new direction in postwar U.S. foreign policy transcended personalities. The United States emerged from World War II as the world's dominant power with global ambitions and responsibilities; regional concerns would be subordinated to the larger task of rebuilding Europe and Japan and containing the Soviet Union.

During President Harry Truman's first term, the Latin American policy of the United States seemed confused and inconsistent. In form, the Truman administration continued to focus U.S. foreign policy on Latin America. At the United Nations Conference on International Organization in San Francisco in 1945, the U.S. delegation, at the urging of the new assistant secretary of state for Latin American affairs, Nelson Rockefeller, agreed with Latin Americans that the United Nations should sanction regional security organizations. This agreement was transformed into Article 51 of the U.N. charter. Thereafter, in 1947, the administration signed a mutual defense pact with Latin America at Rio de Janeiro, and a year later, at Bogotá, Colombia, it joined with Latin Americans in incorporating Pan-Americanism into the charter of the Organization of American States (OAS). These treaties served as models for other regional pacts, such as the North Atlantic Treaty Organization.

The Rio Treaty and the OAS reflected the spirit of the Good Neighbor policy. But they also revealed vastly different perspectives on inter-American relations. With Article 51 the United States was able, in Secretary of War Henry L. Stimson's view, to preserve "the unilateral character of the Monroe Doctrine"; if the United States needed to enforce peace in Latin America, it would not be "at the mercy of getting the assent of the Security Council."[16] In accepting Article 51 President Truman was affirming the views of President Roosevelt, who, during the war, assured Latin Americans that the inter-American system would not be supplanted by a new international organization. But, while pursuing U.S. foreign policy objectives, both Truman and Roosevelt were also acceding to Latin American wishes. Indeed, Latin Americans, led by Mexico and Colombia, vigorously lobbied at the San Francisco conference for the inclusion of regional alliances into the U.N. Charter. Latin Americans believed that Article 51 would help "contain" the United States. With the OAS, Latin Americans would have a forum to influence the United States, a treaty that guaranteed the nonintervention principle, and a vehicle for transferring economic aid.[17]

Although Latin Americans achieved their organizational goals, they were alarmed by the substance of inter-American relations. In the first postwar years the question of intervention again dominated inter-American affairs. After Secretary of State Hull resigned because of poor health in late 1944, the United States reassessed its Argentine policy. The new secretary of state, Edward Stettinius, accepted the arguments of Assistant Secretary Rockefeller and of Latin Americans that Argentina should be admitted to the United Nations in order to maintain regional solidarity. But by the end of 1945, the department had once again changed U.S. policy. The new ambassador to Argentina, Spruille Braden, interfered in Argentine politics: Braden, who had established a reputation as a tough foe of fascism during his wartime ambassadorships in Colombia and Cuba, denounced the military rulers of Argentina as erstwhile sympathizers of Nazi Germany. For his efforts, he reaped the disdain of Argentine military men, popular support in the United States, and a promotion in December 1945 to assistant secretary from the new secretary of state, James F. Byrnes. From Washington, Braden continued his noisy campaign, particularly against the leading presidential candidate, Colonel Juan Perón. Two weeks before the Argentine election, the department published the "Blue Book," a study that purported to document the Fascist proclivities of leading Argentinians. Perón cleverly seized upon Braden's impolitic behavior and turned the election into a campaign against Yankee imperialism; he won a landslide victory on 24 February 1946.[18]

In Braden's view, intervention was a false issue. The United States dominated the hemisphere; "whatever we refrain from saying and whatever we refrain from doing may constitute intervention, no less than what we do or say." Braden therefore feuded with Perón, denounced Rafael Trujillo, and warmly praised fledgling democracies in Peru and Venezuela. He also embraced the Larreta Doctrine: in October 1945 Eduardo Rodríguez Larreta, the foreign minister of Uruguay—one of Latin America's few staunch democracies—had proposed that the Pan-American nations consider multilateral action against any member state violating elementary human rights. The proposal received an indifferent reception from all the Latin American countries except Uruguay and Venezuela; this response was predictable, for repressive, authoritarian governments wielded power in many of these lands, and the Larreta Doctrine raised the specter of intervention.[19]

However, by mid-1947 both Byrnes and Braden had left Washington, and the State Department once again altered its Argentine policy. In January 1947, in a dispute over European questions, President Truman asked Byrnes to resign and appointed General George C. Marshall to be secretary of state. In June 1947 Marshall fired Braden, for he found that his Argentine policy had not weakened Perón and that it endangered hemispheric solidarity by delaying the scheduled defense conference: the Rio Conference had been scheduled to meet in 1945, but Braden had twice postponed it because of the dispute with Argentina.[20] In late 1948, the department officially buried Braden's policies. After extended debate and review, it decided to issue a statement deploring "the use of force as an instrument of political change," even as it recognized the military dictators who overthrew popularly elected governments in Peru and Venezuela.[21]

In part, these oscillations in policy can be attributed to bureaucratic disorder and clashes among strong personalities. In three years, Truman had three secretaries of state and three assistant secretaries for Latin America. But U.S. policy on Argentina and intervention also changed because the imperatives of the cold war had triumphed over the democratic idealism engendered by World War II. Secretary Marshall decided to form a military alliance that would include Argentina, because of the ongoing confrontations with the Soviet Union over Europe and the Middle East: the goal of a united hemisphere outweighed misgivings about Perón's past associations and beliefs. The military rulers in Peru and Venezuela coupled their requests for diplomatic recognition with promises to oppose communism and support the United States at the United Nations. And Rafael Trujillo assured Washington that he had undergone metamorphosis from an anti-Fascist into the hemisphere's most vigorous anti-Communist.[22]

Although the cold war had intruded into inter-American affairs, the Truman administration was not prepared by 1948 to battle communism with every means. At the Bogotá Conference, the delegates denounced international communism and resolved to exchange information on international Communist activities. But the United States opposed "a multilateral inter-American anti-Communist agreement." In what became the first National Security Council (NSC) document devoted exclusively to Latin America, NSC 16, the Truman administration decided that "communism in the Americas is a potential danger, but that, with a few possible exceptions, it is not seriously dangerous at the present time." It feared "that there would be many cases in which such anti-Communist agreements would be directed against all political opposition, Communist or otherwise, by dictatorial governments, with the inevitable result of driving leftist elements into the hands of the Communist organization."[23] It was an apt prediction. Between 1947 and 1952, five Latin American countries, with U.S. approval, severed relations with the Soviet Union. They also simultaneously outlawed Communist activities, a category that often was broadly defined.[24]

The Truman administration's position on intervention and communism, thus, was in evolution between 1945 and 1948. What remained constant was the policy toward economic cooperation with Latin America. Latin Americans expected economic aid from the United States. During the war, Undersecretary Sumner Welles had consistently pledged that the United States would cooperate with Latin America, once the enemy was defeated. Whether the Roosevelt administration would have redeemed those promises is uncertain, but it seems doubtful. In 1944 Cordell Hull twice postponed a hemispheric economic conference because of the imbroglio with Argentina. When the American republics met in Chapultepec, near Mexico City, in early 1945 to discuss "problems of war and peace," Latin Americans were interested in economic questions. They spoke of international commodity agreements, controls on foreign investment, linking the prices of raw materials to finished goods, and economic aid. The U.S. delegation responded indifferently to these overtures, but, in order to avoid a wartime clash, it agreed to explore economic issues at a special conference scheduled for 15 June 1945.[25]

The Truman administration refused to attend an inter-American economic conference. Between 1945 and 1947, the administration argued that economic cooperation could not be discussed until the Argentine issue was resolved. But the State Department feared that an economic conference would be a fiasco, with the United States resisting demands for economic aid and commodity agreements—in early 1946, for example, Brazil requested a five-year $1-billion loan. Latin America would prosper if it implemented free trade and investment principles and prepared for the massive orders of raw materials that would surely come from a rebuilding Europe. By 1946, department officials wanted "to kill" the conference idea but, fearing a stormy reaction from Latin Americans, chose only to postpone it. The United States had reneged on the promises of Sumner Welles, perhaps because, as department officer Louis Halle bluntly put it, with the war over, "the United States no longer desperately needs Latin America."[26]

Latin Americans were dismayed not only by the U.S. position on economic aid but also by its handling of wartime contracts. During the war, Latin America sold its strategic commodities in a controlled market, with prices fixed. Latin Americans accumulated credits of $3.4 billion, because the capital goods they wanted to purchase were scarce in the United States. This influx of money contributed to inflationary pressures, with the cost of living rising over 80 percent in Latin America during the war. In 1945 at Chapultepec, the United States promised not to terminate wartime contracts suddenly and to allocate capital goods fairly. But after the war, the United States abruptly lifted price controls and prices rose rapidly; Latin America quickly exhausted its wartime credits. Chile, for example, by selling its copper and nitrates at artificially low prices and buying goods it wanted for industrial development in a free market, may have lost more than $500 million. In effect, Latin America made a $3-billion non-interest-bearing loan to the United States and could not collect on the principal. The United States answered, however, that it had sacrificed men and matériel in protecting the hemisphere from totalitarianism.[27]

Latin American hopes for economic aid revived in 1947, after Secretary Marshall announced his plan to reconstruct Europe. If the United States was ready to help its former enemies, then a "Marshall Plan for Latin America" might follow. At the Rio Conference, Latin American delegates wanted to focus on economic cooperation, but Marshall persuaded them to wait until the meeting in Bogotá. There, he quashed all hopes of economic aid. In a speech that was greeted by stony silence, Marshall promised only to increase the lending authority of the Export-Import Bank by $500 million. The European Recovery Program would aid Latin America by restoring markets for raw materials and tropical foods. Once Europe rebuilt its industrial plant, Latin America would also have another source of supply for capital goods. Such arguments meant to Latin Americans that their region would be confined to its traditional role of supplying the industrial world with raw materials. In any case, between 1945 and 1952 the twenty Latin American nations together received less economic aid from the United States than did Belgium and tiny Luxembourg.[28]

In lieu of economic assistance, the U.S. prescription for Latin America's economic health included self-help, technical cooperation, liberal trade practices, and, in particular, private enterprise and investment. The State Department repeatedly told Latin Americans that they could have the capital they so desperately needed by creating a "suitable climate" for foreign investors and by not imposing unreasonable barriers to transferring capital and earnings. The Truman administration backed these pronouncements by vigorously opposing economic nationalism. It refused to approve loans to state companies such as PEMEX and the new Brazilian national oil company, PETROBRÁS. The Export-Import Bank would make loans only if they supplemented domestic and foreign private investment. The administration also threatened to reduce Cuba's sugar quota and to cancel Bolivian tin purchases in an attempt to "'put across' U.S. corporation practices and safeguards" to those countries. And it scrutinized Latin American laws and constitutions, such as the Venezuelan constitution of 1947, and forcefully objected if they violated free trade and investment principles.[29]

Latin Americans reacted angrily to these policies, charging that the United States had misled them during the war and now "neglected" them. But although Latin America was the one non-Communist area of the world not under a direct aid program, the Truman administration was not uninterested in the good neighbors. The area remained strategically significant and economically vital. In the early postwar years, U.S. businessmen counted on Latin America for approximately 30 percent of their international trade and nearly 40 percent of their global direct investments. The Truman administration did not develop a Marshall Plan for Latin America because it believed in the efficacy of international capitalism and because it grounded its analyses of inter-American relations on the cold war. Unlike Europe, Latin America did not seem threatened by the Soviet Union. As Ambassador Herschel Johnson explained to the Brazilian press, "the situation might be graphically represented as a case of smallpox in Europe competing with a common cold in Latin America."[30]

By the end of 1948, the Truman administration had decided on its hemispheric policies: it would work with non-Communist governments in Latin America and defend the foreign economic policy of free trade and investment. During Truman's second term the State Department, led by Secretary of State Dean Acheson and Assistant Secretary Edward G. Miller, Jr., continued to apply those policies. What changed was that, under the continuing impact of the cold war, the Truman administration expanded its concept of national security in regard to Latin America. It also began to criticize sharply the attitudes and policies of Latin Americans.

Secretary Acheson set the tone for inter-American relations during Truman's second term when, in September 1949, he addressed the Pan American Society. The speech, which the State Department called "the most complete restatement of Latin American policy in many years," covered familiar ground. Acheson conceded there had been "occasional disappointments," with the overthrow of freely elected governments; yet, he rejected the Larreta Doctrine and reaffirmed a de facto recognition policy. He argued that "our long-range objectives in the promotion of democracy" would be better served by maintaining communication with unelected governments. As for a Marshall Plan for Latin America, Acheson could not have been more unequivocal. The United States "has been built by private initiative, and it remains a land of private initiative." The State Department would not approve loans for development projects, when private capital was available. In any case, he did not "believe that rapid industrialization is good per se." Instead, Latin Americans should increase agricultural productivity and negotiate treaties that attracted and protected international investors. Acheson concluded: "I cannot stress too strongly that progress will come most rapidly in countries that help themselves vigorously."[31]

The State Department was true to Secretary Acheson's words. It continued to postpone indefinitely an inter-American economic conference, and it repeatedly informed Latin Americans that "the greatest single obstacle to economic development in Latin America is the slow rate of private foreign investment." It also unsuccessfully tried to persuade Latin Americans to abolish the Economic Commission for Latin America, a U.N. agency. The commission irritated U.S. officials by issuing reports demonstrating that the prices of raw material and food exports were declining relative to the prices of imported manufactures, and by suggesting that the solution to these declining terms of trade was to attract development capital, presumably from the U.S. government, for industrialization and economic diversification. Ignoring this unsolicited advice, the United States confined its aid to Export-Import Bank loans and technical cooperation. The Export-Import Bank loans were primarily short-term credits to finance the purchase of imports from the United States. Technical cooperation, the "Point Four" initiative of President Truman, amounted to about $25 million a year in grants for agricultural modernization. So limited were U.S. economic efforts in Latin America that the interest the U.S. Treasury collected on Export-Import Bank loans actually exceeded the amount of aid granted to the region.[32] Assistant Secretary Miller dutifully upheld these foreign economic policies, although he was not oblivious to the irony in them. As he wondered in a confidential memorandum: "How is it possible to justify on either moral or logical grounds the extension of U.S. grants to a heavy dollar and gold earner such as Saudi Arabia, when similar assistance is not available to such poverty-stricken, dollar-short countries as Paraguay and Ecuador?"[33]

Miller also, as instructed by Acheson, maintained "channels of communication" with unsavory governments. In particular, he worked hard for a rapprochement with President Perón of Argentina. With the approval of President Truman, Miller went to Buenos Aires in February 1950 to meet with the Argentine strongman. Perón had said that he was anti-Communist and that he would support the United States in a war with the Soviet Union, and he implied that he would send the Rio Treaty of 1947 to the Argentine legislature for ratification. Accordingly, it did not seem "wise to jeopardize this cooperation by making what would probably be an unfruitful effort to inject into the Perón government a respect for civil liberties." The visit appeared successful: Perón agreed to back the Rio Treaty, and a few months later he voted with the United States at the United Nations in condemning North Korea's invasion of South Korea. In return, Argentina received a $125-million credit from the Export-Import Bank. Argentina's return to the fold was, however, short-lived. By the end of 1950 Perón, perhaps responding to domestic pressure, was reasserting Argentina's traditional independence, denouncing both communism and capitalism and upholding the "third ideological position," *justicialismo*.[34]

The Truman administration's position on economic aid and its special efforts toward Argentina, the only neutral nation during World War II, engendered a new wave of complaints and criticisms from Latin Americans. But the problem, as Secretary Miller saw it, was that Latin America wanted to ignore the cold war and return to the 1930s when "the Good Neighbor Policy was virtually our sole foreign policy"; that experience, combined with a consequential high-level attention devoted to Latin America, "had fostered an exaggerated and extreme sense of self-importance on the part of individuals connected with Latin American governments." Miller, whose father owned sugar plantations and mills in Cuba, also told the House Foreign Affairs Committee in executive session that, during the 1930s, "we went too far in the direction of not protecting American interests."[35] Miller kept such views confidential, but he authorized Louis Halle, under the pseudonym "Y," to reveal in the influential journal *Foreign Affairs* the State Department's "impatience with Latin America." In that article, Halle argued that the United States would have to follow the dictates of "noblesse oblige" toward Latin American countries, for they were like children, not yet ready to exercise, for themselves, the responsibility of adult nations. Dean Acheson would later ascribe problems in Latin America to "Hispano-Indian culture—or lack of it."[36]

Although, during its second term, the Truman administration spoke frankly to Latin America, it had not restructured the policies it had developed by 1947–48 on recognition, nondemocratic governments, and economic aid. What was new was a heightened fear and perception of communism in the hemisphere. These anxieties were not based on developments within Latin America. In his speech to the Pan American Society in 1949, Secretary Acheson noted there was not a "direct threat against our independence." In 1950, in a comprehensive review of Latin America, the State Department concluded that the Communists had "lost ground." As late as 1951, Assistant Secretary Miller assured Congress that the Soviet Union's role in Latin America "at this time will not be great." Miller criticized the social and economic policies of Guatemala, but he concluded they could be blamed on President Juan José Arévalo, a "wooly-head." U.S. officials also knew that by 1952 the Soviet Union had diplomatic relations with only three Latin American countries—Argentina, Mexico, and Uruguay—and a minuscule amount of trade in the hemisphere.[37]

Yet, despite its own evidence and its continuing belief that an inter-American, anti-Communist agreement might be used by some governments to "suppress all types of liberal opposition," the Truman administration decided to redefine the Monroe Doctrine and the oas charter. In a speech in April 1950, two months before the outbreak of the Korean War, Miller reviewed the history of intervention. He condoned the decisions of presidents like Theodore Roosevelt, Woodrow Wilson, and Calvin Coolidge, arguing that they had ordered troops into Caribbean nations to forestall European interference and perhaps colonialism—these decisions had been "necessary evils," or "protective interventions." Miller accepted the Good Neighbor policy, the juridical equality of states, but he warned that "if the circumstances that led to the protective interventions by the United States should arise again today, the organized community of American states would be faced with the responsibility that the United States had once to assume alone." The doctrine of nonintervention incorporated in the oas charter of 1948 was not absolute; if a member state was threatened by Communist political aggression, the oas would have to act for the common welfare. This action would be "the alternative to intervention," the "corollary of non-intervention." What Miller left unanalyzed was the policy the United States would adopt, if it could not convince Latin American nations to sanction an intervention against another American republic.[38]

The Truman administration coupled the "Miller Doctrine" on intervention with a decision in 1950 to arm Latin America against communism. Since the middle of World War II, defense planners had wanted Latin America to be militarily dependent upon the United States. Prior to the war, South Americans had purchased their arms and accepted military training missions from Europe, including the Axis nations of Germany and Italy. In order to exclude foreign influence from the hemisphere and to "promote with respect to the American continent, the United States policy regarding the organization of peace and security," defense officials proposed an arms standardization policy for the hemisphere. The United States would provide arms, if Latin America would cooperate in postwar hemispheric defense, make available its military bases to U.S. air and naval forces, and agree not to purchase equipment and training from foreign sources.[39]

Although the Truman administration submitted to Congress in both 1946 and 1947 a military aid package for Latin America, it did not secure funding. Congressional critics managed to delay legislation, arguing that military aid was wasteful, would bolster authoritarian regimes, and would trigger a hemispheric arms race. Officials in the Latin American section of the State Department did not lament the postponement, for they also feared the political effects of military aid. In any case, the United States lacked arms to transfer, because programs such as Greek-Turkish aid, NATO, and support for Chinese nationalist forces took priority over inter-American military cooperation.[40]

But on 19 May 1950 President Truman authorized military aid for Latin America when he approved NSC 56/2, "United States Policy Toward Inter-American Military Collaboration": Defense officials would design with Latin Americans a plan for hemispheric defense; the United States would then provide "such mutual assistance among the American republics as may be necessary to assure adequate implementation of the Hemisphere Defense Scheme." The preparation of NSC 56/2 was done while the Truman administration was conducting the broad review of national security policy that would be tagged NSC 68. Like NSC 68, the new policy on inter-American military collaboration assumed that the United States was locked in a momentous global struggle with the Soviet Union and that "the cold war is in fact a real war in which the survival of the free world is at stake." Yet, neither NSC 68 nor NSC 56/2 explained precisely how the Soviet Union threatened Latin America. And, whereas NSC 56/2 recognized, for example, that Latin Americans might use U.S. weapons against one another, it did not resolve the political and diplomatic issues raised by transferring arms to poor, weak, undemocratic nations. These problems seemed inconsequential, however, after the outbreak of the Korean conflict. As it did with NSC 68, the war helped "sell" NSC 56/2. In 1951 Congress voted $38,150,000 for direct military assistance for Latin America, and in 1952 it added $51,685,750 to that sum.[41]

In expanding its interpretation of the Monroe Doctrine and arming Latin America, the Truman administration was working "to strengthen the free world and frustrate the Kremlin design." As the administration concluded in late 1950, "U.S. security is the objective of our world-wide foreign policy today," and "U.S. security is synonymous with hemisphere security." What the United States wanted from Latin America was for the other American states to "identify with our policy."[42] The Truman administration failed, however, to achieve that "identification." After President Truman declared a national emergency following attacks on U.S. troops in Korea by Chinese forces, Secretary Acheson hastily called an inter-American conference of foreign ministers, which met in Washington between March and April 1951. But, for this war, Latin Americans were willing to give only "rhetorical" support to their northern neighbor. The conference's key resolution, calling for increased production of strategic materials, was tied to a statement citing Latin America's need for economic development. Moreover, only Colombia responded to requests for troops, and with only a token battalion of volunteers.[43]

Latin America did not rally behind the United States in Korea because of the Truman administration's policy on economic aid. Secretary Miller found "apathy and sullenness resulting from the feeling that the United States has abandoned Latin America in the post-war era and is giving priority to new friends in other parts of the world." When he journeyed to Rio de Janeiro in February 1951 to request a division of Brazilian troops for Korea, Miller received a frosty reception. As the Brazilian Foreign Minister João Neves da Fontura observed to Miller, "Brazil's present situation would be different and our cooperation in the present emergency could probably be greater," if Washington "had elaborated a recovery plan for Latin America similar to the Marshall Plan for Europe." Alarmed at the course of inter-American relations, Miller began to argue that the United States would have to grant Latin America at least a small amount of assistance. But the administration was too harried and the economy too strained by the Korean conflict for the United States to consider another economic aid program. Miller's only significant success was to obtain in late 1952 an emergency $300 million loan for Brazil to relieve balance-of-payment and currency difficulties.[44]

In lambasting the Truman administration's Latin American policy, Dwight Eisenhower accurately depicted the disillusionment that Latin Americans felt over inter-American relations. He also correctly charged that the United States was not devoting the same amount of energy and imagination to relations with Latin America that it had in the 1930s. But the presidential candidate exaggerated when he implied that the Truman government did not have a policy for Latin America. President Truman and his advisors wanted to wage cold war, and their policies toward Latin America reflected that overriding objective. The administration's stance on the issues of recognition, military aid, and intervention was designed to build a dependable and secure hemisphere, a region the United States could rely on while confronting the Soviet Union. Whereas its approach toward Latin America was perhaps less conciliatory and sympathetic than that of President Roosevelt, Sumner Welles, and Laurence Duggan, the Truman administration retained the central feature of the Good Neighbor policy. The United States would maintain its hegemony in the Western Hemisphere.

To be sure, the Truman administration would leave President Eisenhower with dilemmas and unresolved issues in inter-American relations. Latin Americans placed a higher priority on economic development and diversification than on winning the cold war. They were being swept up in the nationalist fervor and the "revolution of rising expectations" that characterized nations in Asia, Africa, and the Middle East, as they emerged from colonialism in the postwar world. Latin Americans might begin to identify more with the "Third World" than with Pan-Americanism. Moreover, the Truman administration, in choosing to subordinate human rights issues to security concerns and in deciding to work with and arm dictators, was frustrating, demoralizing, even radicalizing Latin American progressives and reformers who might be natural allies of the United States; the security that a Trujillo could provide in the short term might jeopardize the long-term interests of the United States in Latin America. Finally, in espousing, as it did in NSC 68, the doctrine that every manifestation of communism on the globe was a gain for the Soviet Union and a direct threat to the United States, the administration was ensuring that the issue of unilateral intervention would again arise in inter-American relations. Remembering past violations of their sovereignty, Latin Americans were unlikely to accept Secretary Miller's judgment that collective intervention against communism was an "imperative" of the Monroe Doctrine and the OAS charter. These issues of economic nationalism, human rights, communism, and intervention would be the ones that the Eisenhower administration would encounter in formulating policies for Latin America.

CHAPTER 2

COLD-WAR POLICIES

1953–1954

President Dwight D. Eisenhower decisively established the Latin American policy of his administration. Within two months after taking the presidential oath, he had approved a preliminary statement on "United States Objectives and Courses of Action with Respect to Latin America."[1] Eisenhower and his advisors defined hemispheric solidarity as the key objective in inter-American relations. The United States needed Latin America's support in the struggle with the Soviet Union, and it wanted to eliminate internal Communist subversion from the hemisphere. In pursuit of hemispheric solidarity, the Eisenhower administration would, in 1953 and 1954, offer money, medals, and military support to Latin American leaders who were anti-Communists, including those who were dictators. It would also prepare to destroy a popularly elected government in Guatemala.

Before they assumed office in January 1953, President Eisenhower and his closest advisors had gained some experience in Latin American affairs. As a youth, Eisenhower dreamed of seeking his fortune in Argentina, envisioning it to be like the American West in the 1870s. After graduating from the military academy at West Point, Eisenhower was ordered to Fort Sam Houston in San Antonio, Texas. He remembered his assignment there between 1915 and 1917 as the happiest time of his life. He usually completed his duties by midday and then went deer and dove hunting and horseback riding. The military base also had a gay social life, filled with beer drinking and poker games. And it was at Fort Sam Houston that the young officer met his future wife, Mamie Doud. While stationed in San Antonio, Eisenhower frequently crossed the border for weekend hunting trips in Mexico. These experiences left him with a romantic view of Mexico and a patronizing attitude toward Mexicans. As Ambassador to Mexico Robert Hill recalled, a relaxed Eisenhower once told him: "You know, they're rascals at heart. You can't trust them and so forth, but they're lovable types, and you know, I sure would like to get away on a holiday and go back to relive that youth of mine in the military, those happy days in Mexico."[2]

Eisenhower's only assignment in Latin America was in Panama from 1922 to 1924. Although he received valuable training, neither he nor his wife enjoyed this tropical duty station. Eisenhower was also offended by the discrimination in work and pay that Panamanians suffered in the Canal Zone. Later, at the beginning of World War II, he was briefly involved in securing arms for Latin America under the Lend-Lease program. After the war, he toured Mexico, Panama, and Brazil; this visit left him vaguely concerned with the state of inter-American relations.[3]

During the Truman years, Eisenhower consistently supported military aid for Latin America. As chief of staff, General Eisenhower testified in favor of military assistance, assuring skeptics that defense officials would not supply "guns, tanks, and airplanes indiscriminately to the Latin American countries." He also unsuccessfully tried to convince the Joint Chiefs of Staff to give Latin America special consideration in allocating scarce military resources. Eisenhower judged that Latin America was the "main base" of U.S. war potential and that the negotiation of an inter-American military agreement was essential to national security.[4]

President Eisenhower chose John Foster Dulles to be his secretary of state, a man whose experience with Latin America was primarily in the field of international investment and finance. Dulles and his brother, Allen, the new director of the CIA, were members of the prestigious Wall Street law firm of Sullivan and Cromwell. Sullivan and Cromwell represented numerous U.S. corporations, such as United Fruit Company, in Latin America, and members of this firm typically served in the Latin American section of the Department of State (Assistant Secretary Edward Miller, for example, worked for Sullivan and Cromwell). For his assistant secretary for Latin America, Dulles tapped John Moors Cabot, a career foreign service officer. Cabot, who was from an old and respected family in Massachusetts, had two decades of experience in a variety of diplomatic posts in Latin America.[5]

Eisenhower discussed Latin American affairs with his advisors in several fora. The most significant meetings were those of the National Security Council. Eisenhower used the NSC, which was created by the National Security Act of 1947, to set policy for the cold war. During his two terms the NSC met 366 times, with the president presiding over 339 of these often-lengthy meetings. Members of the NSC—which included the vice-president, the director of the CIA, the chairman of the Joint Chiefs of Staff, and appropriate cabinet secretaries and their deputies—would debate the issues, with Eisenhower usually waiting until near the end of the meeting to offer his views and decide on policy. Papers for discussion were generated by the planning staff headed by the special assistant for national security affairs (in the period 1953–61 there were three special assistants: successively, Robert Cutler, Dillon Anderson, and Gordon Gray). After the NSC had established policy, the Operations Coordinating Board, headed by the undersecretary of state, monitored policy.[6]

Although Eisenhower's NSC apparatus was orderly and efficient, it also had the potential to be ponderous and divisive. To ensure harmony with Secretary Dulles and the State Department, a division was made between national security policy and diplomacy, the day-to-day conduct of international relations. The NSC defined the former; Dulles was in charge of the latter. Eisenhower held Oval Office meetings with Dulles—and later with his successor, Christian Herter—and other State Department officers, such as the assistant secretary for Latin American affairs. These discussions were coordinated by Eisenhower's staff secretary, first General Paul Carroll and then General Andrew Goodpaster. Moreover, Eisenhower often met with Dulles in the late afternoons for drinks and philosophical discussions on foreign policy.[7]

Eisenhower also sought outside advice on Latin America. He listened, for example, to conservative businessmen such as Harry Guggenheim, the former ambassador to Cuba, and William Pawley, the former ambassador to Brazil. But his most influential outside advisor on Latin America was his youngest brother, Dr. Milton Eisenhower. Dwight Eisenhower loved and respected his brother. As he confided to his diary, Milton was "the most knowledgeable and widely informed of all the people with whom I deal" and "the most highly qualified man in the United States to be president. This most emphatically makes no exception of me. . . ."[8] The president designated his brother a special ambassador and had him make two fact-finding tours of Latin America as his personal representative. Milton Eisenhower did not have special training in Latin American affairs, but he had had a rich and varied career. After graduating from Kansas State College in 1924, he served in government in the foreign service, in the Department of Agriculture, and in wartime agencies. Beginning in 1943 he was a college president, serving first as the leader of Kansas State, then of Pennsylvania State University, and then of Johns Hopkins University. The president corresponded with his brother and often invited him to spend weekends with him. Latin American leaders also wrote directly to Dr. Eisenhower when they wanted to bring vital concerns to the president's attention. For Milton Eisenhower, this was a delicate assignment, for he did not want to undercut the authority of cabinet officers, particularly the secretary of state.[9] But whatever mechanism was used, it was President Eisenhower who was at the center of discussion and decision making in foreign policy.

In winning the election of 1952, Dwight Eisenhower and his Republican allies convinced many citizens that U.S. foreign policy was in disarray, that the Truman administration was "soft on communism," and that a new administration could turn the tide against the red menace. During the campaign, vice-presidential candidate Richard M. Nixon accused Democrats of "twenty years of treason" and charged that candidate Adlai E. Stevenson was a graduate of "Dean Acheson's cowardly College of Communist Containment." The Republican party platform labeled Truman's containment policy as "negative, futile, and immoral." John Foster Dulles pledged to audiences that the Republicans would "roll back the Iron Curtain" in Eastern Europe.

The Republicans continued to sound the tocsin during the presidential transition. During his confirmation hearings, Dulles told the Senate Foreign Relations Committee that Soviet communism was "not only the gravest threat that ever faced the United States, but the gravest threat that has ever faced what we call western civilization, or, indeed, any civilization which was dominated by a spiritual faith." As for Latin America, Dulles saw a well-organized Communist movement in most countries and a Fascist apparatus in Argentina. These totalitarians were allied in their "hatred of the Yankee" and were determined "to destroy the influence of the so-called Colossus of the North in Central and South America." Dulles warned that "conditions in Latin America are somewhat comparable to conditions as they were in China in the mid-thirties when the Communist movement was getting started." He concluded: "The time to deal with this rising menace in South America is now."[10]

The Eisenhower administration's actions, of course, often belied its rhetoric. The administration wisely did not try to "liberate" Eastern Europe, although Hungarians tragically believed that U.S. forces would come to their aid during the revolution of 1956. In part, Eisenhower and his aides used militantly anti-Communist rhetoric to hold the support of extremists and zealots in the Republican party.[11] Yet in regard to Latin America, the private discussions and classified policy statements of administration officials differed little from their public positions. President Eisenhower correctly identified the emergence of a vigorous and assertive nationalism throughout the developing world as the most dynamic new feature in international affairs in the postwar world. With nationalism "on the march," the Western powers could no longer hope to preserve the status quo. But Eisenhower analyzed nationalism in cold-war terms. As he confided to his diary in January 1953, "actually what is going on is that the communists are hoping to take advantage of the confusion resulting from destruction of existing relationships and in the difficulties and uncertainties of disrupted trade, security, and understanding—to further the aims of world revolution and the Kremlin's domination of all people."[12]

How to respond to this Soviet threat in the developing world was a central concern of Eisenhower's. Early in his administration, the president gathered the NSC and outside consultants for a day-long discussion on the relationship between federal budget deficits and national security. In essence, the meeting was a review of the ambitious military and economic spending plans outlined in the Truman administration's strategy for cold war, NSC 68 of 1950. Eisenhower lamented the advantages held by the Communists: "since the Soviets are totalitarians they could assign whatever proportion of national income they desire to warlike purposes. We, who are dedicated to raising the standards for all peoples, are inhibited from such methods"—and yet, he opposed "any relaxation of pressure on the USSR." As for Latin America, the United States would have to design policies to "secure the allegiance of these republics to our camp in the cold war."[13]

Secretary Dulles similarly subscribed to a bipolar view of the world. In a telephone conversation, he told his brother Allen that "the Communists are trying to extend their form of despotism in this hemisphere." He informed the cabinet that he would have to convince Latin Americans that communism was "an internationalist conspiracy, not an indigenous movement." In executive congressional hearings, he testified that Latin America needed social change and economic development and that the United States must accommodate those aspirations: "In the old days," he noted, "we used to be able to let South America go through the wringer of bad times, and then when times would get better it was right there where it was; but the trouble is that now, when you put it through the wringer, it comes out red."[14] Assistant Secretary Cabot agreed with his boss; there must be "social evolution without revolution" in order to stop the "spread of communism" in Latin America.[15]

Convinced that Communist aggression directed by the Soviet Union imperiled the world, the Eisenhower administration set out to construct its Latin American policy. In his inaugural address, President Eisenhower made only a passing reference to inter-American relations with the platitudinous statement that "in the Western Hemisphere, we enthusiastically join with all our neighbors in the work of perfecting a community of fraternal trust and common purpose." On 27 January Secretary Dulles, in his first official address to the U.S. people, repeated the campaign charge that the Truman administration had neglected Latin America, and he recited his testimony during his confirmation hearings that a well-organized Communist movement operated in Latin America and that Fascist influences existed "in some quarters."[16] The administration's first substantive discussion of inter-American relations took place, however, on 18 February 1953 at an NSC meeting. The council received an unsettling briefing from CIA director Allen Dulles, who reported that Latin America was "deteriorating not only in terms of cordiality of relationships with the United States but in the economic and political spheres of most of the Latin American states. The Kremlin was exploiting this situation." Dulles compared developments in Latin America with revolutionary movements in the Middle East, with "trends in the direction of economic nationalism, regionalism, neutralism, and increasing Communist influence." In particular, "Communist infection" in Guatemala was "such as to mark an approaching crisis." These developments endangered U.S. access to Latin America's strategic raw materials and were retarding inter-American military cooperation, as set forth in NSC 56/2 of 1950. "Deeply disturbed" by Dulles's report, Eisenhower ordered the NSC staff to prepare expeditiously a paper on Latin America.[17]

A month later, on 18 March 1953, Eisenhower had a new policy for Latin America, NSC 144/1. Described by Undersecretary of State Walter Bedell Smith as a paper "prepared in some haste" and representing a "shotgun approach," NSC 144/1 interpreted inter-American affairs solely within the context of the global struggle with the Soviet Union. The document had little to say about political and social democracy or human rights in Latin America, other than to note that the United States favored "orderly political and economic development" in the region. What the United States wanted was for Latin America to support the U.S. position at the United Nations, eliminate the "menace of internal Communist or other anti-U.S. subversion," produce strategic raw materials, and cooperate in defending the hemisphere, as outlined in NSC 56/2. After cursory debate, Eisenhower approved the paper, ruling also that he would not endorse any new military or economic aid program for Latin America until there was a complete review of policy.[18]

Beyond enumerating U.S. objectives, NSC 144/1 reflected the frustration administration officials felt about Latin Americans' failure to understand the dangers of international communism. In the annex to NSC 144, the staff study that served as the basis for NSC 144/1, the administration recognized the intense pressures for social and economic progress in Latin America; "Cárdenas in Mexico, Arévalo in Guatemala, Figueres in Costa Rica, Gaitán in Colombia, Betancourt in Venezuela, Haya de la Torre in Peru, Ibáñez in Chile, Perón in Argentina, Vargas in Brazil, Grau in Cuba, all achieved their political power by promising change." Yet, many were "immature and impractical idealists," who "not only are inadequately trained to conduct government business efficiently but also lack the disposition to combat extremists within their ranks, including communists." Moreover, they weakened respect for property rights by expropriating the haciendas and plantations of oligarchs, "with inadequate regard for compensating those whose property is taken."[19]

The same staff study went on to state that their preoccupation with domestic problems led Latin American reformers to "court popular favor by sensational, irresponsible acts" and to ignore their international responsibilities. Therefore, the Eisenhower administration was reconsidering the U.S. commitment to nonintervention and the OAS charter. The study noted that "it is probable that the majority of Latin American governments do not yet favor even limited multilateral intervention," and it speculated that collective action "would probably be supported" only if a "clearly identifiable communist regime should establish itself in the hemisphere." The study therefore concluded that "overriding security interests" required the United States to consider acting unilaterally, recognizing that "this would be a violation of our treaty commitments, would endanger the

Organization of American States . . . and would probably intensify anti-U.S. attitudes in many Latin American countries."[20]

With NSC 144/1 as guidance, the Eisenhower administration worked to hold Latin America's support for the cold war and to eradicate Communists in the hemisphere. To demonstrate that the administration did not "neglect" Latin America, officials tried to "dramatize" U.S. interest in Latin America. In 1953 the president dispatched his brother to South America, attended a dinner for Latin American ambassadors, and spoke on Pan American Day at the OAS center in Washington. Eisenhower also considered creating a permanent position of special ambassador for Latin America and asking an influential citizen, like General Lucius Clay or John McCloy, to accept the position. Secretary Dulles persuaded Eisenhower to drop this proposal, however, pointing out that other regions of the world would feel slighted. But the State Department also tried to show that the United States was paying more attention to Latin America by inviting Latin Americans for visits, issuing commemorative stamps, and distributing movies that "would be particularly effective in getting our message to the illiterate masses."[21] Such efforts, Dulles told Eisenhower, were "a very good way of doing things," for "you have to pat them a little bit and make them think that you are fond of them."[22]

The administration coupled its "fondness" campaign with tough anti-Communist measures. Its information and cultural programs were aimed at alerting Latin Americans to "the dangers of Soviet imperialism and communist and other anti-U.S. subversion." The U.S. Information Agency spent about $5.2 million a year producing and distributing such items as 90,000 anti-Communist cartoon books for Central America, anti-Communist comic strips for over 300 Latin American newspapers, and scripts for twenty-six anti-Communist radio shows in Cuba. The administration also opened a 50,000-watt radio broadcast station in El Salvador, which in the State Department's view would be useful both for "overt propaganda and news" and "in the covert propaganda field as well."[23] In addition, the department tried to disrupt what it considered Communist-front conferences, such as youth festivals and student congresses. It asked all Latin American countries to deny visas and passports for travel to Communist-sponsored conferences, noting that under U.S. regulations the department "would not knowingly issue a passport to a United States national to attend one of these conferences." Most countries acceded to the U.S. request, although the large countries—

Argentina, Brazil, and Mexico—declined to issue new regulations, citing constitutional restrictions.[24]

The administration's anti-Communist offensive was also launched on the labor front. One of the objectives of NSC 144/1 was to encourage the development of the regional Inter-American Organization of Workers (ORIT), an anti-Communist trade-union movement in Latin America sponsored by the American Federation of Labor. Further, the United States opposed Peronist organizations and, in particular, the Confederation of Latin American Workers led by labor boss Lombardo Toledano, a political leftist from Mexico. The administration's policies included gathering information on the Latin American labor movement, inviting labor leaders to visit the United States, and investigating the backgrounds of union officials in plants that were to receive technical cooperation under the Point Four program. In implementing these policies, the State Department consulted with U.S. union officials, such as George Meany, the president of the American Federation, and Serafino Romualdi, the American Federation's chief organizer in Latin America. Meany assured department officers that his union's goal in Latin America was "to create friendship and support for the U.S. in opposition to the attempt of the Communists to seek the same support and friendship of Russia." Meany and others added, however, that their task of creating a democratic labor movement would be easier if the United States did not recognize dictatorships and if U.S. firms in Latin America established fair labor practices.[25] Nonetheless, State Department officials were impressed by the anti-Communist fervor of U.S. trade unions, and Assistant Secretary Cabot recommended to Dulles that "we be prepared to supplement the financial contributions of U.S. labor on a highly secret basis."[26]

In addition to sponsoring anti-Communist measures in Latin America the Eisenhower administration tried to arm the region, having accepted the assumptions inherent in NSC 56/2 and the military aid program developed by the Truman government. In 1953 and 1954, when administration witnesses appeared before Congress to ask for military aid for Latin America, they reiterated the arguments that the Truman government had used during the Korean War. They pointed out that the United States had assigned 100,000 troops to guard the Western Hemisphere during World War II—but if Latin America were properly armed, these U.S. troops could be assigned to other theaters of conflict. By providing arms, the United States could also exclude foreign military missions from Latin America. The witnesses assured members of Congress that these weapons would be used solely for hemispheric defense and that the United States was working on a multilateral basis with its southern neighbors in planning continental security.[27] Senators and representatives barely examined this testimony; instead, they accepted the underlying premise that the Soviet Union threatened the Americas.

President Eisenhower heartily backed military aid for Latin America. Recalling his efforts during the Truman years, the president told the NSC that he had "never wholly sympathized with the State Department view that munitions sent to Latin America would be used by the republics for hostilities against each other." Military aid was crucial because the United States needed Latin America's strategic materials and because "we can't defend South America if this Communist war starts."[28] But despite Eisenhower's strong views, the United States could not immediately deliver weapons to Latin America. By mid-1954, $105 million in military aid had been appropriated, but only $20 million in matériel had been shipped. Other regions, such as French Indochina, had a greater claim on U.S. military aid than did Latin America. When informed of the delay, Eisenhower in 1954 instructed the Department of Defense to "investigate the feasibility of accelerating deliveries of military equipment to the Latin American republics." But, although promising to expedite deliveries, the Joint Chiefs of Staff and defense officials resisted giving Latin America priority for U.S. military equipment. Their decision left Latin America, in the words of Undersecretary Smith, "at the bottom of the heap as far as military priorities were concerned."[29]

This decision suggested that fears of Soviet aggression against Latin America were exaggerated. Indeed, the activities of defense planners continually belied the need for inter-American military cooperation. Over 100,000 U.S. troops did serve in the Western Hemisphere during World War II—but virtually all of them were located in the Caribbean, guarding the Panama Canal. According to NSC 144/1, the United States would insist that Latin Americans continue to accept "U.S. military control of the defense of these areas." Moreover, although ostensibly part of a multilateral plan, military assistance agreements were bilateral pacts. The Inter-American Defense Board, which was composed of U.S. and Latin American military officers, had functioned since 1942; but the United States largely ignored the Defense Board, and the Board did not coordinate or supervise the bilateral agreements. In any case, by arming Western Europe, Japan, the Philippine Islands, and South Korea, the United States was moving its lines of defense far from the American continents.[30]

Whereas the strategic benefits of inter-American military cooperation may have been slight, the political advantages of military aid were significant. Training and assistance programs gave the Eisenhower administration access to the Latin American military caste. U.S. Army Chief of Staff J. Lawton Collins, in supporting military aid for Anastasio Somoza's Nicaragua, noted that "the Latin American officers who work with us and some of whom come to this country and see what we have and what we can do are frequently our most useful friends in those countries." Because military officers either ruled or dominated many Latin American nations, this friendship was essential. Ambassador to Paraguay George Shaw reported that the U.S. military mission lent prestige to the Paraguayan military establishment and demonstrated that "the United States is backing the government of Paraguay and the party in power, which remains in power largely because of the military." Ambassador to Venezuela Fletcher Warren advised Washington that the United States should sell sophisticated military equipment to dictator Marcos Peréz Jiménez because he had "broken diplomatic relations with the Soviet Russia and Czechoslovakia, and embarked upon the closest supervision of the activities of Communist front groups." Officials in Washington agreed that the primary purpose of military aid was to maintain "good U.S. military relations with the Latin American military," although they declined to say that publicly when defending aid programs.[31]

Along with military aid, the Eisenhower administration revived another initiative of the Truman government: the normalization of relations with Argentina. When the Republicans took control of the White House, it appeared that U.S.-Argentine relations would be as stormy as they had been during the Braden years. In his confirmation hearings, Dulles charged that there were Fascists in Argentina, although in his first nationwide address he softened that to fascism "in some quarters" in Latin America. And President Eisenhower actively disliked Juan Perón. Like most North Americans, Eisenhower probably still resented the pro-Nazi sympathies of Argentine military leaders during World War II. He told Dulles he did not want his brother to call on Perón, noting, "Why crawl on our knees to a man who kicks us in the teeth."[32] But a shift in President Perón's tactics and the imperatives of the administration's anti-Communist policies combined to soothe relations between the United States and Argentina.

By 1953 the Argentine economy was in disarray and Juan Perón was in political trouble. During the war, Argentina had accumulated substantial credits of $1.7 billion selling its beef and wheat to the Allies. In the immediate postwar years, Argentine products continued to command good prices in a hungry Europe. But Perón squandered this bonanza. In part, Argentina suffered the same fate as its neighbors: the capital goods it wanted to purchase for industrialization were scarce and dear in the early postwar period. This difficulty was compounded by some dubious economic strategies. In order to satisfy Argentine nationalists, Perón purchased Argentine railroads and public utilities owned by British and French investors. He generously compensated the Europeans for these facilities, many of which were in poor repair. But spending on capital goods and utilities meant there was little money left for agricultural modernization, and the heart of the Argentine economy began to deteriorate. Moreover, under the direction of Perón's energetic wife, Eva, Argentina began to build an impressive social welfare state for the Argentine poor or *descamisados*. But by 1952, when beef and wheat prices began to decay, Argentina could no longer afford to finance these ambitious projects. Perón responded by inflating the currency, and the cost of living rose wildly. The problem, as the Economic Commission for Latin America reported, was that "Argentina has sought to increase consumption without sufficiently increasing its production."[33]

Perón looked to the United States for help. Soon after Eisenhower took office, Perón called in the U.S. ambassador, Albert Nufer, and informed him that he wanted to improve relations with the United States, blaming all past tensions on the Truman administration. He followed that by loosening controls on the independent press and by ordering his press organs to limit anti-American attacks and to increase attacks on Communists. He also relaxed restrictions on U.S. investments in Argentina and even suggested that he would welcome foreign investment in Argentine petroleum (although opposition to foreign participation in oil exploitation was a cherished principle of Argentine nationalists).[34] In response to these initiatives, Secretary Dulles gained Eisenhower's reluctant permission to allow Dr. Eisenhower to stop in Buenos Aires in July 1953, during his tour of South America. Perón feted Milton Eisenhower and won his friendship. Thereafter, Perón frequently wrote to the president's brother. Dr. Eisenhower, in turn, accepted Perón's conversion to anticommunism and emphasized to the president that "it would be a serious mistake not to capitalize on President Perón's attitude and offer."[35]

President Eisenhower remained suspicious of Perón, writing Dulles in late 1953 that he wondered whether "the man has really reformed." Dulles agreed that Perón could be a more fervent anti-Communist. Argentina refused to accept the administration's contention that communism in Guatemala was a dire threat to hemispheric security. Dulles also disliked Argentina's 1953 trade treaty with the Soviet Union, although he knew that the hard-pressed Argentines were looking for new markets for their agricultural products. But he concluded that it was "of the greatest importance" to take advantage of Perón's new orientation in order to "develop a sound basis of solidarity with the Argentine Government to prevent its becoming a possible communist threat to inter-American security and solidarity." The Secretary of State probably agreed with intelligence reports that the Perón regime was stable and that there was "little chance that Perón will be ousted by an armed forces coup."[36]

The handling of relations with Perón's Argentina represents one of the few episodes in inter-American relations during the 1950s when Secretary Dulles seems to have overawed the president. By the end of 1954, the United States had sold Argentina a government-owned rolling mill for the production of steel, had agreed to loan $60 million through the Export-Import Bank to help build a new steel mill, and had begun to consider including Argentina in its military assistance program.[37] These efforts to curry favor with Perón gained little, however, for U.S. diplomacy. The Argentine economy continued to flounder and the Perón regime began to disintegrate in early 1955. United States intelligence analysts had badly misinterpreted the Argentine political milieu; Argentine military officers overthrew Perón in September 1955.

During its first two years in office, then, the Eisenhower administration employed a variety of measures to combat communism in the Americas. What was not in its anti-Communist arsenal, however, was a policy to promote democracy and human rights in Latin America. NSC 144/1 had not, of course, listed democracy as an objective of U.S. policy. Perhaps administration officials worried little about such issues because they had been comforted by Milton Eisenhower's optimistic assessment of political developments in the region. Dr. Eisenhower, after returning from South America, reported to his brother that "most American nations which still have degrees of feudalism and dictatorship are moving gradually toward democratic concepts and practices"—a surprisingly inaccurate prediction, for by 1954 dictators were firmly ensconced in power in thirteen of the twenty Latin American nations.[38] In any case, administration officials believed that to raise human-rights issues would constitute "intervention." For example, President Eisenhower suggested testing Perón's sincerity by urging freedom of the press; Secretary Dulles rejected the president's idea, however, arguing that if the United States spoke on behalf of the distinguished newspaper *La Prensa* it would upset Perón and violate "our policy and commitments against intervention in the internal affairs of the other American nations." Labeling it "an internal Venezuelan matter," Assistant Secretary Cabot similarly turned away appeals from U.S. citizens who wanted the State Department to intercede on behalf of the political prisoners rotting in the dungeons of Pérez Jiménez. On the other hand, the State Department pandered to Pérez Jiménez by harassing and threatening to revoke the political asylum of the exiled democrat Rómulo Betancourt.[39]

Communists, not dictators, were the enemies of the United States. Indeed, the Eisenhower administration fawned over some of Latin America's most unsavory tyrants. The president awarded a Legion of Merit, the nation's highest honor for foreign personages, to both Manuel Odría, the military dictator of Peru, and Pérez Jiménez. Both men had earned Washington's gratitude by dutifully following the anti-Communist line. The Venezuelan, for example, received his medal in October 1954 in a grand ceremony conducted by U.S. Ambassador Fletcher Warren. The award's announcement cited the dictator's "indefatigable energy and firmness of purpose" for having "greatly increased the capacity of the Armed Forces of Venezuela to participate in the collective defense of the Western Hemisphere," as well as noting that "his constant concern toward the problem of Communist infiltration has kept his government alert to repel the threat existing against his country and the rest of the Americas."[40] To be sure, the administration did not prefer dictators over democrats. As U.S. Ambassador to the OAS John Dreier later recalled, Secretary Dulles would have been happy to see "flourishing little democracies" in Latin America, but "I think that he was somewhat inclined to feel that governments which contributed to a stability in the area were preferable to those which introduced instability and social upheaval, which would lead to Communist penetration."

Dulles, therefore, was "very tolerant" of dictatorships, "as long as they took a firm stand against communism."[41] José Figueres, the popularly elected president of Costa Rica, was less charitable, however, when, in reviewing inter-American relations in the 1950s, he charged that "our main enemy was Mr. John Foster Dulles in his defending corrupt dictatorships."[42]

President Eisenhower and his advisors based these policies on national security grounds. But their fears about Soviet imperialism in the Western Hemisphere were derived more from inference and analogies from other areas of the world than from dispassionate analyses. Communism did not seem to threaten Latin America any more then than it had in 1948, when the Truman administration, in NSC 16, concluded that communism in Latin America was only a "potential danger." For example, in September 1953 Assistant Secretary Cabot responded to an NSC inquiry about communism in the hemisphere. He conceded that the major source of friction in inter-American relations was not the machinations of the Soviet Union but rather the intense resentment Latin Americans felt about the absence of a Marshall Plan for them. Latin Americans, including political radicals, were absorbed with domestic, not international, problems. As Cabot told the NSC, "we must remember that many of them are essentially native Communists."[43] Soviet economic influence in the hemisphere continued to be similarly minimal. Russia's only trading partners in the hemisphere were Argentina and Uruguay. Russia badly needed their beef, wheat, and wool but had few valuable goods, except petroleum, to sell in return; the bilateral balance of trade favored the Latin Americans. In any case, the trade was small, amounting to only 2.5 percent of the value of Argentina's exports in 1953. Argentina and Uruguay traded with the Soviets because the hemisphere's wealthiest nations, Canada and the United States, did not need their products, for they also produced abundant quantities of beef, wheat, and wool.[44] In sum, the Eisenhower administration, in fearing a Communist conspiracy in Latin America, had injected global concerns into what were purely regional affairs.

By 1954, the Eisenhower administration had made anticommunism the central feature of the Latin American policy of the United States. In doing this, it was retaining policies first adopted during the Truman years. But what distinguished its policies from those of the previous administration was the Eisenhower administration's unabashed embrace of anti-Communist military dictatorships and its unwillingness to criticize, however mutedly, rampant political and civil repression in Latin America.[45] Moreover, it confided to itself that it was prepared to repudiate solemn treaty commitments and intervene unilaterally in Latin America. The administration's next assignment was to wring an anti-Communist resolution out of Latin Americans as diplomatic cover for its campaign to overthrow the government of Jacobo Arbenz of Guatemala.

CHAPTER 3

INTERVENTION IN GUATEMALA

1953–1954

The Eisenhower administration wanted Latin Americans to understand that the cold war was the essential feature of international relations in the postwar world. As mature, responsible members of the world community, Latin American nations needed to defer to U.S. leadership in the momentous confrontation with the Soviet Union and to cooperate with the United States in safeguarding the hemisphere against Communist aggression. In the view of the administration, the inter-American system had to become an anti-Communist alliance. The United States tried to codify that view in 1954 when it obtained Latin American assent to an anti-Communist manifesto, the Declaration of Caracas. Latin Americans refused, however, to apply the Caracas resolution to the internal affairs of individual countries. Judging Latin American behavior irresponsible, the Eisenhower administration then decided to intervene unilaterally to help overthrow what it thought to be a Communist-dominated government in Guatemala.

President Eisenhower and his advisors worried that Communists had penetrated the political and social institutions of every Latin American nation. But, in 1953 and 1954, they especially feared that agents directed by the Soviet Union planned to subvert Guatemala and to turn it into an advance base for Soviet imperialism in the Western Hemisphere. The administration believed that what had started as a middle-class reform effort had been transformed into a radical political movement that threatened U.S. strategic and commercial interests both in Guatemala and throughout the hemisphere.

Guatemala had a history characterized by political repression and economic stagnation. During the nation's first century of independence, personalist leaders—*caudillos*—held sway. One of the most arbitrary and excessive was Jorge Ubico, the strong-man who tyrannized Guatemala between 1931 and 1944. A military careerist from an aristocratic family, Ubico ruled on behalf of social and economic elites. The dictator brutally repressed Guatemalans who proposed reforming the hierarchical social structure. His penal code, for example, recommended the death penalty for anyone found guilty of union organizing. He also issued deceptive vagrancy regulations that forced the rural poor, many of them Mayan Indians, to labor on public works projects. In addition to being a dictator, Ubico was a bizarre and unstable man. He was intensely suspicious and paranoid and had a ferocious temper. He fancied himself another Napoleon, and he pompously strutted around the country in ostentatious uniforms.[1]

Ubico and his military henchman fled Guatemala in the aftermath of mass uprisings in the summer and fall of 1944. The urban middle sectors—schoolteachers, shopkeepers, students, lawyers, and junior military officers—marched, demonstrated, and refused to work. What they wanted was a modern, socially enlightened Guatemala. Like other Latin Americans, they had been inspired by the democratic goals of World War II, as set forth in such documents as the Atlantic Charter. They also envied the progress made by their neighbors to the north. President Franklin Roosevelt had developed a social welfare state in the United States with his New Deal programs. In Mexico, President Lázaro Cárdenas (1934–40) had implemented the Constitution of 1917, redistributing land, nationalizing the foreign-owned oil companies, and empowering labor; with these nationalist actions, Cárdenas had created the conditions for a generation of remarkable economic growth and development in Mexico.[2]

After the flight of Ubico, Juan José Arévalo became the new leader of Guatemala. In 1945, in a fair election, albeit one that was limited to literate males, Arévalo captured more than 85 percent of the vote. The new president was a university teacher who, as an opponent of the Ubico regime, had been in exile since 1935 at the University of Tucumán in Argentina. When he returned, he found an impoverished country. The annual per capita income of agricultural workers—the majority of the population—was less than $100. Approximately 2 percent of the population owned 70 percent of the arable land. Only one-quarter of the land that comprised these vast plantations, or *latifundias*, was under cultivation. The economy was barely industrialized. Seventy percent of the population was illiterate. Among Indians, who constituted about half of the population, illiteracy rates approached 90 percent.[3]

Promising democracy and reform, President Arévalo set about to transform his nation. He extended the franchise to all adult Guatemalans. He abolished forced labor and the vagrancy laws and promulgated a labor code that sanctioned minimum wages and collective bargaining; agricultural wages subsequently rose from less than 25 cents a day to nearly 80 cents a day. He restricted the growth of *latifundias* and redistributed the land confiscated from Germans during the war. And he established a social security agency and a national planning and development ministry and launched a literacy campaign. Such measures outraged the landed elite, the traditional arbiters of Guatemalan life. During his six-year term, President Arévalo survived more than twenty attempts to overthrow him.[4]

The first peaceful transition of power in Guatemalan history took place in March 1951 when Jacobo Arbenz Guzmán assumed the presidency. In November 1950 Arbenz had garnered over 60 percent of the vote, defeating two conservative candidates. The thirty-seven-year-old president was a graduate of Guatemala's military academy who had participated in the overthrow of the Ubico regime and served as minister of defense under Arévalo. A striking, athletic man, Arbenz was married to the dynamic María Vilanova, the daughter of a wealthy plantation-owner from El Salvador. Appalled at the treatment of the rural poor in El Salvador, María Arbenz resigned her role as a member of high society and committed herself to social activism. In her beauty, concern for the poor, and influence with her husband, she reminded many of Eva Perón.[5]

President Arbenz accelerated the pace of change in Guatemala. In his inaugural address, he pledged to create an economically independent, modern, capitalist state. He set about to upgrade the economic infrastructure of the country, building ports and highways. He convinced the legislature to enact a modest income tax, the first in Guatemalan history. But the centerpiece of his program was agrarian reform. He believed that the inequitable distribution of land was the source of Guatemala's backwardness and the greatest barrier to social and economic development. In mid-1952, the legislature enacted a comprehensive agrarian reform bill that empowered the government to expropriate uncultivated portions of *latifundias* and redistribute the land; landowners would be compensated with interest-bearing Guatemalan bonds. Between 1952 and 1954, the Arbenz administration distributed 1.5 million acres of land to 100,000 families. Ironically, even the Arbenz family forfeited land to agrarian reform: the state expropriated 1,700 fallow acres owned by the president and his wife.[6]

The socioeconomic changes that the Arévalo and Arbenz administrations pursued were not outside the boundaries set by twentieth-century reform movements in the West. Guatemala's new social welfare programs were more modest than those advocated by liberal Democrats in the United States and Laborites in Great Britain. The agrarian reform legislation of 1952 was sweeping in its effect, but it was also intricate and a rational response to Guatemalan conditions: it left untouched, for example, estates of up to 670 acres, if at least two-thirds of the land was cultivated; moreover, as appropriate for a mountainous nation, it exempted lands that had a slope of more than 30 degrees. The law, like the nineteenth-century Homestead Act of the United States, was designed to create a nation of individual landowners; the allocated land went mainly to individual families rather than to cooperatives. Agrarian reform in Guatemala was thus more moderate than that pursued by President Cárdenas in Mexico. Indeed, the administrators of the Alliance for Progress program of the 1960s probably would have looked favorably upon the agrarian reform in Guatemala.[7]

The process and pattern of change in Guatemala seemed, however, to threaten the commercial and strategic interests of the United States. The largest landowner in Guatemala, and the country's chief private employer, was the banana-producing United Fruit Company of Boston, Massachusetts. United Fruit, which had operated in Guatemala since the late nineteenth century, had always been linked with the social and economic elite of Guatemala. It had been, for example, an ally of the Ubico regime; in return, it had received from the dictator vast tracts of land and generous tax concessions. As did privileged Guatemalans, United Fruit resisted change. During the Arévalo administration, it engaged in a series of stormy confrontations with its Guatemalan workers, who were trying to exercise their new right of collective bargaining. It also saw its domination of the Guatemalan economy challenged by the port and highway construction projects of President Arbenz: United Fruit owned virtually all of the railroad tracks in Guatemala and controlled Puerto Barrios, the country's major Atlantic port.[8]

But United Fruit particularly opposed agrarian reform. The company owned 550,000 acres of land, 85 percent of which was uncultivated. It argued that it needed vast reserves for crop rotation and soil conservation and as insurance against disastrous hurricanes. The government dismissed these arguments, treating United Fruit like any other landed oligarch. Between 1952 and 1954, the government expropriated nearly 400,000 acres of land. Following the law, it offered approximately $3 an acre for the land as compensation, in the form of guaranteed twenty-five-year bonds bearing 3 percent annual interest. The government had arrived at the $3-an-acre figure by taking United Fruit's declaration of the value of the land for taxable purposes; United Fruit rejected this valuation, claiming that the land was worth at least $75 an acre.[9]

The Eisenhower administration vigorously backed United Fruit's claim. Between 1953 and 1954, the State Department submitted a series of sharp notes to Guatemalan officials. The United States did not consider deferred payment in the form of agrarian bonds as constituting prompt and effective compensation to the company. It also held that the amount of compensation offered was inadequate under well-established principles of international law. It requested that Guatemala negotiate directly with the company or the U.S. government or submit the dispute to international arbitration. In April 1954 the State Department, on behalf of United Fruit, handed the Guatemalans a bill for $15,854,849 for the first 200,000 acres of land expropriated;[10] this was the largest claim submitted to a foreign government by the United States since 1938, when the State Department demanded that Mexico compensate U.S. oil companies for their expropriated properties.

In entering the dispute, the Eisenhower administration believed that it was dealing, not with misguided, irresponsible nationalists, but with ruthless agents of international communism. However, Guatemala's revolution of 1944 had been a spontaneous and indigenous movement of the frustrated urban middle sectors; the only foreign intrusion had been the political ideas of the West, such as freedom of association. Both the Arévalo and Arbenz governments permitted political radicals, including Communists, to organize— but in March 1952, U.S. intelligence officials calculated there were only 500 members of the Guatemalan Communist party, "of whom perhaps one-third are militants," and the next year, the Eisenhower administration estimated Communist strength at "no more than 1,000 members." And yet, despite these small numbers, both the Truman and Eisenhower administrations believed that Communists wielded significant influence in Guatemala. Party members were active in organizing labor and in the agrarian reform movement. President Arbenz accepted the support of Guatemalan Communists and consulted with José Manuel Fortuny, a Communist party official. Another influential Communist, labor organizer Víctor Manuel Gutiérrez, visited Soviet-bloc nations.[11]

Communists did not, however, dominate Guatemala. President Arbenz's ruling coalition in the Guatemalan Congress consisted of 51 deputies, of whom only four were Communists. He did not appoint any Communists to his cabinet, and he did not permit Communists in key departments such as the military, the police, and the foreign ministry. Furthermore, Guatemala did not exchange diplomatic representatives with the Soviet Union, and both Arévalo and Arbenz consistently supported U.S. positions at the United Nations on issues such as the Korean conflict. Moreover, the government retained U.S. military missions. And, even with the expropriation of United Fruit's uncultivated lands, the Guatemalan economy remained tied to the United States: Guatemala sent over 80 percent of its exports to the north.[12]

Both the Truman and Eisenhower administrations repeatedly instructed Guatemalan leaders to sever all relationships with Guatemalan Communists. In January 1954, for example, President Eisenhower informed Foreign Minister Guillermo Toriello that, because the United States was "determined to block the international communist conspiracy," he "couldn't help a government which was openly playing ball with communists." The Guatemalans replied that Guatemala was a democratic country, that Communists could be controlled best in the open, and that their reforms, like the redistribution of land, would undermine the appeal of communism. As they saw it, the key issue between the United States and Guatemala was not communism but the recalcitrance of United Fruit. The Eisenhower administration rejected these explanations, deciding that President Arbenz was either a Communist "dupe" or worse. As Ambassador to Guatemala John Peurifoy put it, after his first conversation with Arbenz, "if the president is not a Communist he will certainly do until one comes along."[13]

Although President Eisenhower and his closest advisors were certain that "Guatemalan Communists are in fact disciplined agents of international Communism, preaching authentic Soviet-dictated doctrine,"[14] some U.S. officials were willing to venture that President Arbenz was a political pragmatist, not an ideologue. Arbenz was threatened by the same powerful groups who had plotted against President Arévalo. In August 1953, the Bureau of Inter-American

Affairs of the State Department noted, in a draft paper prepared for the NSC, that "it is possible that President Arbenz thinks of the Communists in Guatemala only as reformers and useful allies rather than as Soviet agents." Because none of the traditional propertied groups supported him, Arbenz "is probably unwilling to repudiate the Communists and risk the loss of much of his organized political backing." In any case, Arbenz could legitimately claim that his Communist supporters were loyal Guatemalans. The Bureau of Inter-American Affairs found that, "almost without exception," Guatemalan Communists were "indigenous to the area and are Mexico-trained rather than Moscow-trained, although some have visited the Soviet orbit and may have received brief instruction there."[15]

The Eisenhower administration did not distinguish between Latin American Communists, and it pressured President Arbenz to repudiate his Communist allies. In doing so, the administration went beyond the policies of the Truman government. Between 1945 and 1951, the State Department had been befuddled, even mystified, by President Arévalo, his reforms, and his talk of democracy, capitalism, and "spiritual socialism." In 1951, however, Assistant Secretary Edward Miller confidently predicted that the pace of change in Guatemala would slow with the ascendancy of Jacobo Arbenz, for the new president was wealthy and owned coffee plantations.[16] When Arbenz declined to denounce Guatemalan Communists or restore the holdings of United Fruit, the department decided on an approach that would be diplomatically correct but chilly. Without actually threatening Guatemala, the department refused to help Guatemala complete the inter-American highway and to approve the sale of arms to the Guatemalan military. The objective, in the words of Ambassador to Guatemala Rudolf E. Schoenfeld, was "to bring Guatemalans to the realization that they were dependent upon the United States and that if they expected assistance or consideration from the United States it behooved them to adjust their actions vis-à-vis the United States accordingly."[17]

Evidence has appeared—which is both hazy and incomplete—that in the summer of 1952 President Truman discussed and perhaps approved a plan developed by CIA Director Walter Bedell Smith to foment revolution in Guatemala: the United States would clandestinely arm anti-Arbenz Guatemalans, using dictator Anastasio Somoza of Nicaragua as a conduit.[18] But however accurate the account of this plot may be, the Truman administration did not try to overthrow President Arbenz. Department of State officers Dean Acheson, Undersecretary David K. E. Bruce, and Miller flatly opposed intervention and were able to waylay whatever plans existed to arm rebels. In April 1950 Secretary Miller, in pronouncing his "Miller Doctrine," had raised questions about the U.S. commitment to nonintervention in the face of Communist aggression in the hemisphere. But, at least through January 1953, the policy of the United States remained that it "could never condone military intervention on the part of an American State against one of its neighbors."[19]

Because the Truman administration's policy of persuasion and pressure showed, in Ambassador Peurifoy's view, the "inadequacy of normal diplomatic procedures," the Eisenhower administration decided on sterner measures to demonstrate to the Guatemalans their dependence on the United States. Beginning in late 1953, the Department of State began a campaign to convince the other nineteen Latin American nations of the threat that Guatemala posed to their security. Simultaneously, President Eisenhower and his most trusted aides secretly developed a plan to destabilize and overthrow Jacobo Arbenz. They prepared to try, in the words of the Bureau of Inter-American Affairs, "a Czechoslovakia in reverse in Guatemala."[20]

The Tenth Inter-American Conference, which was held in Caracas, Venezuela, between 1 March and 28 March 1954, was intended to focus on economic issues. As they had since the middle of World War II, Latin Americans wanted to discuss with the United States terms of trade, commodity agreements, and economic aid—and the Eisenhower administration answered with the familiar argument that cold-war concerns took priority over inter-American economic cooperation. But now the United States attached a special urgency to its position, for the cold war had come to the Americas.

In late 1953, responding to U.S. pressure, the OAS planning committee had placed an anti-Communist resolution on the agenda for the Caracas conference. The United States wanted the American republics to agree that "the domination or control of the political institutions of any American state by the international communist movement . . . would constitute a threat" to the entire hemisphere and would require "appropriate action in accordance with existing treaties." The appropriate treaty would be, in the U.S. view, the Rio Treaty of 1947, which allowed in Article 6 for the OAS to take action if two-thirds of the member states agreed that the political independence of another member was threatened by "an aggression which was not an armed attack"; the OAS could then decide to impose economic sanctions or to sponsor a collective intervention. What the United States wanted, in John Foster Dulles's words, was to extend "the Monroe Doctrine to include the concept of outlawing foreign ideologies in the American Republics."[21]

By expanding the definition of the Monroe Doctrine, the Eisenhower administration also hoped to prove to Latin Americans that nationalism and communism did not mix. As explained by Secretary Cabot, the U.S. position was that communism was international in scope, that it was directed by Moscow, and that it constituted intervention in the internal affairs of Latin American states. A Guatemalan Communist by definition was a subversive, not a nationalist reformer. Indeed, the United States wanted Latin Americans not merely to "regulate" travel by Communists but to "prevent" it. The legal niceties of suspecting people of subversive acts or proving criminal intent were irrelevant; "it is our position that anyone traveling in the interests of communism is in fact part of the whole subversive program of international communism."[22]

Latin Americans would not only receive at Caracas an education about communism but would also be tested on their hostility to it. In NSC 144/1, the Eisenhower administration questioned whether the United States could be bound by the OAS charter in the midst of cold war. On the eve of the Caracas conference, Undersecretary Walter Bedell Smith reiterated that problem to U.S. diplomats in Latin America. By subscribing to the nonintervention pledge, the most powerful nation in the OAS had "limited its freedom of action" and "given to the relatively weak Latin American states an important voice in determining steps for the protection of U.S. security interests." The United States would now find out if the relationship was a "useful and effective one." If Latin Americans did not support the U.S. resolution on communism, then "some question must be raised regarding the soundness of the OAS relationship." Smith instructed officers to use this information as background in opposing any suggestion from Latin American governments that the United States engage in "horsetrading," exchanging economic concessions for the anti-Communist resolution.[23]

But, before it could test Latin Americans, the administration had to decide whether anticommunism and democracy could coexist. Journalists in both the United States and Latin America pointed out that the anti-Communist conference was to be held in the capital city of Venezuela, the home of the sordid dictator Marcos Pérez Jiménez. Costa Rica, democratic and anti-Communist, would refuse to attend. Moreover, at previous inter-American conferences, anti-Communist resolutions had been tied to denunciations of other totalitarian movements. The Truman administration had declined to back a strictly anti-Communist resolution, predicting that rightist dictators would use it to repress legitimate opposition and tag all reform as "communism."[24] The Eisenhower administration admitted to itself that dictators might misuse the Caracas resolution. It also did not want U.S. policy to be identified with "entrenched, authoritarian governments." But Latin Americans had to concentrate on the Communist conspiracy in Guatemala. The administration opposed putting human rights issues on the agenda, fearing that it would "precipitate a sharp cleavage at the conference between governments having various degrees of political control." And it vowed not to permit democratic governments "who do not have a sufficient appreciation for the dangers of communism" to control the conference.[25]

On the surface, the Caracas conference went well for the administration, and the OAS passed Undersecretary Smith's test. The U.S. delegation, led by Secretary Dulles, fervently pressed the anti-Communist case and, after two weeks of debate, the resolution carried by a vote of 17–1–2. Only Guatemala opposed the resolution; Argentina and Mexico abstained. Guatemala's lone opposition underscored the administration's contention of Communist penetration and proved to be a powerful propaganda point for the United States. The U.S. Information Agency produced a documentary film on the conference and distributed it throughout Latin America. Secretary Dulles publicly proclaimed that the Monroe Doctrine had become a multilateral pact. President Eisenhower applauded the resolution, claiming in his memoirs that the resolution justified U.S. military support for anti-Communist Guatemalans.[26]

Privately, the administration understood that the meaning of Caracas was that the United States could never convince Latin Americans to boycott or invade Guatemala. Secretary Dulles, a skilled international lawyer and debater, met his match in Guatemalan Foreign Minister Guillermo Toriello. In a stirring address, Toriello averred that the issue was United Fruit, not communism. The United States "wanted to find a ready expedient to maintain the economic dependence of the American Republics and suppress the legitimate desires of the peoples, cataloguing as 'communism' every manifestation of nationalism or economic independence, any desire for social progress, any intellectual curiosity, and any interest in progressive and liberal reforms." Latin American delegates warmly applauded his speech.[27] A stunned Dulles counterattacked by "horsetrading." After urgent consultations with the president and the cabinet, Dulles assured delegates that the administration would fight any congressional move to restrict their exports to the United States and would consider expanding the lending authority of the Export-Import Bank. He also promised to schedule the long-delayed economic conference.[28]

Even with these concessions, Dulles had to labor to secure his anti-Communist manifesto. Latin Americans, led by representatives from Argentina, Mexico, and Uruguay, offered fifty-one amendments designed to weaken the resolution. Dulles was able to fend off fifty of the amendments, defeating many of them by votes of 11 to 9. His allies were the Caribbean and South American dictators, something Dulles confessed in executive congressional testimony "was sometimes a bit embarrassing." Dulles was particularly troubled by Mexico's abstention on the final resolution. Foreign Minister Luís Padilla Nervo defended Guatemala, telling Dulles, "I remember the time when Mexico stood alone and we were going through an economic and social reform, a revolution, and if at that moment you had called a meeting of the American States to judge us, probably we would have been found guilty of some subjection to foreign influences." Dulles wildly concluded that Mexico's position was due to "a real infiltration of Communist, or fellow traveller influence into the Mexican Government itself."[29]

Although Dulles obtained his resolution, it lacked, in his word, "vitality." The one amendment that carried seriously weakened the resolution, for, instead of calling for immediate action, it merely recommended that the American states meet to consider the adoption of measures in accordance with existing treaties. In short, the Latin Americans rejected the administration's contention that communism in Latin America constituted external aggression. Moreover, all of the approving countries, except the dictatorships in the Dominican Republic, El Salvador, Nicaragua, Peru, and Venezuela, specified that their approval was based on the understanding that the resolution would not justify unilateral or collective intervention and that it "did not impair the inalienable right of each American state freely to choose its own form of government and economic system." Returning to their original thesis that Latin America needed a Marshall Plan, the Latin Americans also resolved that the most effective way to undermine the appeal of communism was through social and economic progress.[30] Reviewing the results of Caracas, the Department of State told the NSC that, although a substantial majority of Latin American states opposed international communism, they were not willing to transfer their opposition "to the specific threat inherent in the Guatemalan situation." Louis Halle, of the State Department's Policy Planning Staff, opined that the message of Caracas was "that there was more fear of U.S. interventionism than of Guatemalan communism."[31]

The allegiance of Latin America to the nonintervention principle became even more apparent as the Guatemalan crisis intensified. On 10 May 1954 Dulles instructed State Department officials to prepare a case against Guatemala to present to the OAS. Five days later, the U.S. case seemed strengthened when Guatemala received a shipment of arms from Soviet-dominated Czechoslovakia. The United States proposed that the OAS condemn Guatemala and resolve to detain and inspect all ships bound for Guatemala. But, in a straw vote, the State Department found it could count on only eleven Latin American votes, which was short of the two-thirds majority necessary for collective action under the Rio Treaty. Of the popularly elected governments, only Costa Rica and Bolivia firmly endorsed the U.S. proposal, and both countries had been offered U.S. aid to induce their support.[32] The Eisenhower administration particularly wanted Uruguay's vote and proposed that the consultative meeting be held in Montevideo. Uruguay, in President Eisenhower's view, "was the outstanding democracy in South America"; Dulles agreed that "we needed support from others than the Somozas in the hemisphere." But the sturdiest democracy in Latin America could be neither bought nor persuaded to relinquish its commitment to the nonintervention principle.[33]

On 26 June 1954, one day before Jacobo Arbenz fell from power, the United States and ten Latin American states requested an emergency meeting of foreign ministers to consult on Guatemala. The Eisenhower administration invoked Article 51 of the U.N. charter, deciding that the OAS was more responsive to U.S. power than was the Security Council. Guatemala had complained to the Security Council that outside forces based in Nicaragua and Honduras were invading its territory and had received a sympathetic hearing from three permanent members: the Soviet Union, France, and the United Kingdom. Because the Arbenz government was overthrown, the OAS meeting, which had been scheduled for Rio de Janeiro on 7 July, was cancelled on 2 July[34]—but if the OAS had met, it probably would have been an unpleasant experience for the administration. After agreeing to schedule a meeting, the ambassadors to the OAS debated the agenda. Argentina and Uruguay proposed that the foreign ministers consider not just the issue of communism in Guatemala but also "all" interventions that "may interfere with the political, economic, or military sovereignty of any state." The proposal was defeated by a vote of 7–5–8. Only Cuba, El Salvador, Honduras, Paraguay, Peru, and Venezuela—all right-wing dictatorships—voted with the United States. Nevertheless, if the Rio meeting had been held, the United States, as much as Guatemala, would have been on trial.[35]

Based on available evidence, it cannot be determined that the Eisenhower administration listed collective security as an option ahead of unilateral intervention. That is, President Eisenhower did not issue an order to intervene covertly in Guatemala solely because Latin Americans declined to back the United States. The administration had been plotting against President Arbenz since perhaps late 1953. In part, the Caracas resolution was designed to be diplomatic cover and a propaganda tool, to serve, as Eisenhower put it, as a "charter for the anti-Communist counterattack that followed." The Caracas resolution might also, Secretary Dulles circumspectly told his brother Allen Dulles, "make other things more natural."[36] Yet, beginning in March 1953 with NSC 144/1, the administration sharply questioned whether Latin America could be counted on to wage cold war. The Guatemalan imbroglio demonstrated that the influential, more democratic Latin American nations cherished the nonintervention principle and that they did not subscribe to the U.S. version of a monolithic, international Communist conspiracy. Covert intervention offered convenient solutions to both problems: it would eliminate the Arbenz government and preserve the appearance of nonintervention. Thereafter, the administration would promise itself that it would no longer be bound by the OAS charter when it came to communism in Latin America.

The story of how the Eisenhower administration overthrew the Arbenz government has been well told elsewhere, and only the essential details need be recited here for clarity.[37] During the latter part of 1953, President Eisenhower ordered the CIA to organize a program to undermine the Arbenz government. The president had become fascinated with the efficiency and sophistication of intelligence agents and covert operations. During World War II, he had particularly admired how British agents, in the project code-named "ULTRA," had cracked German secret codes.[38] In the summer of 1953, Eisenhower asked eighteen national security officials to convene for six weeks to establish strategy for confronting the Soviet Union. The conference was tagged "Operation Solarium" for the location, a small penthouse on the White House roof where Eisenhower had earlier approved the idea for a study conference. Eisenhower accepted as one of the recommendations of the "New Basic Concept" that the United States "take selective aggressive actions of a limited scope, involving moderately increased risks of general war, to eliminate Soviet-dominated areas within the free world and to reduce Soviet power in the satellite periphery."[39] The first application of the new strategy came in August 1953 with "AJAX," a masterful and subtle operation commanded by CIA agent Kermit Roosevelt: Roosevelt engineered the overthrow of Prime Minister Mohammed Mossadegh of Iran, a leader who, like Arbenz, had accepted the support of local Communists. Roosevelt's "countercoup" helped the pro-American Shah Reza Pahlavi reclaim his peacock throne.[40]

PBSUCCESS was the code name for the CIA operation in Guatemala. As he did with other covert operations, Eisenhower confined knowledge of the conspiracy to his closest advisors. Probably only the president, the Dulles brothers, Undersecretary Smith, and Special Assistant for National Security Affairs Robert Cutler were intimately aware of all the details. Communications from the CIA were classified "top-secret Ita," a unique classification that permitted a document to be read only by those stipulated on the heading; the documents were then destroyed. Eisenhower probably controlled the operation through oral communications with Secretary Dulles. Eisenhower revealed, of course, in his memoirs that once the coup began he approved the shipment of two P-51 fighter-bombers to the Guatemalan rebels.[41]

The administration and the CIA concentrated on turning the Guatemalan military against President Arbenz. Officials always recognized that "the Army is the only organized element in Guatemala capable of rapidly and decisively altering the political situation." Yet, the army was loyal to Arbenz and would act only if they felt threatened by Communists or if "the policies of the Government were to result in extreme social disorder and economic collapse."[42] Accordingly, the administration tried to demoralize the Guatemalan military. It proceeded on the assumption that "the implicit emphasis of Guatemala's ineligibility to receive grant assistance, in the face of tangible assistance to neighboring states, would help establish a political climate in Guatemala of benefit to anti-communist Guatemalan elements, including elements of the Guatemalan armed forces disposed to combat communist domination of the present Guatemalan government." Therefore, between 1953 and 1954 the administration refused to sell Guatemala arms, and it pressured European allies to bar commercial sales to Guatemala. On the other hand, it armed Guatemala's neighbors, Honduras and Nicaragua. By detaining and inspecting Guatemalan ships, it also hoped to generate economic chaos in the nation and induce the army to intervene. CIA agents and Ambassador John Peurifoy and his staff probably also secretly lobbied top officers to plot against Arbenz.[43]

The actual "invasion" of Guatemala began on 18 June 1954 when the forces of Lieutenant Colonel Carlos Castillo Armas, an army officer in exile, crossed the border from Honduras. Castillo Armas and his band of less than 200 men had been recruited and trained by the CIA. The CIA knew that the rebels could hardly hope to defeat Central America's largest army and they did little fighting—the foray was, as CIA Director Dulles reported to Eisenhower, "more dependent upon psychological impact rather than actual military strength." Castillo Armas needed only to "create and maintain for a short time the *impression* of very substantial military strength." The CIA supplemented the invasion with the massive and clever use of radio broadcasting from Honduras that gave panic-stricken Guatemalans the impression that fighting was intense and widespread. The CIA added to the hysteria by having its pilots, who were stationed in Nicaragua, bomb the capital city; the intelligence agency easily controlled the air, because the Guatemalan air force consisted of six antiquated airplanes.[44]

The Guatemalan army initially refused to act, unwilling to defend President Arbenz but unimpressed by Castillo Armas's invasion. The CIA air-strikes, however, seem to have convinced the top officers that the United States was determined to oust their president. Arbenz was badly shaken by the psychological offensive and the bombings and began to drink heavily. He also probably concluded that Eisenhower was prepared to escalate the violence if he did not resign. He turned over control of the government to a military junta on 27 June 1954; he would spend the rest of his life in dismal exile. Over the next week, military officers wrangled over who should lead their nation. After receiving authorization from Secretary Dulles to "crack some heads together," Ambassador Peurifoy arranged on 2 July a settlement that left Colonel Castillo Armas, the CIA's man, the president of the junta.[45]

That the Eisenhower administration toppled the Arbenz government is undisputed. What remain subjects of debate are the motivations that underlay U.S. actions and the implications of a foreign policy of intervention. Eisenhower activated PBSUCCESS a month after Guatemala received arms from the Soviet bloc. The arms shipment seemed to be the final piece of proof that Communists dominated Guatemala and were aiming to expand communism throughout Central America. But the Guatemalans answered that the arms, which they could not buy elsewhere, were for self-defense against the anticipated invasion of Castillo Armas. Indeed, in May 1954 the U.S. ambassador to Sweden reported to Washington that Guatemalans were frantically trying to buy arms in Western Europe. President Arbenz possibly intended to distribute the arms to the population, because he no longer trusted his military commanders.[46] In any event, what is remarkable is that the administration prepared and executed a *golpe de estado*, a coup, when it knew its case against Arbenz was based on "circumstantial" evidence. On 11 May 1954 Dulles admitted to the Brazilian ambassador that it would be "impossible to produce evidence clearly tying the Guatemalan Government to Moscow; that the decision must be a political one and based on our deep conviction that such a tie must exist." In early June, the secretary of state pleaded with the U.S. embassy in Honduras to produce evidence linking strikes against United Fruit in that country to agitation by Guatemalan Communists; the embassy gloomily reported, "facts few, convicting and convincing evidence scarce." After the *golpe*, intelligence agents combed through the Guatemalan archives; but a year later, Assistant Secretary of State for Intelligence W. Park Armstrong informed Dulles that "nothing conclusive" had been found linking Guatemalan Communists with Moscow.[47]

Few in Washington advised the administration to think and act dispassionately. Milton Eisenhower, for example, warned his brother about Guatemala and applauded the fall of Arbenz. Moreover, Congress reacted strongly to the news of arms shipments to Guatemala. At the behest of the administration, the House and Senate resolved that the United States would not tolerate communism in the hemisphere. Senator Mike Mansfield, a liberal Democrat from Montana, represented congressional sentiment when he asserted in executive session that "there is no question of Communist control, there has been contact between Guatemalan leaders and Moscow." Democratic Senator J. William Fulbright of Arkansas, who in the latter half of the 1950s would become the leading critic of Eisenhower's Latin American policy, learned and approved of the CIA intervention.[48] Within the executive branch, apparently only Louis Halle of the Policy Planning Staff questioned the soundness of the case against Guatemala. On 28 May 1954 Halle, who under the pseudonym "Y" had tartly criticized Latin America in a 1950 article in *Foreign Affairs*, submitted a lengthy review of the Guatemalan revolution. His thesis was that the revolution was "nationalist and anti-Yanqui in its own right," a movement for social justice and reform. Guatemalans vented their fury on United Fruit because of the perceived injustices of the past; Communism aggravated this situation, but it did not cause it. Halle's colleagues in Washington did not reply directly to his review. But State Department officer Raymond Leddy summarized their feelings when on 5 June he assured Ambassador Peurifoy that "there is a 100 percent determination, from the top down, to get rid of this stinker [Arbenz] and not to stop until that is done."[49]

Because the Eisenhower administration ignored critics and had only incomplete and tenuous evidence to sustain its claim that it had legitimate national security fears, scholars have argued that the United States overthrew the Arbenz government in order to rescue United Fruit. They point out that, starting with the Dulles brothers, a host of administration officials had either worked for or had a personal interest in United Fruit. Moreover, Castillo Armas promptly returned United Fruit's property and welcomed new investors, such as U.S. oilmen. Indeed, so eager to please was Castillo Armas that he informed Vice-President Richard Nixon in early 1955: "Tell me what you want me to do and I will do it."[50] Administration officials forcibly denied that they were handmaidens of United Fruit. Just prior to Castillo Armas's invasion, Secretary Dulles told journalists that "if the United Fruit matter were settled, if they gave a gold piece for every banana, the problem would remain just as it is today as far as the presence of Communist infiltration in Guatemala is concerned."[51] At an NSC meeting, Dulles also urged the Justice Department to file a long-pending antitrust suit against United Fruit, because "many of the Central American countries were convinced that the sole objective of United States foreign policy was to protect the fruit company."[52]

To emphasize either strategic *or* economic motives in analyzing U.S. policies toward Guatemala is perhaps to draw distinctions without differences. Guatemalan leaders violated both the national security decisions and the foreign economic policies of the United States. The Eisenhower administration encapsulated these concerns when it began a comprehensive assessment of Guatemala with the telling observation that "the current political situation in Guatemala is adverse to U.S. interests."[53] Although it is true that the administration adopted United Fruit's position in toto and that it feared the effect of Guatemala's expropriation on U.S. investments throughout Latin America, it seems that the Eisenhower administration destroyed the Arbenz government because it believed that Guatemala was or soon would be under the domination of Communists loyal to Moscow. President Arbenz's friendship with Guatemalan Communists, the expropriation of United Fruit's land, and the purchase of arms from the Soviet bloc sustained that assumption. In fact, the policy the administration pursued in Guatemala was consistent with the policies it implemented throughout Latin America. As highlighted by the adoption of NSC 144/1, the administration had, in 1953 and 1954, made anticommunism the essential feature of its Latin American policy. The administration had courted rightist dictators, disbursed military aid, meddled in the Latin American labor movement, and launched a propaganda offensive. The CIA intervention in Guatemala was simply the most extreme of these anti-Communist measures.

The administration's anti-Communist zealotry is further evidenced by calculating the extraordinary price President Eisenhower was willing to pay to overthrow the Arbenz government. Eisenhower and his aides trampled on domestic and international law during the Guatemalan crisis. The administration disliked the reports correspondent Sydney Gruson of the *New York Times* filed from Guatemala. Secretary Dulles called Gruson a "dangerous character" and charged that he was following "the Communist line." Eisenhower agreed that "the *New York Times* was the most untrustworthy newspaper in the United States" and authorized Special Assistant Lewis L. Strauss to speak to the newspaper's publisher, Arthur Sulzberger. Sulzberger succumbed to administration pressure and transferred Gruson—who later became an editor of the newspaper—to Mexico City.[54]

The CIA intervention, even though it was a covert operation, violated the OAS charter. But Eisenhower probably was prepared to intervene overtly as well. On 27 May 1954 he approved NSC 5419/1, "U.S. Policy in the Event of Guatemalan Aggression in Latin America." The president accepted the recommendation of the Joint Chiefs of Staff that NSC 5419/1 include the statement that the United States would collaborate with the OAS to the extent feasible but would take military action "unilaterally only as a last resort."[55] What Eisenhower would have done had the Guatemalan army chosen to fight Castillo Armas cannot be determined—but he later confided to his must trusted aide, General Andrew Goodpaster, that he "had gone quite deeply into the Guatemalan situation." The president recalled that he warned his closest advisors that "if you at any time take the route of violence or support of violence . . . then you commit yourself to carry it through, and it's too late to have second thoughts, not having faced up to the possible consequences, when you're midway in an operation."[56]

President Eisenhower further displayed his determination to overthrow the Arbenz government in international fora. After Guatemala received arms from Czechoslovakia, he ordered U.S. warships to seize and inspect, in international waters, ships bound for Guatemala. His legal advisors developed tortured defenses for this order. Press Secretary James C. Hagerty, however, dismissed the lawyers' sophistry; as he told his diary, the United States opposed the right of search of neutral vessels on the high seas, and, "as a matter of fact, we were at war with the British in 1812 over the same principle."[57] Eisenhower also bullied the French and British over Guatemala. The European allies wanted the U.N. Security Council to investigate Guatemala's complaint of aggression. A furious Eisenhower, who blurted that he would "show the British that they have no right to stick their nose into matters which concern this hemisphere entirely," had U.N. Ambassador Henry Cabot Lodge warn the Europeans that if they "felt that they must take an independent line backing the present government of Guatemala, we would feel free to take an independent line concerning such matters as Egypt and North Africa in which we hitherto tried to exercise the greatest forbearance so as not to embarrass Great Britain and France." Lodge reported that his "announcement was received with great solemnity." In case the Europeans were not sufficiently cowed, Eisenhower authorized Lodge to use the first U.S. veto in the United Nations, which would have forfeited the propaganda point that only the Soviet Union vetoed U.N. resolutions.[58]

Eisenhower was immensely pleased that his bold policy had succeeded. The Republicans had alleged that the Truman administration had lost whole areas of the world to communism; the Eisenhower administration was rolling back the Communist tide. Secretary Dulles boasted to colleagues that Guatemala was "the biggest success in the last five years against communism." Eisenhower pointed to Guatemala with pride during the 1956 presidential campaign. The victory also came at a diplomatically opportune moment: it helped draw attention away from the triumph of the Vietnamese Communists in French Indochina. Eisenhower had a grand reception in the White House for the CIA agents. He joshed with them, wondering why they had let Arbenz escape. And he shook everyone's hand, ending with Allen Dulles, and said: "Thanks, Allen, and thanks to all of you. You've averted a Soviet beachhead in our hemisphere."[59]

The reaction in the rest of the Western Hemisphere to the CIA intervention in Guatemala was mixed. The dictatorships acquiesced in the *golpe*. Legislators in Argentina, Chile, and Uruguay, however, passed resolutions either supporting Arbenz or condemning U.S. "aggression" in Guatemala. Student and labor groups in countries such as Bolivia, Cuba, Ecuador, and Mexico demonstrated against the intervention and issued statements of protest. Latin Americans did not, of course, have the power to block the United States. The Department of State was troubled by the reaction, concluding that "we had won a round against the Communists but paid a price in terms of prestige and good-will."[60]

In Guatemala, Castillo Armas oversaw political repression. Under the "Preventive Penal Law Against Communism," he suspended the writ of habeas corpus. He also returned the man who had been chief of secret police during the Ubico regime to his post. Agrarian reform and collective bargaining rights were abolished, and the franchise was again limited to literate Guatemalans. Guatemalans who had received land under Arévalo and Arbenz were driven off their property. By 1956, the American Federation of Labor, which had "rejoiced over the downfall of the Communist-controlled regime in Guatemala," was reporting that agricultural workers were "in conditions of servitude if not actual slavery," working eighty-four hours a week and earning 50 cents a day. Guatemala predictably became a politically polarized society. During the three decades that followed the intervention, perhaps as many as 100,000 Guatemalans died in political violence. Castillo Armas was one of the victims: he was assassinated in 1957 in a plot probably directed by jealous military officers.[61]

The Eisenhower administration hoped for an open, progressive Guatemala, because, as Secretary Dulles noted, "it was important that an example be given to the free world of the success of a people in recovering after a period of Communist rule." Between 1954 and

1957, the administration granted Guatemala $46 million in emergency assistance. It also showered support on Castillo Armas, believing that he stood between "greater instability, a return of open communism, and a return of a more severe nationalistic, anti-American government." Vice-President Nixon toured Guatemala in early 1955, and in November 1955 President Eisenhower hosted Castillo Armas. Eisenhower was generous with his praise, writing to Castillo Armas that "I count myself among those who deeply admire your achievements on behalf of the Guatemalan people and your determination to lead them steadily forward in freedom toward more secure peace and greater prosperity." Eisenhower was shocked by the Guatemalan's assassination and sent his son, John Eisenhower, to the funeral.[62]

Although the administration wished for a humane Guatemala, it did not pressure Castillo Armas to enact reforms, and it deluded itself about the political skills of the Guatemalan leader. CIA agent David Phillips, who had directed the anti-Arbenz radio broadcasts, accurately described Castillo Armas as "a bad president, tolerating corruption throughout his government and kowtowing to United Fruit Company more than to his own people."[63] In any case, the administration hedged its bets. In 1954, it rushed military aid to the Guatemalan military, because "in the final analysis" it was "in the best position to determine the successor government and its orientation." It also found it could work with Castillo Armas's unsavory successor, the archconservative General Miguel Ydígoras Fuentes. In 1953, when it was looking for a candidate to lead an anti-Arbenz army, the CIA had contacted Ydígoras; but the administration thought him too reactionary and unpopular in Guatemala: Ydígoras had brutally enforced Ubico's vagrancy laws. Nevertheless, he was a tough anti-Communist. Eisenhower hosted him in Washington and in 1960 sent him emergency economic aid, assuring him that "it would indeed be a tragedy for us all and a great triumph for Communism if your country having once freed itself of the Communist yoke should again find that yoke reimposed."[64] President Ydígoras Fuentes reciprocated by allowing the CIA to train Cubans in Guatemala for the Eisenhower administration's planned second intervention in Latin America, the overthrow of Fidel Castro.

Within two years after assuming office, the Eisenhower administration had achieved its primary goals for Latin America: it had instituted rigorous anti-Communist measures for Latin America, and it had driven supposed Communists out of Guatemala. But the administration could not rest. Latin Americans continued to expect U.S. economic assistance. Having secured the hemisphere from Communist aggression, the administration focused on inter-American economic relations.

CHAPTER 4

FREE TRADE AND INVESTMENT POLICIES

1953–1954

The Eisenhower administration made the eradication of communism its major foreign policy goal for Latin America. Latin Americans did not, however, share the administration's intense fear of a global Communist conspiracy. They argued that the region's primary need was for economic growth and development. The inter-American system should be a mechanism for economic cooperation, not merely an anti-Communist alliance. Because it wanted Latin America's cold-war support, the Eisenhower administration was forced to discuss the economic demands of Latin Americans and to attend an inter-American economic conference. It also decided, as a cold-war measure, to send economic aid to the leftist government of Bolivia.

Like his predecessors from Woodrow Wilson through Harry Truman, President Dwight D. Eisenhower believed that the key to world peace and prosperity was free trade and investment. In Eisenhower's view, "general world prosperity" meant "general peace and security"—when there was group oppression, mass poverty, or the hunger of children, revolution and social chaos surely followed. And the Communists could be counted on to "reach out to absorb every area in which can be detected the slightest discontent or other form of weakness." The responsibility of the United States, with the world's most dynamic economy, was to lower tariffs and to open markets. Free trade would "allow backward people to make a decent living—even if only a minimum one measured by American standards." Free trade would also secure America's freedom. The United States, Eisenhower wrote in his diary, would increasingly need to import vital raw materials such as tin, cobalt, uranium, manganese, and crude oil. He worried that "unless the areas in which these materials are found are under the control of people who are friendly to us and who want to trade with us, then again we are bound in the long run to suffer the most disastrous and doleful consequences."[1]

Although Eisenhower argued that the United States must assume the burdens of world leadership and facilitate international economic cooperation, he also held that there were limits to the role the United States could play. The president was a fiscal conservative who had pledged during the 1952 campaign to slow the growth of government, and both domestic public assistance and foreign aid strained the federal budget. He was not unalterably opposed to foreign aid; in fact, between 1953 and 1961 the United States would grant or loan nearly $50 billion in economic and military assistance to other countries. But, as Eisenhower told his brother Milton, foreign aid was appropriate only for those areas under direct assault from "the Communist menace." Other areas could garner development capital by expanding foreign trade and attracting private foreign investment. The slogan of the new administration was "trade not aid."[2]

President Eisenhower applied these foreign economic policies to Latin America. When he took office, a $300-million Export-Import Bank loan for Brazil was pending: during its last days, the Truman administration had promised emergency assistance to help relieve Brazil's balance-of-payments and currency problems. Eisenhower wanted to halve the loan, and his secretary of the treasury, George Humphrey, wanted to dump the "inherited mess"—but eventually they agreed that the United States was "hooked," because the money had been promised and the Truman administration had in 1950 loaned $125 million to Brazil's rival, Argentina.[3] Eisenhower urged cabinet officers to learn from this fiasco. The Democrats had put inter-American relations on a "come and get it" basis; if Latin Americans "want our money, they ought to be required to go after our capital." Eisenhower instructed the cabinet to think of new approaches for Latin America, concluding with the observation that "we put a coin in the tin cup and yet tomorrow we know the tin cup is going to be there."[4]

Eisenhower's views on foreign economic policy were also expressed in NSC 144/1 of 18 March 1953. The primary economic objective of the United States was to encourage "Latin American governments to recognize that the bulk of the capital required for their economic development can best be supplied by private enterprise and that their own self-interest requires the creation of a climate which will attract private investment"; in turn, the administration would resist protectionism and work to lower U.S. tariffs on Latin

American products. In discussing the document, Eisenhower agreed with Secretary Humphrey's opinion that businessmen should become U.S. ambassadors in Latin America and remarked that he had "jumped" the Mexican ambassador on the need for Latin Americans to safeguard foreign investment.[5] Eisenhower also subsequently approved Humphrey's plan to limit the lending authority of the Export-Import Bank to short-term credits for the expansion of trade. Both the Roosevelt and Truman governments had permitted the bank to make development loans. With the freezing of long-term lending, the bank's development loans in Latin America fell from $147 million in 1952 to $7.6 million in 1953.[6]

By denying economic aid and preaching that Latin America would find its salvation in private enterprise, Eisenhower seemed certain to rekindle protests that the United States neglected Latin America. This, of course, was the accusation that Eisenhower had leveled at the Truman administration during the presidential campaign. But the debate was postponed both in Washington and in Latin America. NSC 144/1 reflected the administration's cold-war priorities; Eisenhower ruled that economic policies would be reviewed in the future. Moreover, the president promised to send Dr. Milton Eisenhower to South America. Latin Americans expected that there would be a significant shift in U.S. policies after Dr. Eisenhower reported to the president.

Milton Eisenhower's report to the president, which was published in November 1953, was by the author's later admission an orthodox and unimaginative analysis of Latin America's economic problems. In the document, he reiterated the points he had made to Latin American leaders during his fact-finding tour. He recommended to Latin Americans fiscal responsibility, "the maintenance of honest money," and balanced budgets. He opposed economic nationalism, criticizing "industrialization for its own sake" and "creeping expropriation"; instead, Latin Americans needed to practice free trade and investment policies. But he warned that the United States could not induce private capital to flow to Latin America; "it must be *attracted* by the nation desiring the capital."[7]

It is true that Dr. Eisenhower's report was innocuous and conventional. Indeed, Brazilian diplomats privately laughed at it, observing that it could have been written without traveling to Latin America.[8] Yet, despite its modest nature, the release of the report initiated a year of bitter debate within the Eisenhower administration over economic policies. In addition to instructing Latin Americans on the efficacy of international capitalism, Dr. Eisenhower suggested changes in U.S. policies. He recommended the funding of several small-scale development projects, such as a $2.5-million Export-Import Bank loan for airport improvements in Ecuador. The cost of these various projects amounted to only $17 million. But Dr. Eisenhower also asked that the Export-Import Bank resume long-term lending in Latin America, and that the United States expand its stockpiling program—stockpiling would help support the prices of Latin America's raw materials, which were sharply declining as demand engendered by the Korean War subsided.[9] The thrust of these recommendations was that the United States had some limited responsibility for Latin America's economic welfare.

The report received its friendliest reception within the Latin American section of the Department of State. Assistant Secretary of State John Moors Cabot, who had accompanied Eisenhower on his tour, enthusiastically endorsed the report's recommendations. The per capita income of Latin Americans was about one-eighth that of North Americans. In the poorest nations—Bolivia, Ecuador, Haiti—per capita income was perhaps 3–5 percent of that in the United States. Yet, the United States allocated only about 1 percent of its development assistance to Latin America. Cabot warned that "we cannot indefinitely continue the present discrimination against our sister republics in this hemisphere without gravely prejudicing our relations with them." Moreover, he questioned whether foreign investment could resolve all of Latin America's economic problems. Even in countries that had favorable tax and investment laws, foreign investors stayed away because of an inadequate economic infrastructure and poor human resources: transportation and communication systems were primitive, and the impoverished people had limited educational and technical skills. Cabot also worried about the vast disparities of wealth in Latin America, with the upper classes "exercising an almost feudal control." "Trickle-down" economics would not undercut the appeal of communism in Latin America.[10]

Although Cabot's analysis of Latin America's economic and social misery was far-reaching, he proposed to administration officials a relatively modest package for Latin America. He recognized what one of his aides called "the present drive for economy" in the federal government. He supported Dr. Eisenhower's proposals to continue technical cooperation or Point Four, which amounted to about $25 million a year, to fund the small-scale development projects cited by

Dr. Eisenhower, and to assist in the construction of the inter-American highway. He also called for making the Export-Import Bank into an instrument of U.S. foreign policy and assigning $1 billion of loans over five years for long-term development projects. These loans would be dedicated primarily to improving the economic infrastructure of Latin America, which would facilitate private investment. In making his presentation, Cabot noted that he was not recommending grants, loans at concessional rates, or loans repayable in local currencies—so-called "soft" loans. In addition, he pointed out that Latin Americans had excellent credit records: the Export-Import Bank had collected 40 percent of the principal it had lent in the previous two decades and had turned a handsome profit from interest payments. Current interest and principal payments were almost exceeding the amount of new loans flowing to Latin America. Such a policy of economic cooperation, Cabot predicted, would "convince our Latin American friends that our protestations of friendship are more than pious platitudes, that cooperation with us does benefit them and does raise their living standards, and that our democratic capitalism is far better for them than Communism with its rosy promises."[11]

Cabot's plan ran into the determined and relentless opposition of Secretary of the Treasury Humphrey. Humphrey was an Ohio industrialist and a loyal supporter of Senator Robert Taft. On fiscal matters, he was even more conservative than the president. He was also self-assured and loquacious; he was combative at cabinet and NSC meetings, endlessly warning that excessive federal spending would ruin the country. As a nationalist, he argued that the United States could not purchase friends with economic aid. In any case, the U.S. Treasury could not afford Cabot's plan for the Export-Import Bank. Like other conservatives, he was fond of pointing out that during the nineteenth century the developing United States had welcomed foreign capital; Latin Americans should emulate U.S. patterns of development. Although President Eisenhower was often exasperated with Humphrey, he respected and enjoyed him. The treasury secretary was a man of Eisenhower's generation and, though an ideologue, a warm and gregarious fellow; furthermore, he represented a potent wing of the Republican party.[12]

The battle over economic cooperation with Latin America was ultimately decided, however, by the president and by Secretary of State Dulles. Dulles disliked Humphrey's meddling in his foreign-policy bailiwick. He also worried about the ramifications of poverty in

Latin America. He feared that the raw-material–producing econo-mies of Latin America were dangerously sensitive to world market conditions. He wrote to the president that "at times we need their raw materials badly, and then they have feverish prosperity. Then the need falls off and they go into economic decline with unemploy-ment, which, nowadays, the Communists organize against us." In addition, he debated Humphrey at NSC and cabinet meetings, point-ing out that "in the absence of adequate assistance from us the Latin American countries might well go Communist."[13] But despite these beliefs, Dulles gave relatively little attention to economic relations with Latin America or other areas of the world. He was primarily interested in the political side of foreign relations, and he spent much of his time practicing diplomacy. He declined, for example, to take up Cabot's proposals with the president, noting that he was too busy preparing for the Four-Power Conference to be held in Berlin in early 1954.[14]

John Foster Dulles was, of course, obsessed with communism. And he wanted the Latin American states to adopt an anti-Communist resolution at Caracas. Using that argument, he obtained the presi-dent's permission to announce in his speech at Caracas that the United States would again allow the Export-Import Bank to assist "sound development projects." He also promised an economic con-ference.[15] He simultaneously dismissed Assistant Secretary Cabot and sent him into pleasant exile as ambassador to Sweden. Cabot had pushed too hard for his program. Moreover, although he was a fervent anti-Communist and a determined foe of Jacobo Arbenz of Guatemala, Cabot disputed the administration's contention that the cold war was the major issue in inter-American relations: he held that "the most fundamental problem we have in our relations with the Latin American republics is that of their economic develop-ment." Dulles replaced Cabot with Henry F. Holland, a lawyer with minimal diplomatic experience who worked for the prestigious Hous-ton law firm of Baker and Botts. Holland's knowledge of inter-Ameri-can affairs came from representing U.S. corporations in Latin Ameri-ca. In accepting his appointment, Holland assured Dulles that, although Latin America deserved special economic consideration, "I understand that our global foreign policy prohibits such recogni-tion."[16]

President Eisenhower backed Dulles's actions. He reversed his 1953 decision on the Export-Import Bank, because he understood that Dulles needed to bring something to the Caracas conference to encourage Latin Americans to embrace the administration's anti-Communist policies. He also liked the idea of loaning an additional $17 million for small development projects, which would improve relations, without "getting into spending billions."[17] Eisenhower supplemented this by authorizing Dulles to assure Latin Americans at Caracas that the administration would keep U.S. markets open. The president resisted congressional pressure to mandate quotas on oil imports from Venezuela and on lead and zinc imports from Mexico and Peru. He explained that "if we erect stronger barriers against trade with Mexico, I know that the possibility of her turning communist would mount rapidly."[18]

After the Arbenz government was toppled in June 1954, the Eisenhower administration faced the "evil day" of discussing economic issues with Latin Americans and making good on the promises Secretary Dulles had made at Caracas. For a time, Dulles and Holland hoped "things will develop so it won't be necessary to hold it."[19] But the United States had exhausted all credible excuses for not attending a conference that had been postponed repeatedly since 1944. During the summer and fall of 1954, interdepartmental and subcabinet committees constantly met to develop a policy for economic relations with Latin America and to plan for the forthcoming Rio Economic Conference.[20]

While lower-level officials negotiated, the NSC wrote a new policy for Latin America. On 3 September 1954 the president approved NSC 5432/1, which superseded NSC 144/1 and NSC 5419/1, the policy pertaining to Guatemala. The new policy reiterated U.S. goals to expand trade and to encourage Latin Americans "to create a political and economic climate conducive to private investment, of both domestic and foreign capital." But the document also accepted Dr. Eisenhower's recommendation to permit the Export-Import Bank to finance all sound economic development projects and even allowed the possibility of development assistance loans to Latin America. These new policies did not elicit significant debate at the 212th meeting of the NSC. Vice-President Richard Nixon presided over the 2 September 1954 meeting, and the departments were represented by acting or assistant secretaries.[21] President Eisenhower was vacationing in Denver, after a rigorous summer of overseeing crises in Guatemala and Indochina.

Tension did arise, however, at the interdepartmental meetings planning the Rio Conference. The Foreign Operations Administration (FOA), the agency that oversaw U.S. economic assistance, took up Latin America's cause. Going beyond John Cabot's program, it advocated extensive development assistance, food aid, and a regional development bank. It also suggested that the United States help stabilize raw-material and tropical-food prices through stockpiling programs, commodity agreements, and buffer stocks. Harold Stassen, the liberal Republican and former presidential candidate from Minnesota, headed the FOA. Stassen believed that the United States needed to indicate "a social conscience in relationship to the people of Latin America by supporting a progressive approach to an advance in the standard of living of the people as a whole, supporting such things as minimum wages and opposing current semi-slave labor conditions." Both the CIA and the Department of Defense supported the FOA, believing that economic aid to Latin America would increase U.S. security. Treasury Department representatives predictably opposed any new public spending, and Assistant Secretary Holland did not support the FOA.[22]

Arguments over Latin America and the U.S. position at the Rio Conference spilled over into the 224th meeting of the NSC, which was held on 15 November 1954. Secretary Humphrey and Stassen feuded in front of the president. Humphrey, who was heading the U.S. delegation, simply wanted to tell Latin Americans that the United States would remain prosperous and keep its markets open to Latin American exporters. He also asked the president to modify the language in NSC 5432/1 that allowed for Export-Import Bank loans and development assistance. In turn, Stassen predicted that "the proposed U.S. position at the Rio Conference would evoke a very negative reaction" from Latin Americans. An obviously irritated Eisenhower ended the wrangling by saying that he hated "these long drawn-out papers which lay down hard and fast rules for carrying out every detail of a program." To assuage Humphrey, the president agreed to add to NSC 5432/1 the proviso that any grant or soft loan to Latin America must have presidential approval; but the Export-Import Bank would be permitted to operate in Latin America, and its overall lending capacity would be raised by $500 million. Eisenhower reminded Humphrey that U.S. policy in Latin America was "chiefly designed to play a part in the cold war against our enemies." The "United States was not merely doing 'business' in Latin America, but was fighting a war there against Communism."[23]

The restoration of the bank's lending authority was to be the only significant initiative that the U.S. delegation would bring to Rio. The decision seemed to leave George Humphrey in charge of Latin

American policy. Milton Eisenhower protested to both his brother and Secretary Dulles: he doubted that Humphrey would implement NSC 5432/1, and he labeled as "tragic" the choice of Humphrey to lead the U.S. delegation.[24] Ambassador Merwin Bohan, who was responsible for coordinating position papers for the Rio Conference, resigned, explaining that he could not "sell" U.S. policies to Latin Americans. The U.S. stance, Bohan predicted, would contribute to "the widespread belief in Latin America that the principal objective of American policy was to make Latin America safe for American big business."[25]

George Humphrey did not, however, dictate U.S. foreign economic policy. The State Department was satisfied with its triumph on the Export-Import Bank. Its bureaucratic tactic was to let Stassen and Humphrey argue so that "our position would then be put in the most reasonable light as a follow up to the views of the extreme elements." Assistant Secretary Holland opposed development assistance and price-stabilization schemes for Latin America. He even told senators that Latin America did not want U.S. development assistance. On a tour of South America prior to the economic conference, Holland informed Latin Americans that their greatest need was private capital and that private capital was not entering Latin America "because prospective investors are not accorded the protection of contract and property rights, assurances of sound monetary policies, and of opportunities to earn a reasonable rate on their investments." Secretary Dulles fully supported Holland and the U.S. position at Rio and found no reason to attend the economic conference.[26]

President Eisenhower was pleased with U.S. policy. He sent a personal message for Secretary Humphrey to read at the conference. Eisenhower wanted, in Dulles's words, to dispel the "widespread gossip to the effect that there is a split between George Humphrey and Milton, and that Milton really represents our policies and if the present Conference fails, then Milton will take over with more liberal policies."[27] Eisenhower knew that his brother was disappointed with the outcome of the year-long struggle over Latin America. But Milton had to understand geopolitical realities. "Countries like Burma, Thailand, and the remaining parts of Indochina are directly open to assault. This does not apply in South America." The United States wanted an enduring "good partner" relationship with Latin America, which could be encouraged by loans instead of grants; this would "apply whether or not the Communist menace seems to increase or decrease in intensity." In Asia, however, "if the Communist menace should recede in the area, we would consider ourselves still friendly, but we would feel largely relieved of any obligation to help them economically or militarily."[28]

However persuasive President Eisenhower may have been with his brother, he could not sway Latin Americans. As they had during the Truman years, Latin Americans complained that the United States neglected them. Brazilian Ambassador João Carlos Muniz reminded Henry Holland that, during World War II, Latin Americans had believed that "the vast resources of the United States were going to be brought to bear on wide and rapid economic development in Latin America"—but since the war, "there has been an intense process of disillusionment throughout Latin America." Moreover, Latin Americans remained puzzled by U.S. strategy. As the Brazilian Foreign Ministry saw it, the United States fought communism in Asia and Europe with economic aid and depended on "politico-police" methods in Latin America.[29]

Latin Americans were envious of the aid received by others. Their case for development assistance rested, however, more on historical reasoning and contemporary economic analysis than on special pleading. During the nineteenth century, Latin America had been a laboratory for liberal economic theories. The newly independent governments signed trade treaties with Europeans and welcomed British, French, and German investors. But foreign investment did not guarantee sound economic development. Although the infusion of capital helped create modern cities—such as Buenos Aires, Rio de Janeiro, and Mexico City—with efficient public utility and transportation systems, it also seemingly left Latin America's economic destiny in the hands of foreigners. Nationalists charged that investments such as the British financing of railroads had not integrated their economies and developed internal markets but rather facilitated European access to their raw materials and foodstuffs. Moreover, European investors allied with plantation and hacienda owners to preserve traditional patterns of trade; they stoutly defended liberal trade treaties and worked to defeat tariffs that might nurture nascent industries. As a result, Latin American nations still were barely industrialized and most had monocultural economies, relying on the sale of one crop or raw material for their prosperity.[30]

Trading from comparative advantage was an essential component of liberal economic theory. But Latin American economists began to challenge free-trade principles. Latin America was thoroughly integrated into the international capitalist system and dependent upon robust sales to Europe and North America for any semblance of prosperity, and during the first half of the twentieth century, normal trading patterns had been disrupted by the two world wars and the economic depression of the 1930s; national economic planning was impossible, with the prices of exports fluctuating wildly. Furthermore, Latin Americans, led by the Argentine economist Raúl Prebisch, questioned the fairness of the trade between Latin America and its industrialized customers. Prebisch produced studies demonstrating that in the twentieth century the "terms of trade" moved against raw-material producers: relative to the price of manufactures, the prices of foodstuffs and raw materials had declined. The process accelerated in the 1950s. Between 1952 and 1962, the combined price index of commodities sold by Latin America—coffee, wheat, corn, tin, cotton, sisal, lead, zinc, nitrates, sugar—declined every year but one.[31]

Latin Americans passionately believed that these trade and investment patterns explained the poor quality of life in Latin America. In the early 1950s, per capita income in Latin America was less than $250 a year. In impoverished rural areas, many lived outside of a cash economy. Life expectancy in Latin America was 43 years; it was 68 years in the United States. The average North American consumed about 3,100 calories a day, whereas caloric intake for a Latin American was approximately 2,300. A Latin American child typically attended only two years of primary school. Over 60 percent of the population in the extremely poor Central American and Caribbean nations were illiterate. And gains in productivity and economic output were being eroded by an annual population growth that was averaging 2.5 percent in the postwar years.[32]

What Latin Americans were reluctant to admit was that chaotic political conditions and inequitable distributions of land and wealth were also responsible for rampant poverty. In Colombia, for example, perhaps 100,000 people died between 1948 and the mid-1950s in *La Violencia*, political warfare between Colombian Liberals and Conservatives over issues that seemed arcane to outside observers. Excluding Mexico, where far-reaching land reform was carried out in the 1930s, Latin America's agrarian structure followed a uniform pattern: the landed oligarchs, a minuscule percentage of the population, owned most of the arable land. In Peru, 1.1 percent of the farmers controlled 82 percent of the land. The vast majority of the rural population tried to survive on tiny plots, *minifundios*, and by providing seasonal labor for abysmal wages to the *latifundios*. The distribution of income in Latin America was as inequitable as the landholding patterns: in Brazil, the top 1 percent of the population earned 19 percent of the income.[33]

As daunting as the region's social and economic problems were, Latin American economists confidently analyzed them. A wealth of statistical information was being generated by the Economic Commission for Latin America (ECLA), a U.N. agency headed by Prebisch. Individual Latin American nations had traditionally lacked the money and the educational and research facilities to conduct economic surveys of their countries. The ECLA held that Latin America's basic need was for development capital. Its studies purported to show that in the early 1950s there was a net outflow of capital from Latin America, with interest and principal payments and profit remittances exceeding the amount of new public loans and private investments. Economic growth was a meager 1 percent a year.[34] In order to stimulate growth, ECLA economists held that Latin America needed to absorb $1 billion a year for ten years. Approximately 70 percent of this money would come from international lending institutions. The ECLA planned for the Export-Import Bank and the International Bank for Reconstruction and Development, or World Bank, to loan $600 million a year to Latin America. The commission also hoped that the United States would fund a new inter-American development bank, which would provide an additional $100 million in capital. The rest of the money would come from private investors.[35]

This development capital, combined with domestic savings, the ECLA believed, would increase annual economic growth by 2 percent and would diversify Latin American economies. The commission's plan called for the state to be actively involved in development, operating some enterprises and using tariffs, taxes, and subsidies to promote industrial diversification. The ECLA particularly hoped that the proposed inter-American bank would specialize in promoting industrial development in Latin America. In order to stabilize their agricultural and mineral bases, Latin American nations also needed agreements that would stabilize prices and address terms-of-trade problems.[36]

Latin America naturally looked to the United States for assistance. During the twentieth century, North Americans had supplanted Western Europeans as the chief traders and investors in Latin America. By the early 1950s, U.S. capitalists had invested about $6 billion in Latin America, which represented nearly 40 percent of U.S.

direct investments in the world. The bulk of this money was in extractive industries, such as Chilean copper and Venezuelan oil. Annual trade between the United States and Latin America amounted to approximately $7 billion, with the balance of trade slightly favoring the United States. The United States conducted over 25 percent of its international trade with Latin America, buying raw materials and tropical products, especially coffee, and selling processed foods and manufactures.[37]

The Latin Americans hoped that the Eisenhower administration would welcome their proposals. President Eisenhower reported to Dulles that at a dinner party the Brazilian ambassador had told him that Latin Americans expected "great things from the Rio Conference" and that they hoped "the United States will come there with an *Eisenhower Plan*."[38] The administration rejected, however, both the proposals and the philosophy of the ECLA: state enterprises had the potential to become bloated with bureaucracy and responsive to political whims rather than to sound economic analyses. The role of government, Henry Holland asserted, was to "create conditions favorable to the investment and growth of private capital and enterprise." Industrialization was desirable, but not at the expense of agriculture. In Argentina, Juan Perón was sacrificing beef and wheat production, the heart of the country's economy, to his national development schemes. The ECLA's plans also failed to emphasize internal reform. In any case, administration officials, starting with President Eisenhower, were firmly wedded to free trade and investment policies. And economic aid for Latin America was not part of U.S. cold-war strategy. As Eisenhower replied to the Brazilian ambassador, "I said we would be friendly—understanding and helpful—but that our world commitments were heavy."[39]

The Rio Conference, which met between 22 November and 2 December 1954, did not witness a stormy confrontation between the United States and Latin America. Assistant Secretary Holland had already dashed expectations, in the fall of 1954, in a series of speeches and meetings with Latin American leaders, when he emphasized that the United States would grant neither a Marshall nor an Eisenhower Plan for Latin America.[40] The Latin Americans were, of course, deeply disappointed; they had been waiting for ten years to discuss economic cooperation with the United States. A Costa Rican official observed that the U.S. "ideas are well known, and they have been repeated since Mr. Mellon's days to the present." A Colombian diplomat added that the U.S. decision to limit its actions to expanding the lending authority of the Export-Import Bank by $500 million "unfortunately does not reflect the aspirations of Latin America nor does it wholly meet the responsibility of the United States as the leader of the free world."[41] At Rio, the United States abstained on eight of forty-nine resolutions on economic cooperation, refusing to vote on issues involving development assistance, terms of trade, and an inter-American bank. Because no significant agreements emerged from the conference, the final declaration merely emphasized "the energy and frankness which characterized the discussions."[42]

Eisenhower administration officials were relieved that the United States was not publicly embarrassed at Rio, and they judged the conference a success. Treasury Secretary Humphrey reported to the president that Latin Americans were satisfied with the U.S. position at Rio, although they complained about U.S. aid to Asia. The president responded by reminding his cabinet that "we cannot allow them to be judges of our interests" and by reiterating his opposition to development assistance programs for Latin America.[43] Officials outside of Eisenhower's inner circle, however, were less charitable than Humphrey in assessing the Rio Conference. Disgruntled observers like John Cabot and Merwin Bohan considered the conference a noteworthy failure. State Department officer R. Richard Rubottom, who became assistant secretary of state for Latin America in 1957, termed Rio "one of the worst failures of any conference that we've ever had."[44] By intervening in Guatemala and by ignoring Latin America's economic needs, the Eisenhower administration appeared to be reviving attitudes and practices that had characterized the Latin American policy of the United States during the first third of the twentieth century.

By the end of 1954, the Eisenhower administration had firmly established its foreign economic policy for Latin America. But when it came to relations with Bolivia, the administration seemed to ignore its own precepts on nationalism and economic aid. Between 1953 and 1961, the United States gave Bolivia $192.5 million in economic assistance, $178.8 million of that in grants. The small, landlocked nation of 3.5 million people received, on a per capita basis, more economic aid from the United States than did any other country in the world. In 1957, for example, the Eisenhower administration supplied nearly 40 percent of Bolivia's national budget. Until the late

1950s, Bolivia was the only Latin American country, other than Guatemala, that received development assistance from the United States.[45]

Remarkably, this aid went to a revolutionary government. In April 1952, in a bloody, mass uprising, the Movimiento Nacionalista Revolucionario (MNR), or National Revolutionary Movement, took control of Bolivia. In 1951 the MNR's candidate, Víctor Paz Estenssoro, had been elected president, but the Bolivian army had disallowed the election and seized power. The MNR represented a vast array of disaffected Bolivians, including middle-class intellectuals, small businessmen, junior military officers, the rural poor, and mine workers. They believed that Bolivia's traditional rulers—large landholders, senior military officers, and mine owners—were inept and corrupt and had left Bolivia the poorest and most backward country in South America. Led by President Paz Estenssoro, the MNR set out to topple Bolivia's oligarchic socioeconomic structure. It purged the army, established its own militia, enfranchised illiterate Bolivians, nationalized tin mines, and redistributed land.[46]

When asked to explain why it assisted a movement whose policies seemed remarkably similar to those of the Arévalo and Arbenz governments in Guatemala, the Eisenhower administration responded that it opposed communism, not change and reform. Indeed, Bolivian leaders, in seeking U.S. economic assistance, told administration officials that Bolivia's revolution presented the United States with an opportunity to show that it was not wedded to dictators and the status quo.[47] But, in aiding the Bolivian revolution, the Eisenhower administration was not motivated primarily by a need to answer critics of its Guatemalan policy: it used economic aid to keep Bolivia non-Communist and to force the MNR to adopt free trade and investment policies. Thus, the administration's Bolivian policy was consistent with its approach toward the rest of Latin America, even though the United States had to spend money in Bolivia.

As it did in Guatemala, the administration deplored economic nationalism in Bolivia. But it recognized that it could not depend on Bolivian conservatives and the Bolivian military to undermine the revolution: the Bolivian oligarchy had been discredited by its greedy and repressive policies, and the army had been defeated and shattered in the April 1952 uprising. U.S. intelligence analysts predicted that a right-wing coup would plunge the country into chaos. Radicals might then take advantage of the turmoil, and "we might virtually have a Communist state in the heart of South America."[48] In any case, the administration decided that it could influence President Paz and his vice-president, Hernán Siles Zuazo. Both leaders represented the moderate, middle-sector wing of the MNR, which wanted change, reform, and development. Although they wanted the state to play a leading role in economic development, MNR moderates did not subscribe to theories of class conflict or envision a revolutionary, socialist society. The MNR's agrarian reform, for example, did not involve collectivization of agriculture or, as it did in Mexico, the establishment of communal landholdings or *ejidos*; rather, expropriated land was redistributed in small parcels to peasants who became subsistence farmers on *minifundios*. By strengthening Paz and Siles, the Eisenhower administration hoped also to undermine the left wing of the MNR, led by Juan Lechín, the leader of the mine workers.[49]

Not only did the administration perceive the political dynamics of Bolivia to be different from those of Guatemala, it also understood that the U.S. economic stake in Bolivia was minimal. U.S. direct investments in Bolivia amounted to about $10 million. The only substantial holding by North Americans was a minority interest in the Patiño Tin Mining Company, one of three tin companies Bolivia nationalized in October 1952. The United States valued, of course, Bolivia's tin, a strategically vital metal—President Eisenhower once remarked that "it would be much better to have tin in Fort Knox than gold." But in the post–Korean War period, world tin supplies were abundant; the price of tin plunged from a high of $2.00 in 1950 to below 80 cents a pound in the mid-1950s.[50] Whereas the U.S. industrial complex did not need Bolivia, the South American nation was dependent upon the United States: the export of tin normally accounted for 70 percent of Bolivia's foreign exchange and 90 percent of government revenue. Bolivia lost $700,000 every time the price of tin declined by one cent. The United States bought half of Bolivia's tin exports, and a government-owned smelter in Texas City, Texas, was the only major smelter that could take Bolivia's low-grade tin.[51]

The economic power of the United States was used by the Eisenhower administration to curb political radicalism and economic nationalism in Bolivia. As authorized by the president, the administration agreed in 1953 to stockpile Bolivia's tin for a year at above-market prices. But the State Department insisted that the Bolivian government compensate the owners of the expropriated tin mines with funds earned from the stockpiling program; the department wanted the principle of prompt, adequate, and effective compensation upheld to protect U.S. investments in other lands, such as Venezuela.[52] At Milton Eisenhower's urging, the administration also rushed emergency food assistance to Bolivia in 1953. In the aftermath of the revolution and the land redistribution program, agricultural production declined precipitously and Bolivia had to import 50 percent of its food; the U.S. intercession forestalled mass starvation and political upheaval in Bolivia. It also left the Eisenhower administration in the position to tell Bolivia that additional aid awaited "further economic and political stabilization."[53]

The administration achieved that "stabilization" in subsequent years. In 1955, Bolivia signed an investment guarantee treaty with the United States, signaling that Bolivia was again open to foreign investment. The following year the MNR adopted a new oil code, which permitted foreign oil investments. In 1937, Bolivia had expropriated U.S. oil holdings and established a national oil company. Then, starved for capital, the national company's production declined, and Bolivia began to import large quantities of oil in the early 1950s. Continuing the policy of the Truman government, the Eisenhower administration repeatedly denied Bolivian requests for loans; instead, wanting to protect private oil investments in Venezuela and to discourage other national oil companies, such as PETROBRÁS in Brazil, the administration provided a Point Four loan to pay a U.S. law firm to write a new oil code for Bolivia. The code pointedly barred national oil companies from other countries from operating in Bolivia. Assistant Secretary of State Holland closely monitored the writing of the oil code, and, after he left Washington, he represented U.S. oil interests in Bolivia. By the end of the decade, ten North American oil companies, including Gulf Oil, held leases in Bolivia.[54]

After 1956, U.S. influence in Bolivia increased rapidly. Even with U.S. aid, the Bolivian economy nearly collapsed during President Paz's term (1952–56). Wanting to improve the lot of poor Bolivians and to diversify their nation's economy, Paz and his MNR followers established costly social-welfare and economic-development programs. But tin revenues declined, and the country continued to be short of food. President Paz responded by inflating the currency: the cost of living soared by 900 percent a year, and the Bolivian currency, the boliviano, became virtually worthless on foreign exchanges.[55] The desperate new president, Hernán Siles Zuazo, was forced to accept the Eisenhower administration's demand that Bolivia stabilize its economy as a condition for future aid. Washington dispatched George Eder, a brusque and intemperate economist from the International Cooperation Administration, to reorganize the Bolivian economy. Eder vowed to "return Bolivia to a free market economy," ensuring that it was "permanently enjoined from any further expansion of government enterprise." He publicly criticized Bolivian leftists, such as Juan Lechín, who opposed him. His plan called for a balanced budget, a 40 percent cut in government expenditures, restrictions on subsidies to national companies, the termination of subsidies for consumer goods, and a wage freeze. In return, Bolivia received $25 million from the United States and the International Monetary Fund to stabilize its currency.[56]

The Eder plan marked the end of economic nationalism in Bolivia. It halted national development and economic-diversification projects, hurt the poor, and favored private over public interests. Vice-President Nuflo Chávez, who was allied with leftist groups, resigned in protest, and Lechín led a general strike. President Siles, who believed that the stabilization plan would save the country from disaster, broke the opposition by going on a hunger strike. The president commanded enormous respect in the country, for he had led the the April 1952 uprising. He subsequently chose to rebuild, with U.S. assistance, the Bolivian army in order to control militant miners.[57] With the adoption of the Eder plan, the United States dominated the political economy of Bolivia: it demanded that Bolivia resume payments on the foreign debts of $56 million that it had defaulted on in 1931, during the world economic depression; and it vetoed domestic-spending and economic-development programs. As a State Department officer candidly remarked about one Bolivian development plan, "we had to tell the Bolivian Government that they couldn't put their money into it and we weren't going to put ours into it."[58]

Although the Eisenhower administration had successfully deradicalized the Bolivian revolution, it had also saved it. Presidents Paz and Siles admitted that their governments would not have survived without U.S. aid. The administration had helped to preserve constitutionalism and land reform and had averted mass suffering in Bolivia;[59] but what it had not done was help Bolivia create an economy with a future. The essence of the Eder plan was for Bolivia to have an export-led economy. But after 1954, the administration declined to stockpile any more tin and closed the Texas City smelter. And because the tin mines were now national companies, they could not secure loans from the United States to modernize operations. In any case, the prices of metals plunged in 1957–58 when the United States went into a deep economic recession. Bolivia, which had earned $151 million from exports in 1951, earned only $63 million in 1958. Yet, true to its free trade and investment principles, the administration insisted that Bolivia use its scarce capital to compensate the tin mine owners and repay foreign bondholders. Such good-faith measures would presumably attract private foreign investors to Bolivia. U.S. food shipments and budgetary support kept the Bolivian government afloat. As President Siles saw it, however, "the United States has given me just enough rope to hang myself."[60]

President Eisenhower supervised U.S. policy for Bolivia. His brother, Dr. Eisenhower, became close friends with Presidents Paz and Siles and grew convinced that the Bolivian leaders were moderates and pro-Western. Dr. Eisenhower successfully urged the president to assist the Bolivians as a humanitarian gesture and as a way of preventing communism. The president also kept in touch with Bolivian affairs during golf games with Víctor Andrade, the Bolivian ambassador. Andrade, who was closely linked with Paz and Siles, was a charming and colorful raconteur who tirelessly lobbied for assistance for his country. After one encounter with Andrade at the Burning Tree golf club, President Eisenhower told his golfing partner, entertainer Bob Hope, that "I can only bet one dollar, for I have just lost two million dollars to the Bolivian ambassador."[61] Yet, although appreciative of Bolivia's moderation and cold-war support and sympathetic to Bolivia's economic plight, the president was unwilling to abandon fundamental components of his foreign economic policy. In a 1956 meeting with President Siles, Eisenhower rebuffed requests for new stockpiling programs and money for national development companies. Two years later, Vice-President Nixon brought the same message to La Paz, informing Siles that the United States would provide emergency relief, but not long-term development assistance. Bolivia's salvation was in free trade; it could expect to export more tin, when the U.S. economy recovered from recession.[62]

By the end of its second year in office, the Eisenhower administration had a concise and coherent policy for Latin America. It wanted the region to be secure, stable, and non-Communist so that the United States could marshal its forces for cold war with the Soviet Union. Because Latin America was not directly imperiled by the Soviet Union, it did not need emergency assistance. Consistent with its own domestic preferences, the administration affirmed that private enterprise could meet Latin America's development needs. The administration was prepared, of course, to take extraordinary measures, as it did in Guatemala and Bolivia, to meet any Communist challenge. But, confident of their strategy, President Eisenhower and his advisors saw no need, over the next four years, to alter the basic tenets of their Latin American policy.

CHAPTER 5

ANTICOMMUNISM AND INTERNATIONAL CAPITALISM

1955–1958

Between 1955 and mid-1958, the Eisenhower administration resolutely conducted its Latin American policy. Upholding the principles it had enunciated at the inter-American conferences at Caracas and Rio, the administration concentrated on eliminating communism from the hemisphere and expanding U.S. trade and investment. It warmly supported Latin American regimes that were anti-Communist and capitalist. It also challenged a move by the Soviet Union to expand its commerce in Latin America. Complacent administration officials believed that they had established an unprecedented era of good will and confidence in inter-American relations. Critics in both North and South America charged, however, that the administration fawned over ruthless dictators and ignored Latin America's crushing poverty. They warned that Latin America was ripe for revolution.

The mid-1950s seemed to be a time of peace and prosperity for the United States, a period dubbed the "Eisenhower equilibrium."[1] After a short, post–Korean War recession, the U.S. economy rose sharply: unemployment rates were falling and the cost of living was holding steady. Cold-war tensions subsided, with President Eisenhower meeting Russian leaders at a summit conference in Geneva in 1955. The president also secured the withdrawal of Russian troops from Austria. Eisenhower faced difficult crises in 1956, when the Soviet Union invaded Hungary and when British, French, and Israeli forces attacked Egypt and the Suez Canal—but he seemed a capable and steadfast leader, and he kept the United States out of war. U.S. voters heartily approved of Eisenhower's leadership, rewarding him with a convincing reelection victory in November 1956. The public was impressed also by the president's fortitude: during the mid-1950s, he survived a major heart attack and a minor stroke and weathered an emergency operation, after being stricken by an ileitis attack.

The relations of the United States with Latin America gained scant public notice during the mid-1950s. During the presidential campaign, for example, inter-American relations did not become a major issue. The administration continued to point proudly to the defeat of communism in Guatemala. And, with some hyperbole, it claimed that the Caracas Declaration was the foundation for trust and good-will in the Americas and "as significant for our generation as was the Monroe Doctrine at the time of its proclamation."[2] Democratic candidate Adlai Stevenson briefly tried to make relations with Argentina an issue, criticizing the president for permitting his brother to call on Juan Perón in 1953 and for approving loans to Argentina. The latter charge was embarrassing, for the administration had committed the loans just a few months before Perón was overthrown in September 1955. Secretary of State John Foster Dulles deftly parried Stevenson, reminding reporters that the Truman administration had also loaned money to the Argentine.[3]

Although inter-American relations were not subjects of widespread concern, the administration continued to address the serious issues of human rights, military aid, and communism. Military dictators ruled in a majority of Latin American countries; nevertheless, citing the nonintervention principles of the OAS, the administration conducted relations with all regimes. At a news conference in 1956, Secretary Dulles explained he realized that "the American Republics are much divided among themselves on the question of democratic governments as against so-called dictator governments." But he added that, whatever U.S. views, he did not think it "wise or profitable to carry those views into the current conditions of our relations with those countries."[4] Assistant Secretary Henry Holland assured his boss that he was implementing the correct policy. In Holland's view, "the genius of the Eisenhower administration was to get along with all countries." To denounce dictators would be "going back to Bradenism."[5]

The administration, particularly President Eisenhower, probably preferred to work with leaders who protected civil and human rights. At an NSC meeting in February 1955, the president rejected Secretary of the Treasury George Humphrey's argument that the United States "should back strong men in Latin American governments," because "whenever a dictator was replaced, Communists gained." Eisenhower pointed out to his advisors that he "firmly believed that if power lies with the people, then there will be no aggressive war." "In the long run," therefore, "the United States must back democracies."[6] Indeed, Eisenhower quietly worked to expand democratic practices in Latin America. He privately congratulated President Carlos Ibáñez of Chile for combating communism in his country through constitutional and legal means, and assured him that this was "the only possible way to handle this question without falling into the same class as the communists." Eisenhower also authorized the State Department to inform General Gustavo Rojas Pinilla privately that public opinion in the United States would be aroused if the dictator persisted in suppressing the Colombian newspaper, El Tiempo. And the president was gladdened by Juan Perón's downfall; he had never been comfortable with the view held by Dulles and Dr. Eisenhower that the United States should work with Perón because he was anti-Communist. He was not being self-serving when, in 1957, he told Dr. Gainza Paz, the editor of the distinguished Argentine newspaper La Prensa, that "nothing had pleased him more than the removal from the American scene by the Argentine people of the Perón dictatorship."[7]

In addition to these confidential statements, the Eisenhower administration openly supported a democracy when it rushed four P-51 fighter planes to Costa Rica in early 1955. A bitter personal feud between President José Figueres of Costa Rica and Anastasio Somoza, the strong-man of Nicaragua, had erupted into war, with Nicaragua aiding an invasion of Costa Rica by dissident Costa Ricans. In siding with the popularly elected Figueres, the administration was assisting an acerbic critic of its Latin American policy and spurning Somoza, a long-time ally.[8]

But even President Eisenhower could be ambivalent about dictators. He had previously bestowed the Legion of Merit upon Manuel Odría of Peru and Marcos Pérez Jiménez of Venezuela. In July 1956, Eisenhower attended with the leaders of the other American republics a ceremonial inter-American conclave in Panama; he also met individually with each leader. He did not raise questions of human and civil rights with any dictator. Instead, he confided to his diary that Somoza and General Alfredo Stroessner, the military dictator of Paraguay, "stood out" among those he had met. Stroessner had perhaps earned Eisenhower's admiration by assuring him that "Paraguay was one-hundred percent anti-communist and would continue to be so." The obsequious Somoza told Eisenhower that "if the United

States desired a canal in Nicaragua, it was all right with him." Thereafter, the president denounced in unusually vehement terms the September 1956 shooting of Somoza by a young Nicaraguan poet and dispatched an airplane to Nicaragua to carry the dying dictator to a U.S. hospital in the Canal Zone.[9] Eisenhower's merciful action was an ironic comment on the condition of medical facilities in Somoza's Nicaragua.

The Eisenhower administration not only worked with "so-called dictator governments" but also effusively supported them. Veteran foreign-service officer and Ambassador to Costa Rica Robert Woodward alleged that at a staff meeting Secretary Dulles had "laid down with vigor" the policy to "do nothing to offend the dictators; they are the only people we can depend on."[10] Woodward, a critic of the administration's policies, may have been unduly cynical, but other ambassadors adhered to such a policy. Ambassador to Venezuela Fletcher Warren flattered Pérez Jiménez, and Ambassador to Cuba Arthur Gardner became "intimately cordial" with dictator Fulgencio Batista. Gardner and his wife were frequently seen in the social company of the Batistas. Ambassador to the Dominican Republic William Pheiffer characterized Rafael Trujillo, in a speech, as "an authentic genius who thinks and labors, primarily, in terms of the best interests of his people." On the other hand, Ambassador to Colombia Philip Bonsal maintained contact with democrats such as Alberto Lleras Camargo, a future president of Colombia; for his diplomacy, Ambassador Bonsal earned the wrath of the dictator Rojas Pinilla and reassignment orders from the Department of State.[11]

The same stance on dictatorships was evident during Vice-President Richard Nixon's tour of Central America in early 1955. In briefings, State Department officers advised Nixon not to raise questions of civil liberties with Central American tyrants; he should, however, urge them to guard against communism. In regard to Batista, for example, the department noted its disappointment that the Cuban leader did not hound Cuban Communists but added that "his continuance in office is probably a good thing from standpoint of U.S."[12] The vice-president obeyed his instructions. Before cameras, he gleefully embraced Trujillo and Batista. And in a toast to Batista, he compared the Cuban to Abraham Lincoln.[13] When Nixon returned to Washington, he proudly reported to the cabinet; he called Batista "a very remarkable man" and found that Trujillo had given his people clean, drinkable water, an obsession with progress, and pride on being on time, although the price of this was dictatorship. In any case, as Nixon saw it, "Spaniards had many talents, but government was not among them."[14]

Whereas expressions of affection from the hemisphere's preeminent power proved politically useful to Latin American dictators,[15] a more tangible sign of U.S. support was military assistance. Through the mid-1950s, with the exception of economic assistance for Bolivia and Guatemala, military aid remained the administration's major budgetary item for Latin America. The military aid program was not, however, operating flawlessly. In overseeing the administration of military aid, the Operations Coordinating Board (OCB), an arm of the NSC, found two significant problems. First, because it was not threatened by Soviet attack, Latin America continued to receive the lowest priority in allocation of arms, and the United States was unable to achieve its objective of being the sole source of arms for Latin America; for example, only 12 percent of jet aircraft in Latin America were made in the United States, the rest coming from Western Europe. And second, even if the United States could accelerate deliveries, Latin American military rulers would not be satisfied; they wanted advanced weapons systems to enhance their prestige and power. The OCB recommended that administration officials review the military aid program.[16]

President Eisenhower and his foreign policy advisors examined those issues at a meeting of the NSC on 6 September 1956. Secretary of State Dulles began by presenting the view that had been held by career foreign-service officers since 1944, when military officials first proposed postwar inter-American military cooperation. Dulles questioned whether "the United States really wanted to build up large military establishments in these Latin American Republics." He observed that, given the unstable nature of some governments, the United States could not "estimate reasonably what use they will make of larger military establishments." Perhaps one republic would use U.S. arms to threaten another. In fact, the State Department was receiving reports from officers in the field that "much of the military equipment maintained by Latin American countries is obtained in an effort to counter equipment which they fear might be used against them by some rival country." Dulles suggested that the United States "would be better off if by itself it undertook to protect the sea lanes of communication and the Panama Canal."[17]

Admiral William Radford, of the Joint Chiefs of Staff, replied "with emphasis" to Dulles: if the United States drastically changed its military aid policy, it would be difficult to "keep the Latin American Republics in line," for they would purchase arms elsewhere and perhaps establish foreign military missions; moreover, because Congress authorized military aid for hemispheric defense, the Joint Chiefs had to define a military role for Latin America. In the face of the admiral's assault, Dulles quickly retreated from his position. He admitted that Radford was correct about the terms of the Mutual Security Act, and he conceded that it was "better that such additional armament come from U.S. stocks than from some foreign sources."[18]

President Eisenhower saw merit in both views. He recalled that most of the Latin American leaders he had met in Panama wore military medals, which were "struck for their own purposes," and that "only two or three of the leaders of the Latin American Republics wanted to be called by other than some military title." He did not wish to encourage further dependence on the military. He also doubted the ability of the armed forces of Latin America to contribute to hemispheric defense. Yet, he "agreed with Admiral Radford that what we want to preserve above all is the good will of the Latin American Republics" and "to assure their internal security, without which their good will would be useless to us." Eisenhower therefore instructed the NSC to rewrite the military paragraphs of NSC 5613, the administration's latest statement on U.S. policy for Latin America, on an "honest" basis, setting forth the military levels that each Latin American nation should maintain. The United States would then recognize that it might raise those levels for "political or hemispheric defense reasons."[19]

The revised document, NSC 5613/1, which was approved on 25 September 1956, did not clarify the purposes of military aid. Over the next year, administrators in agencies such as the Bureau of the Budget and the Mutual Security Program debated whether the United States intended to expand or restrict military aid. How should the United States respond to repeated Latin American requests for "prestige" equipment like jet aircraft and cruisers? Did the NSC intend "that internal security be considered as a mission for which the U.S. will make equipment available?" How would it be determined what is an "exceptional" case in furnishing equipment above desirable levels?[20] That such confusion would arise was predictable. The president and his closest advisors had discussed inconsistencies and contradictions in military aid to Latin America; they had not resolved them. But the transfer of arms and the training of Latin American officers and soldiers continued, because the administration wanted powerful, anti-Communist friends in Latin America. The United States even began to train Latin American police forces for anti-Communist duty. One of these security forces, Cuba's Buró para Represión de las Actividades Comunistas (BRAC) became notorious for its use of torture against Batista's opponents.[21]

Debates over military aid and U.S. policy toward dictatorships were not new. Defining national security as anticommunism, the administration decided to bolster repressive, often murderous, governments. What was different in the mid-1950s was the perception that the United States faced a new, ominous threat from the Soviet Union. On 16 January 1956, Soviet leader Nikolai Bulganin offered to expand diplomatic, economic, and cultural relations, extend technical assistance, and conclude trading arrangements with Latin American nations. Bulganin's offer was part of a Soviet "economic offensive" to expand its influence in the developing world. Soviet officials toured newly independent nations like Egypt, India, and Indonesia, promising lavish economic assistance programs. The new strategy also reflected a decision by the leaders of post-Stalin Russia, as revealed in the Twentieth Communist Party Congress of 1956, to temper cold-war tensions and to compete peacefully with the West for the allegiance of Asian, African, and Latin American peoples.[22] Bulganin's announcement followed a dramatic increase in Soviet trade with Latin America. In 1955 the value of trade had increased 34 percent to $340 million, with Cuba becoming a new Soviet trading partner; that year, Cuba sold over 500,000 tons of surplus sugar to the Russians.[23]

The Eisenhower administration judged Bulganin's offer to be another Communist attempt to penetrate Latin America. As NSC 5613/1 charged, "the Soviet bloc is seeking broader trade and economic and cultural relations with Latin American countries not only for economic reasons but in order to disrupt our friendly relations with Latin America, to subvert the countries in the area, and to destroy the inter-American system." President Eisenhower added that "the new Communist line of sweetness and light was perhaps more dangerous than their propaganda in Stalin's time."[24] The administration met the Soviet challenge on both economic and political fronts. The president and his advisors resisted congressional pressures to close U.S. markets to Latin American exports. An important victory was the 1956 Sugar Act, which preserved Cuba's special access to the U.S. market; the legislation cut Cuba's share of the market, but because domestic consumption of sugar was growing there would be no reduction in Cuba's sales. With metal prices collapsing around the world, the administration was, however, less successful in maintaining lead and zinc imports from Mexico and Peru. In 1957, to protect domestic producers, the president proposed excise taxes on lead and zinc imports. A year later, he imposed import quotas.[25]

Beyond trying to uphold liberal trade policies, the administration responded to "the intensified Soviet challenge and new Soviet tactics in Latin America" by stiffening its resolve to combat communism. Declaring that "closer relations between the Soviet Union and Latin America are against the security interests of the United States," the NSC, in September 1956, wrote into NSC 5613/1 the following statement (paragraph 16-e):

> If a Latin American state should establish with the Soviet bloc close ties of such a nature as seriously to prejudice our vital interests, be prepared to diminish governmental economic and financial cooperation with that country and take any other political, economic, or military actions deemed appropriate.[26]

It was the Joint Chiefs of Staff who suggested this bold language. The statement, which seemed to codify and extend to Latin America the interventionist policies pursued against Guatemala in 1954, evoked little debate among NSC members. Secretary Dulles initially objected, believing the language to be "so broad as not to give very clear guidance to those who were obliged to carry out the policy." But after some minor changes and Eisenhower's observation that "this issue struck him as largely a matter of semantics," the president ruled that he favored the Joint Chiefs' recommendation.[27]

The administration did not immediately need to fulfill its pledge to take any "political, economic, or military actions deemed appropriate" to sever Soviet ties with Latin America, because the Soviets' economic offensive in Latin America foundered. Latin American businessmen and consumers found Soviet merchandise unattractive and of poor quality. The ugly invasion of Hungary also damaged Russia's image. And trade with Argentina, a traditional trading partner of the Soviet Union, declined; the Argentines, trying to recover from the excesses of the Perón years, had less to buy and sell. The value of Soviet–Latin American trade fell to approximately $230 million in 1956, down $110 million from its 1955 high. Through the rest of the 1950s, Soviet trade with Latin America stagnated, amounting to only about 1.5 percent of the value of Latin America's international trade. Until 1960, the Soviets continued to have embassies in only Argentina, Mexico, and Uruguay.[28]

By the end of 1957 and early 1958, administration officials were satisfied that they had blunted the Soviet offensive and secured the hemisphere from communism. In November 1957 Secretary Dulles assured journalists that, although Communists could be counted on to make trouble, "we see no likelihood at the present time of communism getting into control of the political institutions of any of the American Republics." The administration's confidential analyses confirmed the Secretary of State's public optimism. Reviewing the progress of NSC 5613/1, the OCB concluded that "there are at present no critical or strategic problems or difficulties which are major threats to United States security or which seem likely to cause changes in the generally satisfactory status of United States relations with the area." In February 1958, in executive congressional testimony, CIA Director Allen Dulles agreed with his brother and the OCB that, although there were "soft points," communism in Latin America was not "a situation to be frightened of as an overall problem."[29]

Because it was winning the cold war in Latin America, the Eisenhower administration saw little need to refashion its foreign economic policies. Its principal economic objective for Latin America, as expressed in NSC 5613/1, remained "the development by private initiative of sturdy, self-reliant economies in Latin America which do not require continuing grant assistance from the United States." Assistant Secretary of State Henry Holland constantly defended that policy in meetings with Latin American officials and in speeches in the United States. As Ambassador to Brazil Ellis Briggs wryly observed, the Eisenhower administration borrowed "pages out of Poor Richard's Almanac" in urging Latin Americans to balance budgets, attract foreign investment, and "work harder amigos."[30] The administration also restricted economic assistance to Latin America. In early 1958, for example, it asked Congress to provide, under the Mutual Security Program, $113.5 million to the region for the next fiscal year; in that request, $54 million were allocated to military assistance, $35 million to technical cooperation, $23 million to emergency assistance for Bolivia, Guatemala, and impoverished Haiti, and $1.5 million to support the OAS. As usual, Latin America would receive a tiny percentage of the $2.1 billion in economic assistance that the administration wanted to spend throughout the world.[31]

Although the administration's policy on inter-American economic cooperation was unchanged, its attitude shifted markedly, as it decided that it no longer wanted to be in the passive position of resisting entreaties for economic assistance. During the mid-1950s the administration aggressively pressed its views on international capitalism. Assistant Secretary Holland developed the new tactics. It was essential that the United States counter the main argument of the Economic Commission for Latin America that the basic problem in Latin America was a shortage of public capital. When the United States granted a credit to a government agency, it gave "impetus to a basic trend toward socialist economies which have developed throughout Latin America." Therefore, in lieu of "a massive and socialistic U.S. financial aid program," the administration would use Export-Import Bank loans to encourage capitalist endeavors. In particular, the administration would counter economic nationalism by encouraging "private investors to ask for Export-Import Bank loans for sound industrial projects which we learn are being considered by their governments as invasions of the field of private enterprise." Such an approach would contribute toward the proper "attitudes of mind" in business and government circles. It would also accomplish U.S. goals "with a minimum of cost to our Government."[32]

Holland's superiors implemented his recommendations. At the request of Secretary Dulles, President Eisenhower, in mid-1955, delayed issuing an invitation to President Adolfo Ruíz Cortines of Mexico to visit Washington: Mexico restricted foreign investments and operated state enterprises. A visit by Ruíz Cortines would have an unfortunate effect on Latin America "where we are trying with considerable success to develop a climate which is receptive to private capital." The president also retained the policy of refusing to assist state companies like PEMEX because, in the State Department's view, "such a loan would afford dangerous encouragement to governments elsewhere in the world to follow the pattern of Mexico and expropriate foreign oil investments."[33] Instead, the administration worked to undermine state companies. In 1955 it successfully pressured Argentina to revise its laws on foreign investment, and it obtained Juan Perón's approval for U.S. oil companies to enter Argentina. In return, the Export-Import Bank was authorized to offer Argentina $60 million in credits for a steel mill. The appearance of U.S.

oil companies in Argentina aroused nationalist ire, and Perón's military successors renounced the new oil contracts. The administration continued to pressure Argentina, however, and by mid-1958 U.S. oil companies were invited back. Argentina subsequently received additional loans from U.S. agencies.[34] The United States also underwrote, as we have seen, the cost of preparing Bolivia's new oil code. And in 1956, President Eisenhower urged Brazilian officials to open their country to private oil development, eagerly offering to send a North American oilman on a secret mission to Brazil to explore possibilities with government officials.[35]

The administration's campaign for capitalism included advertising the role of foreign investment in Venezuela. When he took office in 1953, Secretary Dulles had requested Assistant Secretary John Moors Cabot to point to one country as "a showcase of what American economic cooperation could do, if permitted to operate fairly and freely." Cabot declined, because no country "fit the bill" of being democratic, honest, and hospitable to U.S. investors. Cabot argued that a "showcase" policy would prove embarrassing, unless the administration chose a country "which would commend itself broadly both in the United States and Latin America."[36] Secretary Holland proved more amenable to Dulles's request: he and other officials held up Venezuela as a model for the rest of Latin America. In 1956–57 dictator Pérez Jiménez, after years of prodding from the administration, had agreed to allow U.S. oil companies to expand their holdings in Venezuela. U.S. direct investments soared to $2.5 billion, representing about one-third of U.S. investments in Latin America. Holland constantly praised Venezuela, telling U.S. legislators that "Venezuela is a sort of showcase of private enterprise" and that it had a standard of living far exceeding that of any other Latin American country. Dulles added that if other nations emulated Venezuela in creating "a climate which is attractive to foreign capital . . . the danger of communism in South America, of social disorder will gradually disappear."[37]

In reality, neither Venezuela nor any other Latin American country enjoyed economic prosperity. Despite the influx of foreign capital, Venezuela remained a poor country, dependent on the sale of one product for its solvency. Per capita income was a meager $500 a year, and Pérez Jiménez squandered the nation's revenues on military spending and showy public works programs while allocating only 5 percent of the budget to education. Predictably, about half of Venezuela's adults were illiterate.[38] Venezuela's neighbors also stayed poor.

The ECLA estimated that, between 1956 and 1958, Latin American economies grew less than one percent a year. The prices of metals continued to decay and, in particular, the price of coffee beans—the principal export of Brazil, Colombia, Costa Rica, Guatemala, Haiti, Nicaragua, and El Salvador—fell sharply. The price of Colombian coffee, for example, steadily declined from 80 cents a pound in 1954 to 52 cents a pound in 1958.[39] The United States bought 70 percent of Latin America's coffee exports, but the administration ruled out joining any arrangement to stabilize prices. The position of the State Department and the Council on Foreign Economic Policy, a White House agency, was that "the institution of heavy governmental and intergovernmental intervention in price formation in coffee would be injurious to consumers and to the long-range interests of producers."[40]

The administration reiterated that policy when it met with Latin Americans in an economic conference held in Buenos Aires in August 1957. The purpose of the conference was to negotiate an inter-American economic treaty to complement the Rio Treaty and the OAS charter. U.S. officials cavalierly prepared for the meeting, expecting it to fail. As Secretary Dulles informed the president, "an economic treaty is not necessary to further our objectives in Latin America."[41] The head of the U.S. delegation, Robert Anderson—the new Treasury Secretary—stayed only briefly in Buenos Aires. The United States attached nineteen separate reservations to the forty-five articles of the draft treaty, objecting to any tampering with free trade and investment. To avoid a debacle, the delegates finally decided to issue an innocuous Economic Declaration of Buenos Aires. A Uruguayan official observed that the conference had "produced nothing better than a 10 percent increase in the anthology of inter-American resolutions."[42]

President Eisenhower and his key advisors were not oblivious to world poverty. Beginning in 1954, after the French defeat at Dien Bien Phu, Eisenhower gradually decided that the United States needed to promote economic development in order to promote stability and anticommunism. He increasingly lectured conservative nationalists in his party, like Treasury Secretary Humphrey, about international responsibility; concepts of "personal rights" and "personal freedom" had little attraction for starving people. In 1957, for the first time in his tenure, Eisenhower asked Congress for more economic than military aid. That year, he also persuaded Congress to establish a Development Loan Fund, an agency authorized to make soft loans for basic public works projects. The administrations's new slogan would become "trade and aid."[43] Yet Eisenhower continued to exclude Latin America from U.S. programs. He bristled whenever a Latin American official complained to him about the lack of U.S. aid, and the administration told Congress that it did not want any Development Loan Funds earmarked for the region.[44] The administration was devoted to its free trade and investment principles and did not perceive any threat to hemispheric stability.

The Eisenhower administration was proud of its Latin American policy. And U.S. actions generated few objections from Pérez Jiménez, Stroessner, or Trujillo. But, beginning in the mid-1950s, the administration was subjected to intense public criticism, emanating from both Latin America and the United States. In part, these were the same complaints that had been registered since 1945. Latin American democrats like José Figueres denounced Secretary of State Dulles for "defending corrupt dictatorships." Former Colombian president Eduardo Santos deplored military aid programs, pointing to incidents such as the one in 1957 when Colombian troops, armed with U.S. weapons, were photographed beating demonstrators. And economists associated with the ECLA continued to produce studies showing the terms of trade moving against Latin America; they resumed their call for commodity agreements and an inter-American development bank.[45]

But starting in 1956, Latin American critics of U.S. policies had a new, influential spokesman: the president of Brazil, Juscelino Kubitschek (1956–61). The energetic and ebullient Kubitschek, the former governor of the state of Minas Gerais, captured the imagination of Brazilians with his motto, "Fifty years of progress in five." He constantly preached that Brazil's and Latin America's social and economic maladies could be cured with economic growth. He stimulated the economy with deficit spending, launching national development programs and new state enterprises such as a Brazilian automotive industry. Kubitschek also gained international attention by pushing through the old Brazilian dream of building a capital city in the interior: in four years, Brazilians amazed the world by building Brasília, a glittering city with audacious, modernistic architecture. During Kubitschek's presidency, Brazil had hectic economic growth—accompanied, however, by severe inflation.

Prior to taking office, Kubitschek had brought his visions to Washington. In his January 1956 meeting with Eisenhower, the Brazilian stressed that he was a conservative and that he welcomed foreign investment. But he also needed foreign aid to accomplish his "fifty years of progress." He warned that "liberty is merely a word for those who live in extreme poverty." And he told U.S. journalists that "police repression is no way of changing a man's opinion." The "way to defeat leftist totalitarianism" was "to combat poverty wherever it may be encountered."[46] The administration was unmoved by Kubitschek's appeals. Secretary Dulles emphasized that Brazil must intensify its anti-Communist program at home, and Eisenhower stressed the necessity of doing "everything possible to reassure private initiative of the great possibilities which exist in Brazil." The president liked Kubitschek but badly underestimated him, doubting "his stamina if he gets into a real battle."[47] Rebuffed in 1956, the Brazilian would resume his campaign for U.S. assistance in the late 1950s.

Although unable to sway the Eisenhower administration, Latin Americans received a sympathetic hearing from U.S. legislators, particularly Democratic members of the Senate Foreign Relations Committee. The anti-Communist hysteria engendered by the Korean War and McCarthyism had subsided; legislators were again willing to debate inter-American policies. Moreover, in January 1955 the Democrats regained control of the Senate and would strengthen their hold in subsequent elections. Their leader was Senator J. William Fulbright, the dominant member and, beginning in 1959, chair of the Foreign Relations Committee. Senator Wayne Morse, the maverick Oregonian, headed the subcommittee on Latin America. Fulbright and Morse were backed by other powerful Democrats on the committee, including Mike Mansfield, Hubert Humphrey, John Kennedy, and Frank Church. These mainly liberal Democrats did not question the basic tenets of U.S. policy: anticommunism, free trade and investment, and the hegemony of the United States in the Western Hemisphere. Their differences with the administration were over means. By supporting military dictators and denying economic assistance, the administration might be forcing desperate Latin Americans to turn to radical solutions. Some Republican senators—such as George Aiken of Vermont, Homer Capehart of Indiana, and Bourke Hickenlooper—were also distressed, although they declined to criticize the president publicly. Hickenlooper, the conservative from Iowa and the ranking Republican on the subcommittee on Latin America, confessed that "we treated the Southern Hemisphere as sort of in the nature of the traditional old witch's stepchild."[48]

The Foreign Relations Committee focused on military aid, methodically examining administration witnesses. Senator Fulbright wondered, for example, whether the $6 million proposed for Cuba in 1956 was "to keep Batista in power or repel the Russian air force?" He discovered, in executive session, that the $6 million would support a battalion of 800 men and three squadrons of airplanes, but no jet aircraft. A Defense official conceded that this force would not "be effective in actually repelling the Russians." Other witnesses disclosed that hemispheric defense plans had not been carefully reviewed since 1951. Perhaps nettled by Fulbright's relentless questions, the administration by early 1958 was offering different explanations. Secretary of Defense Neil McElroy testified that military aid was "primarily for internal security." McElroy's subordinate, Mansfield Sprague, added that, whereas it was not U.S. policy to prevent elections or support dictatorships, he was "afraid from time to time it does have that effect." Yet the administration rejected the committee's recommendation that military aid be limited to democracies: overlooking its own testimony about the results of military aid, it told incredulous senators that to discriminate between democracies and dictatorships would suggest that the United States was meddling in the internal affairs of other countries and would thereby violate the inter-American principle of nonintervention.[49]

Democratic senators were similarly frustrated over the administration's position on economic aid. Reviewing the budgetary requests for 1956, Senator Humphrey noted that "it seems the three places you have made substantial grants-in-aid are where the Communists have taken over [Guatemala], where the industries have been socialized [Bolivia], and where there has been destruction from a hurricane [Haiti]." Humphrey asked: "Is that what we are waiting for?"[50] Accepting Brazilian President Kubitschek's contention that economic growth was the best way to fight communism, Democratic committee members called for development assistance programs for Latin America. Senator George Smathers, a conservative Democrat from Florida, became the spokesman for Latin America on the Senate floor. Smathers was not a member of the Foreign Relations Committee, but because of his constituency and his state's geographic position, he had a natural interest in Caribbean affairs. In 1956 and 1957, over administration objections, Smathers convinced the legislators to allocate a small amount of money, less than $20 million, for development assistance in Latin America. The administration's opposition was ironic: it annually had difficulty convincing legislators, particularly Republicans, to vote for foreign aid.[51]

Although the Democrats embarrassed administration witnesses, they did not convince President Eisenhower and his key advisors to review critically the Latin American policy of the United States. Nor did the senators feel confident enough to challenge the administration and launch independent congressional investigations. The region was quiet and free of Communists. And the public was satisfied with the president's foreign policy.

During the mid-1950s, the policies the Eisenhower administration "deemed appropriate" for preventing communism in Latin America included befriending dictatorships and belittling economic nationalism. Whereas these anti-Communist policies achieved the administration's primary foreign policy goal for Latin America, they also reinforced a dismal status quo in the region. Most Latin Americans were poor, living in countries with monocultural, export-dependent economies. Their aspirations for change were stymied by military dictators who ruled on behalf of socioeconomic elites. But in the late 1950s, frustrated Latin Americans would topple repressive regimes, call for sweeping social and economic reforms, and challenge U.S. policies in the hemisphere—and the embattled Eisenhower administration would respond by finally heeding its critics from North and South America.

CHAPTER 6

THE NIXON TRIP

1958–1959

The Eisenhower administration's smug confidence in its Latin American policy was abruptly shaken in May 1958, when Vice-President Richard Nixon, who was touring South America, was greeted by angry protestors throughout the continent and was nearly killed by a howling mob in Caracas, Venezuela. The vice-president found Latin Americans bitter over U.S. policies and furious that his government backed regimes that blocked social change. He also heard the familiar refrain that the United States "neglected" Latin America. Fearing that Latin Americans would no longer defer to U.S. leadership, the Eisenhower administration hastily adjusted its policies on the issues of democracy, human rights, and economic and military aid.

It was the new assistant secretary of state for Latin American Affairs, Roy Richard Rubottom, who initiated the decision to send Vice-President Nixon to South America. Rubottom, a career foreign-service officer, replaced Henry Holland, who left the State Department in September 1956 and returned to private law practice, representing U.S. corporations in Latin America. Secretary of State Dulles chose Rubottom after resisting political pressures to appoint Robert Hill, an archconservative politician from New Hampshire who had served in the State Department and as ambassador to Costa Rica during Eisenhower's first term. Dulles apparently believed that Hill would not be sufficiently loyal and deferential to him, and Hill was named Ambassador to Mexico instead. In tapping Rubottom, Dulles chose a cautious man, but one whose views on inter-American relations were similar to those of John Moors Cabot, whom Dulles had previously dismissed. Like Cabot, Rubottom held that the United States should focus on economic and social issues in formulating policies for Latin America. Although his was an uncontroversial appointment, Rubottom experienced difficulty in gaining confirmation from the Senate. Senator Wayne Morse, the chair of the subcommittee on Latin America of the Foreign Relations Committee, subjected Rubottom to lengthy interrogations during confirmation hearings, using the public sessions to denounce the administration for pandering to dictators like Rafael Trujillo. After Morse had made his point, the Senate confirmed Rubottom on 18 June 1957.[1]

Rubottom implicitly questioned the administration's contention that inter-American relations were cordial and solid. In the last week of 1957, he urged Dulles to tour Latin America in February 1958. He noted that "the economic situation in the whole area has deteriorated," with coffee prices declining and a "catastrophic price drop in metals." The administration had responded to the economic crisis by recommending that Latin Americans slash government expenditures, reduce arms expenditures, and delay economic development programs. Latin Americans found such advice "highly unpalatable." Rubottom warned Dulles that Communists might take advantage of these economic troubles.[2] Secretary Dulles forwarded Rubottom's memorandum to President Eisenhower, with the notation that he wanted to visit South America but that he was already scheduled to attend conferences in Europe, the Middle East, and Southeast Asia in the first half of 1958. Replying that "I urgently believe something should be done," Eisenhower suggested sending Vice-President Nixon. Eisenhower ventured that, after Nixon's tour, Dulles and possibly even the president himself might visit South America.[3]

Richard Nixon did not relish his assignment, which was finally scheduled for May 1958. The vice-president had previously toured Central America in 1955 and attended Brazilian President Kubitschek's inauguration in 1956. He told aides that he did not plan to make written or oral reports on his trip and did not want press interviews. Upon returning to Washington, he would not report to the CIA, NSC, or State Department; instead, he would talk informally with Secretary Dulles. As Nixon emphasized, "I cannot be loaded down with people who are interested in South America."[4] The primary purpose of the trip was to attend the inauguration of Arturo Frondizi, the popularly elected president of Argentina: the administration wanted to make amends for its past support of Juan Perón. In addition, Nixon would visit Peru and Venezuela, where dictators had been recently overthrown. An irritated Nixon also learned that the State Department insisted that he visit other Spanish-speaking countries in South America.[5]

The trip to South America proved to be one of the momentous "crises" in Richard Nixon's political career. Nixon was harassed by law students in Montevideo, stoned by university students in Lima, and assaulted by a mob in Caracas. The demonstrators blamed the United States for Latin America's social ills: the Eisenhower administration had supported repressive regimes, had denied Latin America economic assistance, and was now imposing tariff barriers against Latin American exports. Venezuelans, for example, denounced the administration for its past connivance with the deposed Marcos Pérez Jiménez and its present harboring of the fugitive dictator and his chief of secret police, the notorious Pedro Estrada. They also correctly feared that, in order to protect domestic oil producers, the United States was about to limit imports of Venezuelan fuel oil. The ugly incident in Caracas was particularly unsettling for the administration: the vice-president was nearly killed in the "showcase" of U.S. policy in Latin America.[6]

The effect of the unhappy Nixon trip was to spark a debate about the Latin American policy of the United States. The Eisenhower administration initially focused on identifying the demonstrators. In his report to the cabinet, Nixon stressed that the extremists "without any doubt were Communists." The fact that the protestors all chanted the same slogans "was absolute proof that they were directed and controlled by a central Communist conspiracy." The vice-president conceded in a speech, however, that although "Communists spearheaded the attack, they had a lot of willing spear carriers with them." Secretary of State Dulles took up Nixon's Communist conspiracy theme, telling the cabinet that the Soviets had cleverly infiltrated mass political movements in Latin America.[7] But CIA Director Allen Dulles thought it too facile to blame the international Communist movement. He sharply rebuked his brother, informing the secretary of state that "there would be trouble in Latin America if there were no Communists." Moreover, his agency could find no evidence that Moscow had inspired or directed the attacks on Nixon. Indeed, in a mid-1958 study, the CIA concluded that Moscow considered Latin America an appendage of the United States and that therefore "the bloc leadership has been reluctant to allocate to Latin America any substantial proportion of the bloc's total political, economic, and propaganda resources devoted to foreign penetration activities."[8]

The debate within the administration was echoed in Washington and throughout the country. Both the Senate and the House of Representatives launched investigations into the Nixon trip and inter-American relations. Latin American critics of the administration's policies, including José Figueres and Pedro Beltrán, the future prime minister of Peru, were invited to testify. Legislators such as Morse and Senator George Aiken went on study trips to South America. The president called Dr. Milton Eisenhower back into government service, sending him this time on a fact-finding tour of Central America. The U.S. Information Agency surveyed the media in Latin America, seeking to plumb the depths of anti-American sentiment.[9] Businessmen also scrambled to analyze the trouble. The Business Advisory Council's Committee on Latin America, which was composed of representatives from such major U.S. corporations as Chase Manhattan Bank, DuPont, General Motors, International Business Machines, Texaco, and Pan American Airways, concluded that "serious political and economic problems exist and constitute obstacles to U.S. private investment." Individual businessmen like Harry Guggenheim and Lamar Fleming (of Anderson, Clayton and Company) agreed, warning Eisenhower that he must pay more attention to Latin America.[10]

The concern over Latin America merged into a wider debate in 1958 about the United States' position in the world and the quality of President Eisenhower's leadership. The nation had been stunned, in late 1957, when the Soviet Union launched into earth orbit an artificial satellite or "sputnik." The Soviets' scientific and technological triumph shattered the confidence of the U.S. public; it also suggested that the Soviets would soon threaten the United States with new nuclear weapon delivery systems. The administration was further beset by cold-war crises in Lebanon, Berlin, and Quemoy and Matsu. At home, the administration had deep political problems, as the U.S. economy went into a severe recession: unemployment rates rose to 7 percent, and the nation's industrial output fell by 14 percent. President Eisenhower, who had an approval rating from fellow citizens of 79 percent in early 1957, saw his approval ratings plunge below 50 percent in 1958.[11] The attack on Vice-President Nixon seemed part of a nightmarish series of setbacks for the country. On the day Nixon was attacked in Caracas, violent anti-American protests erupted in Algeria, Burma, and Lebanon. A distraught Eisenhower told his secretary, Ann Whitman, "I am about ready to go put my uniform on." In fact, he dispatched the Sixth Fleet to sail toward Lebanon and ordered 1,000 troops to be readied for a rescue mission in Venezuela.[12]

While publicly blaming Communists for the attacks on Nixon, the administration knew it needed a new approach to restore public confidence and to assuage the Latin Americans. Vice-President Nixon called for a revised recognition policy. Within the government and in public addresses, he argued that the United States should adhere to the nonintervention principles of the OAS but should make it clear that it preferred to work with democracies. As he cleverly put it, "a formal handshake for dictators; an *embraso* for leaders in freedom."[13] Nixon's suggestion was both artful and brazen—during his 1955 tour of Central America, he had, of course, hugged Fulgencio Batista and Rafael Trujillo. In any case, the vice-president had to overcome the opposition of Secretary Dulles. In a meeting with the president, Dulles mocked Nixon's idea, asserting that it was "not possible in a brief trip to many countries to come back with a formula for a solution." Dulles also held that, when uneducated masses took over, they were "not going to practice democracy as we know it"; instead, he foresaw "dictatorships of the proletariat" or populist dictators "of the Nasser type."[14] Dulles lost the argument. After mid-1958, it was politically unacceptable to claim that socioeconomic elites could best protect the interests of the United States in Latin America. As one congressional committee investigating the Nixon trip reported, the United States had to stop creating the impression in Latin America that it was "indifferent to the sufferings of oppressed people."[15] The secretary of state's influence was also waning as cancer sapped his physical strength. In February 1959, President Eisenhower approved NSC 5902/1, which called upon the United States to give "special encouragement" to representative governments.[16]

The new approach was not only politically appealing but also realistic, for between 1956 and 1960 ten military dictators fell from power, in a process that one journalist hopefully tagged "the twilight of the tyrants." The dictators had not been able to produce the stability and economic growth they had promised. Latin Americans tired of the rampant repression and corruption that characterized military rule. Notably, the Roman Catholic church, a traditional ally of the oligarchy and the military, began to criticize military dictators. The church, under the leadership of Pope Pius XII and Pope John XXIII, had begun to defend social reform movements. In several countries, such as Venezuela, mass protests followed the reading of a pastoral letter denouncing corrupt, repressive rule. The dictators were also undermined by the collapse of their economies. The

U.S. recession reverberated throughout the hemisphere: eleven Latin American countries had per capita incomes of less than $200 per year. The dictators were replaced by leaders, such as Argentina's Arturo Frondizi, whose political base was among urban middle sectors and whose programs included land reform, popular education, social services, and constitutionalism.[17]

Instead of awarding medals to dictators, President Eisenhower began to express publicly his preference for political democracy and respect for human rights. In August 1958, in a ceremony that received a wide notice throughout the hemisphere, the president heartily welcomed the new Venezuelan ambassador and declared that "authoritarianism and autocracy of whatever form are incompatible with ideals of our great leaders of the past." Eisenhower's statement marked the first time that a high administration official had openly and unequivocally recommended representative government for Latin America. Over the next two years, the president repeatedly reaffirmed that position. In 1959 he told Arturo Frondizi that he wanted to help, noting that "the Argentines were the same kind of people we were and the Argentine government and President Frondizi stood for the same things that we stood for." In addition, Eisenhower met with an influential Argentine officer, General Pedro Aramburu, and congratulated him for respecting constitutional processes. The president also wrote open letters of support to embattled democratic leaders and authorized the State Department and the Immigration Service to begin deportation proceedings against Pérez Jiménez, who was residing in Florida.[18]

Although it supported popularly elected leaders, the administration in 1958–59 carefully adhered to its nonintervention pledge, rejecting calls that it recognize *only* representative governments. The new Venezuelan president, Rómulo Betancourt, proposed in 1959 that members of the OAS recognize only "regimes born of free election and respecting human rights." The Betancourt Doctrine, which resembled the Larreta Doctrine of 1945, was founded on the premise that it was "nonsensical" to denounce totalitarian regimes in Asia and Europe and yet to tolerate despotic governments in the Western Hemisphere. Betancourt had been particularly incensed when the United States insisted in 1954 that the American states adopt an anti-Communist resolution, the Declaration of Caracas, while meeting in Pérez Jiménez's Venezuela.[19] Betancourt specifically asked the OAS to exclude Rafael Trujillo from the inter-American community: the Dominican dictator had been meddling in Caribbean and Central

American affairs and assisting ousted right-wing groups, including Venezuelan military officers. In August 1959, OAS foreign ministers met to discuss the Dominican issue and the turmoil throughout the Caribbean basin. The new U.S. secretary of state, Christian Herter, stoutly defended the OAS charter, observing that "history has shown that attempts to impose democracy upon a country by force from without may easily result in the mere substitution of one form of tyranny for another." Herter's position was enthusiastically backed by foreign ministers from influential states like Argentina and Mexico. Most Latin Americans flatly opposed compromising the nonintervention principle. The foreign ministers overwhelmingly rejected the Betancourt Doctrine, refusing to break diplomatic relations with the Dominican Republic.[20]

The Eisenhower administration was sufficiently flexible to have modified its stance toward dictators, but it was unwilling to abandon a mainstay of its Latin American policy: military aid. It was forced, however, to defend the program. In the aftermath of the Nixon trip, congressional critics were emboldened to challenge the administration publicly. Led again by Senator J. William Fulbright, Democrats on the Senate Foreign Relations Committee wrote an open letter to Eisenhower in August 1958. They reminded the president they had just voted for a Mutual Security Act, as they had loyally done in previous years—but they believed that "with respect to the less developed countries there is a serious distortion in the present relative importance which is attached to military and related aid on the one hand and technical assistance on the other." Military assistance had bolstered unrepresentative regimes, created a militaristic image of the United States, and built and perpetuated hierarchies that "endanger the very values of individual freedom which we seek to safeguard." The Democrats implored Eisenhower to reconsider military assistance.[21]

The president responded in November 1958 by appointing William Draper, a retired general, to review U.S. military assistance programs. The Draper Committee was charged to "undertake a completely independent, objective, and non-partisan analysis," but its conclusions seemed preordained: of the committee's nine members, three were retired generals, one a retired admiral, and one a former assistant secretary of defense.[22] Moreover, Dulles advised Eisenhower to appoint the committee and have it issue a public report so as to put military assistance "on a sound long-term basis." As Dulles told Fulbright in early 1959, although he shared the senator's concerns about excessive military aid, "if we carried out our theory too rigidly the practical result would be that many friendly governments would collapse and Communism would take over."[23]

The Draper Committee, which issued its final report in August 1959, predictably endorsed the administration's view and categorically rejected the Democrats' charges. Economic and military assistance were interchangeable, for "without internal security, and the general feeling of confidence engendered by adequate military forces, there is little hope for any economic progress." Military assistance actually promoted economic progress by improving the educational and administrative skills of officers and men. And through training programs, U.S. military officers inculcated democracy by "promoting an appreciation of the values of our civilization and way of life."[24] The committee arrived at its conclusions after listening to official witnesses. Military officers informed the committee that the Soviet Union posed no military threat to Latin America—but Acting Secretary of State Herter, writing for the ailing Dulles, found that irrelevant. The key question was: "Is the country on our side?" Communism threatened the United States; therefore, "a more urgent value—security and survival—must take precedence over an absolute commitment to the promotion of democracy."[25]

During its last years in office, the Eisenhower administration cited the conclusions of the Draper Committee in defending military assistance. Indeed, the administration expanded military aid programs, asking for over $160 million for Latin America in 1959–60. As Secretary Rubottom told members of the Senate, contact with the military was "crucial in the context of our total relations with a country": the military could protect fledgling democracies from subversion and violence. Rubottom pointed out that, because military dictators had been recently overthrown, the popular charge that U.S. military assistance kept dictators in power could not be sustained. And in countries such as Argentina and Colombia, military officers had overseen the transition to civilian rule. Rubottom also suggested that, by granting military aid, the United States was indirectly providing Latin Americans with more capital for socioeconomic development. Responding to this "frustrating" testimony, Fulbright and his colleagues amended the Mutual Security Act to read that U.S. military assistance could not be used for internal security requirements. Even so, the amendment allowed the president to make exceptions.[26]

The Eisenhower administration refused to abandon its military aid program because it did not want to jeopardize its anti-Communist policies. The administration now warmly praised civilian leaders in Latin America, but it did not trust them to keep the region free of communism. By supplying arms and training, the United States maintained leverage and influence over a bulwark of anticommunism: the corps of Latin American military officers. As Richard Nixon argued, military officers were "a great stabilizing force" and were essential in protecting governments from "the highly trained subversive cadres maintained by the Communists." Ambassador to Peru Theodore Achilles agreed, warning the State Department that military aid was "needed to maintain the armed forces as a strong stabilizing and anti-communist element." The administration incorporated those views in NSC 5902/1, the new comprehensive statement on Latin American policy. The United States should strive to be the sole supplier of military hardware to Latin America as "a means of maintaining U.S. influence over Latin American military forces and through such forces on the political orientation of Latin American governments."[27]

The ambiguous and contradictory positions of its critics enabled the Eisenhower administration to have its way on military aid. Senators on the Foreign Relations Committee understood that military aid had no hemispheric defense purposes; in John Kennedy's words, money allocated was "down the drain in a military sense." They also agreed with Russell Long, a conservative Democrat from Louisiana, that "all you are going to get" for military aid "is to provide some dictators with tanks and planes with which to murder their own people when their people try to throw them out." But only Senators Morse and Frank Church of Idaho were willing to eliminate the program. The legislators did not want to be blamed for losing the cold war. They recalled that the Guatemalan military had helped oust Communists. Senator Fulbright summarized majority sentiment when he grudgingly observed that, although he opposed military aid, "the only disciplined and effective organization in many of these countries is the military." Accordingly, congressional critics of military aid continued to vote for it.[28]

Latin American leaders similarly acted against their own desires. In 1958, Costa Rica, the sturdy democracy that had abolished its army in 1948, proposed an arms control treaty for Latin America. Ambassador Gonzalo Facio asked OAS members to admit the obvious: Latin American nations were not capable of playing a meaningful role in hemispheric defense and were dependent on the United

States. Money saved on arms expenditures could be dedicated to economic development. The proposal predictably met a frigid reception; Latin Americans were unwilling to proclaim their military impotence.[29] But Latin American democrats privately agreed with Costa Rica's argument. For example, diplomats confidentially informed members of the Senate Foreign Relations Committee that they opposed military aid for their region. In early 1960, Chilean and Peruvian officials asked the United States to limit arms sales to Latin America and to promote hemispheric disarmament—but they simultaneously asked for destroyers and submarines, explaining that they needed to preserve the appearance of military parity with their neighbors and to placate their own armed forces.[30] As did the Eisenhower administration, Latin American civilian officials understood that military officers were dominant political forces in their countries.

Beyond altering its stance on dictatorships, the Eisenhower administration had also to modify its foreign economic policy for Latin America. While the attacks on the vice-president captured international attention, Nixon's private meetings with South American leaders centered on what most troubled Latin Americans. President Camilo Ponce Enríquez of Ecuador opened his discussion with Nixon by asserting that "Ecuador's principal problem was that of raising the living standards of the people." President-elect Alberto Lleras Camargo of Colombia warned that, "if a better way of life could not be available to the people, an 'explosion' was inevitable." President Hernán Siles Zuazo of Bolivia confessed to Nixon that he feared he would be assassinated by his countrymen if he could not resolve Bolivia's mounting social and economic problems. To these laments, Nixon could only respond by observing that Latin Americans needed to stimulate private investments, and by reiterating U.S. opposition to commodity agreements, loans to state enterprises, and development assistance for Latin America. Despite concern over Latin America's economic woes the administration had not, prior to May 1958, reexamined its policies. The vice-president had been instructed to uphold the traditional foreign economic policy of the United States in Latin America.[31]

The warnings and pleas that Nixon heard were reiterated for the administration by the redoubtable president of Brazil, Juscelino Kubitschek. Knowing that both Eisenhower and the U.S. public were now paying attention, the Brazilian pressed the case that he had first argued in 1956. Two weeks after the riot in Caracas, Kubitschek wrote a letter (which was subsequently published) to Eisenhower, in which he deplored the attacks on Nixon, noting that "before world opinion, the ideal of Pan American unity suffered serious impairment." He vowed that "something must be done to restore composure to the continental unity." Alleging that he had no comprehensive plans, Kubitschek called, however, for a "thorough revision" of hemispheric programs.[32] The harried Eisenhower responded by sending Rubottom and then Dulles to Rio de Janeiro to meet with Kubitschek. The Brazilian president emphasized to U.S. officials that "the problem of underdevelopment will have to be solved if Latin American nations are to be able more effectively to resist subversion and serve the Western cause." In specific, Kubitschek thought the United States should pledge $40 billion in foreign aid to Latin America over the next twenty years. His program, dubbed "Operation Pan America," was, of course, the enduring hemispheric quest, the Marshall Plan for Latin America. Over the next two years, the persistent Kubitschek often wrote to Eisenhower, prodding him to send U.S. aid to Latin America.[33]

Although few U.S. officials supported President Kubitschek's grandiose plans, his views and the private letters to Eisenhower of other desperate Latin American presidents strengthened the position of those who believed that the administration had to alter its foreign economic policies.[34] These officials included Rubottom, Dr. Eisenhower, John Moors Cabot, State Department economic officer Thomas Mann, and Undersecretary of State for Economic Affairs C. Douglas Dillon. These men opined that the United States was unwittingly jeopardizing its security by ignoring Latin America's economic needs. Dillon, Mann, and Rubottom had attended the 1957 inter-American economic conference and were appalled by the administration's arrogant rejection of Latin American proposals. Mann, for example, predicted disaster for the hemisphere if the price of coffee was not stabilized. They also questioned whether private enterprise alone could address development needs. Cabot, who had returned to the hemisphere as ambassador to Colombia, repeated his view that foreign investors would not enter countries that had primitive roads and harbors and illiterate, malnourished people. This poverty and underdevelopment now threatened the United States. Dictators were falling and the region was "on the verge of upheaval." To prevent extreme, left-wing revolutions, the United States needed to aid Latin American democrats who favored orderly reform. As Dr. Eisenhower observed, Latin America was being engulfed by "a surging, swelling, revolutionary demand, not just for aid, but for rapid social revolution in country after country."[35]

The leader of this group calling for economic assistance for Latin America was Douglas Dillon. Dillon came from a powerful and wealthy New York banking family with extensive international ties. In 1957, Secretary Dulles appointed Dillon, who had been ambassador to France, to head the economic section of the State Department—Dulles had belatedly recognized that his anti-Communist crusade needed an economic component. Dillon proved an adept bureaucrat, limiting the influence of the Treasury and Commerce departments over foreign economic policy. That the formidable George Humphrey had resigned and had been succeeded by the less doctrinaire Robert Anderson, a Texas oilman, surely made Dillon's work easier. After Dulles resigned in early 1959, Dillon became Christian Herter's undersecretary of state and an influential advisor to the president on inter-American affairs. He continued to help formulate Latin American policy in the early 1960s, serving as secretary of the treasury in the Kennedy administration.[36]

Dillon's first accomplishment in inter-American affairs was to modify the U.S. position on commodity agreements. Codified in 1955, the policy ruled out U.S. participation in arrangements to stabilize markets or prices. As Clarence Randall, director of the Council on Foreign Economic Policy, explained, the United States needed a rigid policy, because "you cannot compromise with the basic principles of the system of private initiative and free markets," for "every dilution takes you further toward socialism." The United States did indulge in such socialism, however. As a major producer of wheat, it had participated in an international wheat agreement since 1949. It subsidized exports of cotton, and it regulated trade in sugar with three client states—Cuba, the Dominican Republic, and the Philippine Islands.[37] Two weeks after Vice-President Nixon returned from South America, the administration further relaxed its opposition to commodity agreements. Secretary Dulles, who had been pressured by Dillon and Thomas Mann, obtained the president's and the NSC's consent to give a "liberal interpretation" to the clause in the trade policy that permitted discussions about commodity problems. Thereafter, Dillon vigorously pushed through that loophole, warning that additional declines in coffee and metal prices portended social instability, revolution, and communism in Latin America. By the end of 1958, the United States had joined inter-American "study groups" on coffee and on lead and zinc. Dillon had cowed opponents by threatening to "appeal to the President if necessary." He also had been aided by decisions of the Business Advisory Council and the National Coffee Association to support an international solution to coffee problems. His work culminated in September 1959, when most major coffee producers signed an agreement pledging to support prices by limiting coffee exports.[38]

The administration's second significant economic initiative came in August 1958, when Dillon announced, at a meeting of the Inter-American Economic and Social Council, that the United States would support a regional development bank. Latin Americans had waited nearly seventy years for this decision. Secretary of State James G. Blaine had first broached the idea in 1889 at a Pan American Conference, and Latin Americans thought that they had received a solid commitment for a bank from Undersecretary of State Sumner Welles during the emergency meeting of foreign ministers held in Rio de Janeiro in early 1942. Dillon's dramatic announcement represented another triumph for officials who believed that the United States needed to assist Latin America's development. (Realistically, the administration could no longer deny Latin America. In 1957 the European Economic Community had established a development fund for Africa. And a day after Dillon's announcement, President Eisenhower promised in a speech at the United Nations to sponsor a regional development bank for the Arab world; this promise followed his July decision to land U.S. marines in Lebanon.)[39] In April 1959 an inter-American agreement was reached to set the initial capitalization of the bank at $1 billion, with the United States supplying 45 percent of the capital. The bank would be permitted to dedicate 15 percent of its capital to a special fund for soft loans. After more than a year of fund raising and planning, the Inter-American Development Bank began operation in October 1960; it made its first development loan in February 1961.[40]

The public decisions to support commodity agreements and an inter-American bank were undergirded by a moderate shift in the administration's philosophical approach toward Latin America. In NSC 5902/1, which Eisenhower approved on 12 February 1959, the administration restated its traditional goals of expanding U.S. trade and investment, promoting capitalism, and discouraging economic nationalism—but, for the first time, it told itself that "Latin America is and must be dealt with primarily as an underdeveloped area." Latin Americans' aspirations for democracy, industrialization, and higher living standards were "rising more rapidly than they are being satisfied." Moreover, the region might not be able to replicate North American patterns of development—they might need, for example, a free enterprise system "adapted to local conditions." Therefore, to assist Latin Americans and to assure political and economic stability in the hemisphere, the United States might have to move beyond the Export-Import Bank and the new regional bank and, in "exceptional circumstances," grant development assistance. Whatever the solution, NSC 5902/1 concluded that in the past the United States had "not made efforts in all fields commensurate with the magnitude of the problems" and that it was "clear that a consistent and continuing major effort will be required."[41]

However, even though, in the aftermath of the Nixon trip, the Eisenhower administration had begun to focus on Latin America and to propose new initiatives, it had not radically restructured its policies. It still did not believe, for example, that "a consistent and continuing major effort" meant spending vast sums in the region. Its proposal for an inter-American development bank was modest, especially compared to President Kubitschek's suggestion of an initial capitalization of $5 billion for the bank.[42] Moreover, the administration saw few "exceptional circumstances" that called for development assistance; in 1959, Congress was asked for only $25 million in development assistance, with the bulk of that assistance again going to Guatemala and Bolivia. The administration now permitted the Development Loan Fund to consider Latin American loan requests— but the agency favored South Asia, the Far East, and Africa; by early 1960, Latin America had received only 8 percent of the loans.[43] In lieu of development assistance, administration officials suggested stabilization loans from the International Monetary Fund. In return for that aid, hard-pressed Latin American leaders in Argentina, Chile, Colombia, and Peru had to reduce government payrolls, delay development projects, and devalue their currencies, and such austerity measures inevitably fanned popular discontent with these new constitutional governments. Only President Kubitschek of Brazil spurned fiscal conservativism, because, as one U.S. government memorandum disapprovingly noted, he had "the theory that 'underdevelopment' is the root cause of the country's problems."[44]

The failure of the Eisenhower administration fundamentally to change its Latin American policy was due to the resistance of its two senior officials to change, and also to the fact that they and others believed that the region, although tumultuous, was still secure.

President Eisenhower was stunned and angered by the ferocious criticism his foreign policy was subjected to in 1958—even his beloved brother, Milton, chided him for granting "special" recognition to dictators. The president called 1958 "the worst [year] of his life." But he was undissuaded, continuing to hold that Latin Americans needed to attract private investment and to root out radicalism. At a cabinet meeting in February 1959, for example, Eisenhower received a briefing from Thomas Mann on Operation Pan America; he responded by remarking that he approved of Latin American leaders who "battled" their people and then noted that he had given Adolfo López Mateos, the new president of Mexico, a book on the dangers of communism.[45] Secretary of State Dulles agreed with his president. Although he had brought Douglas Dillon into the State Department, Dulles never wavered from his almost purely political approach to foreign policy. When, in the summer of 1958, he went to confer with Kubitschek, Dulles tried to turn the subject of conversation away from underdevelopment to communism. Upon returning to Washington, Dulles reported to the president that he was mystified by the Brazilian's "reluctance to have used the word 'Communism' in our communique." For his part, Kubitschek called Dulles "a tenacious, intransigent debater, almost incapable of compromise."[46]

Eisenhower and Dulles rejected Kubitschek's program because they discounted the region's vulnerability to Communist penetration. To be sure, the administration's reflex response to Nixon's troubles was to blame it on the international Communist movement. And it perceived its military aid program as an anti-Communist insurance policy. But Eisenhower and Dulles, backed by intelligence analysts, did not believe that the Soviet Union had immediate plans for Latin America. After the overthrow of the Arbenz government in Guatemala, Secretary Dulles concluded that Moscow had altered its strategy, believing that Communists had "learned from their Guatemalan experience that, even if opportune, an isolated Communist seizure of control tends to undercut over-all Communist objectives for the area by alarming and rallying the hemisphere against international communism." Citing pronouncements by Nikita Khrushchev and Mao Zedong, Dulles predicted that the Communists would go "the indirect aggression" route with a "national front" strategy. They could be expected to unite with political groups advocating socially progressive causes such as economic development, national economic independence, labor unity and freedom, and agrarian reform. By exaggerating nationalist objectives and setting unrealistic timetables for fulfilling legitimate aspirations, the Communists would then arouse anti-American feelings in the region.[47]

The CIA and the NSC accepted this analysis. Moscow was "somewhat restrained" and "cautious" in regard to Latin America. Bulganin's 1956 offer to expand contacts with the region had not materialized; in 1958, Latin America conducted barely one percent of its trade with the Soviet bloc. Moreover, Latin American Communists had little ideological appeal in their countries and no chance of coming to power. Accordingly, their strategy was "to camouflage revolutionary aims" and "to identify themselves with nationalist aspirations," hoping "to disengage Latin America from its traditional alignment with this country." Their short-term goal was the development of " 'neutralist' governments on the model of Nasser's Egypt, Nehru's India, and Sukarno's Indonesia." The "fundamental objective" of the United States, therefore, must be "to retain its ascendancy as the leader of the Western Hemisphere and to undercut efforts of International Communism to disengage Latin America from its traditional alignment with this country."[48]

In view of these findings, administration officials remained sanguine about inter-American relations. They actually concluded that the vice-president's unhappy experience had had salutary effects, for it had alerted them and the U.S. public to potential dangers. The administration pledged not to relax its attention toward Latin America and to play a constructive role in assisting the area to attain higher political and economic standards, but its basic assumptions about Latin America remained static. Until 1960, the Eisenhower administration continued to hold that a secure and stable hemisphere could be achieved basically with free trade and investment policies, military aid, and admonitions to Latin Americans not to form ties with Moscow or with local Communist parties.

In 1958–59, in pursuit of the "fundamental objective" of asserting U.S. leadership in the Western Hemisphere, President Eisenhower modified his Latin American policy. By praising representative governments and by encouraging commodity agreements and a regional development bank, the president and his advisors hoped to mollify Latin Americans and restore calm and stability to inter-American relations. But although the administration had been profoundly embarrassed by protests and political upheavals in Latin America, they believed that the danger was not grave. U.S. officials questioned whether the Soviet Union was capable of challenging the regional hegemony of the United States, and thus the Eisenhower administration altered its Latin American policy without substantially refashioning it. A thorough revision of policy awaited a reassessment of the appeal and strength of communism in Latin America.

CHAPTER 7

THE CASTRO-COMMUNIST THREAT

1959–1960

In early 1960, the Eisenhower administration suddenly feared that the United States could lose the cold war in Latin America. Cuba, under the fiery leadership of Fidel Castro, had been abruptly transformed from a client of the United States into a radical, bitterly anti-American nation. Moreover, U.S. officials speculated that Castro might allow the Soviet Union to use Cuba as a beachhead for Communist expansion throughout the Western Hemisphere. Confronted by this "Castro-Communist" challenge, the Eisenhower administration rapidly revised its Latin American policies. It prepared to overthrow Castro and dismantle the Cuban Revolution. It also decided that, to prevent radicalism from spreading, it had to underwrite a thoroughgoing reform of Latin America's political, social, and economic institutions.

In the first days of 1959, the rebels of the 26th of July Movement took control of Cuba and its capital city, Havana. Their triumph marked the end of a guerrilla war against Fulgencio Batista, the Cuban strongman who had dominated the island's political life since 1934 and had directly ruled since 1952, when he seized power. With his army and police in disarray, the vicious and venal Batista hustled his relatives onto an airplane and flew to the safety of the Dominican Republic, the home of dictator Rafael Trujillo. The news of Batista's flight set off wild New Year's Day celebrations throughout Cuba. The savage war was over, and another Latin American tyrant had fallen from power.

Fidel Castro, the privileged son of a sugar planter, commanded the rebel army. As a youth, Castro was an outstanding athlete and an excellent student, earning a law degree from the University of Havana. He was active in student politics and a fervent admirer of the

Cuban national hero, José Martí. Like other educated young Cubans, he denounced Batista's 1952 overthrow of President Carlos Prío Socarrás. Castro first came to national attention on 26 July 1953, when he led a band of 165 students in a disastrous storming of the army barracks at Moncada in the southeastern city of Santiago. He received a fifteen-year jail sentence for his rebellion, but he was freed from prison in 1955 by Batista who was feeling secure and wished to burnish his international reputation by releasing the young rebels. Castro and his brother Raúl fled to Mexico to plan another assault on the Batista regime. In 1956, Fidel Castro and eighty-one other men struggled ashore after their leaky ship, *Granma*, beached on Cuba's eastern shore. Again, their attack proved futile; within a few days, Batista's army had killed most of the insurgents. The survivors, who included the Castro brothers and Argentine revolutionary Ernesto "Ché" Guevara, retreated into the Sierra Maestra, the mountains of southeastern Cuba. Castro steadily rebuilt his forces and launched hit-and-run attacks against the Batista regime. The determination and courage of the guerrillas inspired other Cubans, and by 1958 the insurgency had spread from rural areas into the cities. By the end of that year, support for Batista had evaporated.

What Castro and the 26th of July Movement intended for Cuba was unclear in early 1959. The manifesto of the movement was Castro's long, rambling, "History Will Absolve Me" speech, which he gave at his trial and subsequently rewrote in prison, and in which he promised the restoration of the liberal and progressive Cuban Constitution of 1940, agrarian reform, profit sharing for agrarian and industrial workers, and administrative honesty. During the two years spent in the Sierra Maestra, he released letters and issued public declarations that suggested his movement was libertarian and democratic, but also reformist and perhaps socialistic. Those thoughts were also conveyed in a dramatic interview that he gave to *New York Times* correspondent Herbert Matthews, who was spirited to Castro's mountain hideout in February 1957. Although his statements were vague and ambiguous, Castro was probably not trying to deceive; his plans for post-Batista Cuba were inchoate and evolving. Prior to 1960, he almost certainly was not a Marxist-Leninist or an agent of the Soviet Union. He had no ties with international communism. Indeed, the Cuban Communist Party, one of Latin America's largest with 17,000 members, denounced both the attack on the army barracks and Castro's armed return to Cuba. Cuban Communists, adhering to Moscow's line, thought political conditions were not ripe for revolution—in fact, they frequently collaborated with Batista. They also helped sabotage Castro's April 1958 call for a general strike. Soviet periodicals similarly criticized Castro for "terroristic acts and adventuristic activities."[1]

Castro may have been a political unknown, but Cubans, desperate for change, wildly cheered him on his triumphant march through Cuba to Havana. Compared to the rest of Latin America the island nation was relatively prosperous, with a per capita income of approximately $400. But there were grave structural imbalances in the Cuban economy. The nation's major industry, sugar production, required a sizeable labor force only during the harvest period, or *zafra*; most of the year, during the *tiempo muerto* or "dead time," rural workers were unemployed. Accordingly, 25 percent of the Cuban work force was either unemployed or underemployed. The poorest of Cubans were Afro-Cubans, who comprised about one-third of the population and suffered the further indignity of being subjected to racial discrimination and segregation. In the cities, workers labored in sweatshop conditions and resided in ghastly slums, derisively named *llega y pon* ("come and settle"). Discontent was not limited, however, to the poor. Urban middle sectors, intellectuals, the young were disgusted by the corruption, brutality, and inefficiency that characterized Cuban political life. Their country seemed morally bankrupt. The political system produced only tyrants like Gerardo Machado (1925–33) and Batista or weak, inept leaders like Ramón Grau San Martín (1944–48) and Prío Socarrás.[2]

Cuba's unique relationship with the United States accentuated the country's problems. Living only ninety miles away from the coast of Florida, Cubans admired and envied the quality of life in the United States. It was small comfort to frustrated Cubans that they were more affluent than Haitians or Hondurans. And yet, while longing to emulate their northern neighbor, Cubans blamed the United States for their country's failures. Their political immaturity could be ascribed to the constant U.S. meddling and intervention in their political system. Under the aegis of the Platt Amendment (1903–34), the United States had monitored Cuba's political development. Then, after renouncing intervention, the United States replaced the Platt Amendment with reciprocal trade agreements and sugar acts that guaranteed Cuban sugar producers access to the U.S. market at a subsidized price. In 1959, this handsome subsidy amounted to $150 million—but the trading arrangement reinforced the one-crop nature of the Cuban economy, with Cuba depending on sugar sales for 80 percent of its foreign exchange. The trading agreements also gave the United States leverage over the Cuban economy and ensured that U.S. firms would supply most of Cuba's imports. Indeed, the balance of trade normally favored the United States. Moreover, North American investors dominated Cuba's domestic economy. With approximately $900 million invested in Cuba, which was the second largest U.S. direct investment in Latin America, U.S. investors accounted for 40 percent of the country's sugar production and controlled 36 of the 161 sugar mills. U.S. companies also operated two of Cuba's three oil refineries, 90 percent of its public utilities, and 50 percent of its mines and railroads. And North Americans ran Cuba's other major industry, tourism. In view of such foreign influence, significant changes in Cuba's political economy would inevitably impinge on the long-standing power and privileges of the United States in Cuba.[3]

During the 1950s, the Eisenhower administration practiced the traditional U.S. policy of supporting Cubans who kept the island secure and stable and protected U.S. investments. Deeming Batista's rule "a good thing from the standpoint of the U.S.," the administration rewarded the dictator with good-will trips; a U.S. ambassador, Arthur Gardner, who fawned over him; $16 million in military aid; and help in organizing his secret police. Such actions were consistent, of course, with the administration's approach toward other Latin American dictators. In turn, Batista faithfully backed U.S. international positions and cooperated with U.S. investors. In one notorious case, he granted the Cuban Telephone Company, a subsidiary of the U.S. firm International Telephone and Telegraph, a 20 percent rate increase. Whereas the rate hike outraged Cuban consumers, it enhanced the dictator's political and personal fortune. In appreciation, the telephone company, accompanied by Ambassador Gardner, presented Batista with a "golden telephone." The company also allegedly contributed to a media slush fund, which Batista used for propaganda purposes.[4]

By 1957, the administration had to tone down its public support for Batista. Ambassador Gardner's unseemly friendship with the dictator was embarrassing the administration; furthermore, Castro had made a favorable impression with the U.S. public in his *New York Times* interview. The State Department replaced Gardner with Earl E. T. Smith, a Wall Street financier and a political supporter of President Eisenhower, who was instructed to "alter the prevailing notion in Cuba that the American Ambassador was intervening on behalf of the government of Cuba to perpetuate the Batista dictatorship." Shortly after arriving in Cuba in mid-1957, Smith unveiled the new policy. When he witnessed Cuban police attacking a group of Cuban mothers who were demonstrating against the regime, the ambassador publicly deplored "the excessive police action." He may actually have exceeded his instructions. President Eisenhower thought it "not a good idea for any Ambassador to make statements about local conditions." Secretary of State Dulles assured the president, however, that Smith's reaction, although "technically incorrect," was the "human thing to do."[5]

Unsettled though they were by Batista's repression, neither Ambassador Smith nor the State Department knew what course to chart for Cuba's future. Smith was convinced that Castro would not honor international obligations or U.S. investments and that only Communists would benefit from Batista's collapse. Pinning his hopes on Batista's promise to hold fair elections, the ambassador advised Washington to stick with Batista until an alternative to Castro could be elected. His plan collapsed in November 1958, when Batista rigged an election in favor of his handpicked candidate, Dr. Andrés Rivero Aguero. Smith was deeply disappointed by Batista's fraud; nevertheless, he considered Rivero Aguero preferable to Castro and unsuccessfully urged Washington to recognize Batista's man.[6] The State Department shared Smith's distrust of Castro. But in 1958 international criticism of the administration's past connivance with dictators was mounting—highlighted by the Nixon trip. In March 1958 the administration cut off arms shipments to Cuba, after Batista's U.S.-supplied air force began inflicting heavy civilian casualties in bombing attacks on rebel positions. Following the election farce, the State Department dispatched William Pawley, former ambassador to Brazil and Peru and a friend of Caribbean dictators, to urge Batista to capitulate and appoint a military junta to govern Cuba. Batista refused, countering with the demand that he receive an official U.S. request to leave and a pledge that the United States would maintain the military junta in power. The wily dictator was trying to have the United States assume responsibility for the Cuban civil war. Finally, on 17 December 1958, under instructions from Assistant Secretary R. Richard Rubottom, Smith informed Batista that "the United States will no longer support the present government of Cuba and that my government believes that the President is losing control."[7]

The Eisenhower administration was opposed to the 26th of July Movement, but they did not yet perceive it as a threat to U.S. national security. On 23 December 1958, Undersecretary Christian Herter informed Eisenhower that, although Communists were utilizing the movement "to some extent," "there is insufficient evidence on which to base a charge that the rebels are Communist-dominated." The State Department was not even certain that Castro and his followers had enough support to take control of Cuba. On 31 December 1958, the day Batista fled Cuba, Assistant Secretary Rubottom testified to the Senate Foreign Relations Committee in executive session that, although "I would not be happy with Castro solely in command, I cannot quite visualize that at this step."[8] The CIA was less sanguine about the rebels. On the same day that Herter wrote his report, CIA Director Allen Dulles told Eisenhower and the NSC that Communists could be expected to participate in a Castro government—but the CIA was primarily worried about Raúl Castro and Ché Guevara. In late January 1959 Dulles assured senators that Fidel Castro had "shown great courage" and that he was not a Communist agent. Over the next year, the intelligence agency would continue to hold that Communists would be unable "to force Fidel Castro to adopt policies to which he is opposed."[9] These analyses were accurate. In 1959, Castro probably did not subscribe to the dictates of Marxism-Leninism.

The administration prepared to work with the new Cuban regime, despite President Eisenhower's expressed misgivings. Eisenhower claimed in his memoirs that he was disturbed by Allen Dulles's report of 23 December 1958, remarking that it was the "first time" he had heard of possible Communist penetration of Castro's movement. But by the end of 1958 he had little choice but to accept the rebels' victory.[10] The State Department quickly recognized the new government and recalled Ambassador Smith to Washington; Undersecretary Herter convinced a reluctant Eisenhower to replace Smith with Philip Bonsal, the ambassador to Bolivia. Smith was unacceptable to the rebels due to his criticism of Castro; Herter also apparently questioned Smith's personal conduct, referring to him as a "playboy extraordinary." Eisenhower worried, however, that Smith, his friend, would be "crucified" by liberal newspapers for the pro-Batista policies of his administration.[11]

In sending Philip Bonsal to Havana, the State Department was choosing a career foreign officer and a political liberal who favored socioeconomic change in Latin America. Bonsal had helped negotiate the Venezuelan oil law of 1943, which forced U.S. oil companies to share their profits with the government. And he had praised the

Eisenhower administration's economic aid program in Bolivia, calling it "a solitary outpost of American thinking in this field."[12] Like other North Americans in early 1959, Bonsal was optimistic about Cuba's future under Fidel Castro. Batista's fall and Castro's triumph had been widely hailed in the United States. The Cuban Revolution seemed part of a process that was bringing democracy and social justice to Latin America. Even veteran cold warriors like Dean Acheson believed that Castro was a democrat and a social reformer.[13]

Castro's honeymoon with the North Americans was short-lived. In January, he legalized the Communist party and delivered a series of anti-American speeches. He also ousted political moderates whom he had initially appointed to office, and on 13 February 1959 he declared himself Premier of Cuba. Two weeks later he announced that elections would not be held for two years. But what particularly distressed North Americans were the public trials and executions of about 550 of Batista's supporters; Castro often presided at these revolutionary courts, where verdicts were rendered with frenzied crowds shouting *paredón!* (to the wall!). The administration's reaction to these opening developments was mixed: it worried about Communists operating "openly and freely" in Cuba, and it deplored the drumhead trials; but officials decided that this revolutionary fervor would diminish. Allen Dulles compared Cuba to the French Revolution, philosophically noting that "you kill your enemies." In any case, Dulles judged that the people being shot had been "cruel and oppressive" during the Batista years. Rubottom predicted that Cuba would be tumultuous for a time, but that U.S. businesses would ultimately profit, if the revolution gave Cuba its first honest government. He still believed that there was "potential greatness in the Cuban Revolution."[14]

The Eisenhower administration had an opportunity to test its theories about Castro when he came to the United States in April 1959, at the invitation of the American Society of Newspaper Editors. During his hectic eleven-day tour, in speeches, media interviews, and conversations with U.S. officials Castro projected a sincere, progressive image. Cuba needed far-reaching change, particularly agrarian reform. Castro conceded that such reform would adversely affect U.S.-owned properties, but he declared he would not make Cuba into a Communist state. The State Department was cautiously satisfied with Castro's pronouncements. Christian Herter, who was now secretary of state, reported to Eisenhower that the revolutionary leader was on his "best behavior." He had allayed fears in the press and the public by indirectly indicating that "Cuba would remain in the Western camp." Moreover, "he is clearly a strong personality and a born leader of great personal courage and conviction." Castro's weakness, however, was his determination to value results over process and procedure. He did not share "the same idea of law and legality as we have in the United States" and he "confused the roar of mass audiences with the rule of the majority in his concept of democracy." Herter concluded that Castro remained an "enigma" and that the administration should watch and wait "before assuming a more optimistic view than heretofore about the possibility of developing a constructive relationship." Herter's report apparently did not alarm Eisenhower. He wrote by hand on the margin of the report, "*File,* we will check in a year!!"[15]

During his April visit Castro also met for three hours with Vice-President Nixon, who stood in for Eisenhower because the president, angry about the executions in Cuba, refused to see Castro. Nixon later claimed in his 1962 memoirs, *Six Crises,* that after that meeting he urged the administration to take a strong line on Cuba, rejecting the State Department position "to get along with Castro."[16] Indeed, Nixon eventually sided with those—such as FBI Director J. Edgar Hoover, Ambassadors Gardner and Smith, Ambassador to Mexico Robert Hill, State Department officer Thomas Mann, and William Pawley—who believed that the Castro regime endangered the United States. But in April 1959, Nixon seemed remarkably sympathetic to Castro. He echoed the State Department's view that Castro was too easily swayed by the crowd; he also concluded, after debating with him the efficacy of the free-enterprise system, that Castro wanted socialism for Cuba; but he did not believe that he was a Communist. Instead, Castro was naive and uninformed about communism; "he sounded almost exactly like Sukarno had sounded to me when I visited Indonesia in 1953." Castro also had those "indefinable qualities which make him a leader of men," and the prescient Nixon predicted that he was "going to be a great factor in the development of Cuba and very possibly in Latin American affairs generally." Given Castro's appeal, the vice-president recommended that the United States try "to orient him in the right direction."[17]

The United States found it impossible to point Castro in the "right direction." Between April 1959 and early 1960, he continually shocked North Americans. Upon returning to Cuba he promulgated his Agrarian Reform Law, expropriating farmlands of over 1,000 acres, with compensation to be paid in Cuban currency bonds and based on the land's declared value for taxes in 1958. Sugar barons, both domestic and foreign, had predictably undervalued their land in Batista's Cuba. The new law—which was to be administered by a Cuban Communist, Antonio Núñez Jiménez—also prohibited foreigners from owning agricultural land. While socializing the Cuban sugar industry, Castro also gathered power in his own hands, purging many of his erstwhile liberal allies; some were jailed, while others fled to Miami to warn North Americans that Castro was a Communist. Soon these exiles were flying missions from Florida, firing cane fields and dropping antirevolutionary leaflets. Castro angrily and repeatedly denounced the United States for these incursions and warned Cubans that the United States planned to invade Cuba and restore Batista to power. In September 1959 he returned to the United States to address the United Nations; he now projected the image of an aggressive radical, holding the United States responsible for Cuba's poverty and extolling neutralism as the proper stance for developing countries in the cold war. Finally, in February 1960 Castro hosted a Soviet trade fair and signed a commercial agreement with Soviet Vice-Premier Anastas Mikoyan: the Soviets agreed to purchase one million tons of Cuban sugar over each of the next five years and to provide the Cubans with a $100-million credit to purchase Soviet equipment.

Why Fidel Castro turned to radicalism, to anti-Americanism, and to the Soviet Union has been a matter of partisan and scholarly debate since 1959. Opponents of his regime have argued either that he was a Communist agent from the beginning of his revolutionary days or that he evolved from reformer to totalitarian to enhance his power and prestige. Castro "betrayed" those anti-Batista Cubans who wanted a progressive, democratic nation.[18] Those sympathetic to the Cuban Revolution have held that its leader's anti-Americanism was a response to the Eisenhower administration's resistance to social change and economic reform: the United States left Castro with little choice but to ally with the Soviet Union in order to save Cuba's revolution.[19] Such debates perhaps reveal more about the political beliefs of the intellectual combatants than about the conduct of Castro and the course of the Cuban Revolution. In analyzing Cuban-American relations during the Eisenhower years, it is essential to view developments chronologically and to separate the issue of revolutionary nationalism from Castro's decision to seek assistance from the Soviet Union.

During the last months of the Batista regime, the Eisenhower administration tried ineffectually to keep Castro from assuming command of Cuba. But, through most of 1959, the administration did not deliberately provoke Castro or try to undermine the revolution. Key officials—Herter, Rubottom, Bonsal, even Allen Dulles—wanted to work with Castro. Indeed, they seemed fascinated by the bearded revolutionary. They often overlooked his wild charges, declining to add to the acrimony. And the administration worked to prevent hostile actions against Castro in 1959. It arranged for Batista to move from the Dominican Republic to Europe, so that the dictator would not have a convenient base from which to menace the revolution. It also tried, by increasing the security at airports, to prevent Cuban exiles from using Florida as a base for counterrevolutionary operations. President Eisenhower remarked to his advisors that he thought the Cubans should "just shoot the airplanes down."[20]

While restraining its hostility to Castro and his followers in 1959, the administration established parameters for the Cubans' behavior: Cuba was to stay closely tied to the United States. In extending diplomatic recognition to the 26th of July Movement, the State Department decided that Castro could be "politically compatible with U.S. objectives."[21] As Ambassador Bonsal explained, "Cuba belonged to an area where the economic and political influence of the United States was dominant; it seemed desirable for both countries that this continue to be the case." To preserve U.S. hegemony, the administration was prepared to offer Castro economic aid. During Castro's trip to Washington in April 1959, his aides were assured by Assistant Secretary Rubottom that the United States was willing to be helpful financially.[22] In essence, the State Department probably hoped that the Cuban Revolution could be channeled in the same direction as the Bolivian Revolution. The Eisenhower administration had defused the Bolivian Revolution, ensuring its survival with economic aid while insisting that Bolivian leaders accept free trade and investment principles. The administration signaled its desire for the same outcome in Cuba by selecting Bonsal, its representative in La Paz, for Havana.

The national aspirations of the Cubans exceeded, however, the Eisenhower administration's goals for their nation. Cubans wanted more than the dubious independence they had enjoyed since 1898. They wanted, for example, a capital city known more as a center of government than as a tourist playground featuring illicit drugs, gambling, and prostitution. Furthermore, they questioned whether simple reforms would undo the unacceptable status quo: resolving the problem of *tiempo muerto* would require a radical restructuring of the sugar economy. Cuba could not afford, as the United States insisted, to compensate North American planters for their expropriated land in dollars at market prices, a total sum of perhaps $500 million. Aid from the United States could ease Cuba's problems—but it would increase Cuba's historic dependence on its powerful neighbor. Castro decided not to ask for aid when he came to the United States in April 1959, because he wanted to show Cubans that he would be the first leader, since José Martí, not to become subservient to the United States. He understood that Cubans wanted their national dignity restored. He also sensed that his anti-American diatribes provided emotional satisfaction to the Cuban masses and enhanced his popularity.[23]

By the end of 1959, the Eisenhower administration had essentially decided that it could no longer abide Castro or Cuban nationalism, which threatened U.S. leadership and endangered, by example, U.S. investments throughout the hemisphere. It was Secretary of State Herter who initiated the process of undermining the Cuban Revolution. He had previously backed his subordinates, Rubottom and Bonsal, who believed that the United States could work with Castro. But on 5 November 1959 Herter recommended to Eisenhower that the policies of the United States should thenceforth "be designed to encourage within Cuba and elsewhere in Latin America opposition to the extremist, anti-American course of the Castro regime." Herter now believed that Castro would not "voluntarily adopt policies and attitudes consistent with minimum United States security requirements." The Cuban tolerated, even encouraged, the infiltration of Communists into key government institutions. Moreover, Castro's neutralist foreign policies, if "emulated by other Latin American countries, would have serious adverse effects on Free World support of our leadership, especially in the United Nations on such issues as the Chinese representation problem." Castro, by nationalizing the Cuban economy, also damaged U.S. business interests and mocked the free trade and investment policies that the administration was promoting in Latin America. Therefore, the objective of the United States should be to make Cuba compatible with U.S. policies by the end of 1960. In particular, the administration should foster a "coherent opposition" to Castro. Herter was not, however, explicitly calling for the overthrow of Castro, but suggesting either "a reformed Castro regime or a successor to it." President Eisenhower approved Herter's recommendation.[24]

Secretary Herter wanted to keep the control of Cuban policy within the State Department, reminding Eisenhower that the administration must not arouse Latin American fears of intervention. But in late December Eisenhower accepted National Security Advisor Gordon Gray's argument that the discussions about Cuba had to be broadened. As Gray explained, "the Vice-President and other members of the Council [NSC] felt that Cuba and its problems had gone far beyond the question of pure diplomatic operations and it had begun to involve the Congress and other elements of society."[25] Other agencies quickly joined the debate. In January 1960 Allen Dulles began calling for Castro's overthrow, acting on a recommendation from Colonel J. C. King, head of the CIA's Western Hemisphere Division. King, warning that a "far left" dictatorship now existed in Cuba, asked that "thorough consideration be given to the elimination of Fidel Castro." At a 13 January meeting of the 5412 Committee—a special committee created by Eisenhower in 1955 to oversee covert operations—Dulles "noted the possibility that over the long run the U.S. will not be able to tolerate the Castro regime in Cuba, and suggested that covert contingency planning to accomplish the fall of the Castro government might be in order."[26]

Similarly strong views were expressed by President Eisenhower. At two January meetings with State Department officials, a furious Eisenhower labeled Castro a "mad man" and "one who is going wild and harming the whole American structure." He spoke of blockading the island, building up U.S. forces at Guantánamo Bay, or quarantining the island, so that "if they (the Cuban people) are hungry, they will throw Castro out." But after these outbursts, the president conceded that he did not want to punish the Cuban people for Castro's actions.[27] He approved a public statement reiterating the U.S. commitment to nonintervention and offering to negotiate differences with Cuba. However, the statement seemed designed primarily to sway international opinion; the administration believed that productive diplomacy with Castro was at an end.[28] President Eisenhower was talking about Fidel Castro in the same way that he and his advisors had spoken about Jacobo Arbenz of Guatemala.

The administration's attitude hardened and its anti-Castro plotting accelerated in February 1960, after the results of the Mikoyan visit to Cuba were announced. The Cuban-Soviet trade-and-aid agreement had the same impact on the U.S. government and public as had the shipment of Czechoslovakian arms to Guatemala in May 1954: legislators began to pressure the administration to remove or contain the Castro menace. Even the administration's critics, like Senator Wayne Morse, deplored Castro's abusive behavior. Only a few elected officials, such as Senator Fulbright, counseled restraint, warning that the United States must not "be accused of another Hungary."[29] State Department officials were divided: Ambassador Bonsal thought that any economic pressure on Castro would redound to the Cuban's political benefit; Secretary Rubottom predicted that the Cubans would overthrow Castro, once he was exposed as a Communist; Thomas Mann and Ambassador Hill, however, argued that the United States could not afford to wait, asserting that "the days of this regime have to be numbered."[30] Eisenhower agreed with the hard-liners. On 18 February he told Senator George Smathers of Florida that he would blockade Cuba, if the OAS asked the United States "to do something about Castro." Unfortunately, Eisenhower believed that everyone favored clandestine action against Castro, a policy "approximating gangsterism." Yet, he assured Smathers that he found the situation "intolerable," and he urged Smathers to stress that point, remarking that "a senator can speak more freely than a member of the Executive Branch." Smathers complied, telling senators in executive session that he favored initiating policies "right now to somehow squeeze this fellow out."[31]

A month after his conversation with Smathers, Eisenhower authorized a program to overthrow Castro. His 17 March 1960 decision came after extensive discussions about Cuba by a CIA task force on Cuba, the 5412 committee, and the NSC. The resulting document, "A Program of Covert Action Against the Castro Regime," presented a four-part program of attack: (1) "creation of a responsible and unified Cuban opposition to the Castro regime located outside of Cuba"; (2) "a powerful propaganda offensive" against Castro; (3) creation of a "covert action and intelligence organization within Cuba," responsive to the exile opposition; (4) "the development of a paramilitary force outside of Cuba for future guerrilla action."[32]

President Eisenhower would later insist that this did not constitute a "plan" against Castro, only a "program." A "program" presumably represented a general approach, whereas a "plan" set forth specific actions. In interviews that he gave in 1965 in conjunction with the publication of his memoirs, Eisenhower categorically denied any responsibility for the Bay of Pigs invasion, arguing that "there was no tactical or operational plan even discussed." To ensure that historians accepted his argument, Eisenhower had, in June 1961, requested Gordon Gray, his national security advisor, to excise the word "planning" from notes that covered the 17 March meeting.[33] It is true that Eisenhower's March decision was not an irrevocable commitment to invade Cuba—but the authorization of a "plan" or "program" definitively ended any possibility of a rapprochement between the Eisenhower administration and Castro. After 17 March 1960, administration officials focused on how they could harm Castro and Cuba.

The discussions and decisions of early 1960 were based on an anticipation that Cuba would threaten the national security of the United States. But as Secretary of State Herter informed Eisenhower on 17 March, "we lack all of the hard evidence [of Communist domination] which would be required to convince skeptical Latin American Governments and the public opinion behind them."[34] Moreover, Cuba's commercial agreement with the Soviet Union was not, by itself, an ominous development. Batista had sold 500,000 tons of sugar to the Soviet Union in 1955; the Russians now agreed to buy 1,000,000 tons a year, about one-sixth of Cuba's crop. This would leave plenty of sugar for the United States, which traditionally purchased about one-half of Cuba's crop. In agreeing to a long-term contract, the Russians, in Ambassador Bonsal's words, drove a "hard bargain": they would pay a below-market price of only 2.78 cents a pound, significantly less than the 5 cents a pound the United States paid; and only 20 percent of the payment would be in currency, the rest to be in Soviet goods.[35] Furthermore, these terms were in line with commercial agreements that the Russians were negotiating, in late 1959 and early 1960, with anti-Communist governments in Brazil and Chile.[36] Nevertheless, the administration had made anticommunism the central feature of its Latin American policy. It knew that Communists operated in Cuba, and it had grave suspicions about the leader of the government. This type of evidence had been sufficient, six years previously, for the administration to persuade itself to destroy a government in Guatemala.

Although the administration admitted privately that it could not prove that Castro was working for international communism, it was certain that the Cuban Revolution, if permitted to survive, would imperil U.S. interests throughout the hemisphere. After the upheavals of 1958, administration officials were nervous about the security of Latin America and the safety of U.S. investments. Now, they feared that "the Cuban revolution has precipitated a threatening situation simply by bringing to a head social revolutionary forces which have been gathering for years." In Thomas Mann's view, the effect of the revolution was to encourage "left-wing elements in the other American republics." U.S. diplomats such as Ambassador to Mexico Hill and Ambassador to Costa Rica Whiting Willauer warned Washington that, if Latin Americans "see them getting away with taking the property in Cuba, it will happen . . . in other Latin American areas." President Eisenhower saw the opposite danger, predicting that U.S. investors would become frightened and withdraw from Latin America. Actions against Cuba, Eisenhower reasoned, would benefit Latin Americans.[37]

Within days after Eisenhower's 17 March decision, Fidel Castro had undoubtedly learned something of the program to overthrow him. His agents probably had penetrated the exile community, and Cuban exiles were notably indiscreet.[38] The year 1960 was also a decisive period in the history of the Cuban Revolution: Castro nationalized the economy, launched egalitarian socioeconomic programs, took absolute control of Cuba, and assumed a pro-Soviet stance in international affairs. Cuba took an increasingly radical course as the United States became more belligerent. That relationship provides compelling evidence for analysts who have blamed the United States for the radicalization of Cuba and the breakdown in U.S.-Cuban relations. But U.S. actions probably influenced the *pace* of revolutionary change in Cuba more than its ultimate direction. In 1959–60 Castro, although conscious of international developments, concentrated on domestic issues. He faced fierce internal opposition; as Ambassador Bonsal observed, by December 1959 "Castro's own chances of escaping death from assassination or accident appeared poor."[39] The Cuban Communists, on the other hand, finally rallied to Castro's side. By legalizing the party and incorporating Cuban Communists into his coalition, Castro expanded his political base, particularly among urban workers, and gained an effective apparatus for rallying mass support. He had not, however, surrendered to the Partido Socialista Popular (PSP), the Cuban Communist party; leaders of the party, like Blas Roca, were not given influential roles in the revolution. Castro also purged ideologues from the party. As one scholar has pointed out, "Castro took over the Communists, not the reverse."[40]

Castro was hardly a prisoner of the PSP, but he did eventually declare himself a Marxist-Leninist. However, his movement toward communism, like his embrace of the PSP, had its pragmatic features. Castro and his advisors believed that Cuba's problems were urgent and that, to bring about change, power had to be centralized. As he explained to Vice-President Nixon, "a man who worked in the sugar cane fields for three months a year and starved the rest of the year wanted a job, something to eat, a house and some clothing and didn't care a whit about whether he had freedom along with it."[41] The Cuban revolutionary elite probably also concluded, as it grappled with Cuba's depressing realities, that tinkering with Cuba's institutions would not accomplish fundamental social change. Communism, on the other hand, seemed to offer a solution to problems of development. Third World leaders were impressed that the Soviet Union had built a modern, scientific society in four decades. Even Latin American reformers who wanted to retain a capitalist character to their economies—like Rómulo Betancourt, Juscelino Kubitschek, and Raúl Prebisch—believed that the state had to play a leading role in promoting economic growth and development. Once persuaded that socialism could both work in Cuba and justify the revolutionary elite's continuation in power, Castro and his adherents probably gradually convinced themselves of socialism's doctrinal truth. By December 1961, Castro was ready to announce his conversion to Marxism-Lenism.[42]

A better case can be made for the argument that the United States forced Cuba to seek assistance from the Soviet Union than for the proposition that the Eisenhower administration dictated the course of the Cuban Revolution. Latin American radicals understood what had happened to Guatemala. Indeed, Ché Guevara was in Guatemala in 1954 and witnessed the CIA-directed counterrevolution. From the outset of their revolution, Castro and his advisors indicated by their actions that they feared U.S. intervention. Realizing that the United States had toppled Arbenz through the Guatemalan army, Castro took care in 1959 to dismantle the Cuban army and to trust in his revolutionary forces. Thereafter, he created a militia of approximately 200,000 Cubans under his command and a civilian defense force, the Committees for the Defense of the Revolution. The mission of these new forces was to guard against an invasion and to watch for saboteurs.

How to equip these forces became a central problem for Castro. The United States continued the arms embargo it had imposed on Batista, and in late 1959 the Eisenhower administration also insisted that its allies, like Great Britain, not sell military equipment to the

Cubans. The British bowed to U.S. pressure, but they predicted to Secretary Herter that if they did not sell to the Cubans, "the Russians will"[43]—and indeed, by the second half of 1960, as U.S. plans to overthrow Castro accelerated, Cuba began to obtain both equipment and rhetorical support from Soviet Premier Nikita Khrushchev. But the Cubans had to fend for themselves when the exiles invaded in April 1961, for the Soviets remained cautious in their support of Castro during the Eisenhower presidency and the first months of the Kennedy administration. An ironclad Soviet-Cuban alliance emerged only during the Kennedy and Johnson years.

Whether, therefore, Castro initially turned to the Soviets for essentially pragmatic purposes is a complex question. The Eisenhower administration certainly limited the Cuban's options. Some have even argued that Castro accelerated and expanded the revolution at home in order to entice the Soviets to his side.[44] Yet, Castro understood the history of inter-American relations; he was aware that his verbal assaults and domestic measures, such as the agrarian reform law, would provoke a conservative administration in Washington. Perhaps the Cuban decision to seek Soviet assistance can be linked to the evolution of Cuba's political economy. As Castro pushed Cuba leftward, cooperation with the world's most powerful socialist nation increasingly seemed both legitimate and necessary. The decision by the Eisenhower administration to undermine the Cuban Revolution fortified those convictions.[45]

After 17 March 1960, the Eisenhower administration plotted the overthrow of Fidel Castro. But U.S. problems in Latin America would not disappear with Castro. The charismatic Cuban had stirred the Latin American people, who now demanded economic development and social justice. The Eisenhower administration decided that it could no longer afford the easy luxury of simply being anti-Communist: the United States would have to reform the archaic political, economic, and social structures of Latin America. By early 1960, U.S. officials believed that the choices for Latin America were either reform or revolution.

CHAPTER 8

THE NEW INTERVENTIONISM
1960

The year 1960 witnessed a dramatic shift in the Latin American policy of the Eisenhower administration. Alarmed by the course of the Cuban Revolution and the widespread popularity of Fidel Castro in Latin America, the administration responded quickly and decisively to contain the revolutionary ferment. It devised an extensive economic assistance package for the region. It also decided that it had to lead and direct a reform of Latin America's basic institutions. The administration now called for an interventionist policy: the United States needed to intervene in Latin America both to overthrow radicals and to eliminate conditions that might spawn future Fidel Castros in the Western Hemisphere.

In the aftermath of Vice-President Richard Nixon's tour of Latin America, as we have seen, the Eisenhower administration modified its policies: it distanced itself from dictators and praised democratic leaders; it also supported a commodity agreement to stabilize the price of coffee and agreed to fund a regional development bank. It is possible that even without the shock of the Cuban Revolution, the administration would have continued to develop policies to foster economic growth and development in Latin America. Such influential figures as Douglas Dillon, Thomas Mann, and Milton Eisenhower wanted to build on the initiatives of 1958. Dr. Eisenhower, in particular, insisted that the new approach to Latin America antedated the Cuban Revolution and grew out of a genuine desire for democracy and social progress in Latin America.[1] But the policies the administration would implement in 1960 would differ significantly, in both intent and scope, from previous initiatives. In 1958, the goal was to calm angry neighbors; by 1960, the United States was battling communism in Latin America.

Through most of 1959, the administration relied on the policies it had devised in the previous year. No new public funds were allocated for Latin America. The fledgling Inter-American Development Bank was not expected to make its first loan until fiscal year 1962. The Development Loan Fund continued to focus its energies and money on Asian nations such as India and Pakistan. In early 1960, Congress was asked to appropriate $131 million for Latin America for the upcoming fiscal year, of which $67 million, more than one-half of the funds requested, was to be assigned to military assistance—and the administration wanted special assistance to continue to go only to the perennially destitute nations of Bolivia and Haiti. As usual, only about 2 percent of U.S. foreign economic aid was to be devoted to Latin America.[2]

Even as the administration was preparing and presenting its traditional economic program for Latin America, however, it was reassessing hemispheric developments. Shortly after receiving Secretary of State Christian Herter's 5 November 1959 warning that the United States must oppose the Castro regime and rally Latin America against Cuba, President Eisenhower created the National Advisory Committee on Inter-American Affairs. This committee, which was chaired by Herter and Assistant Secretary Richard Rubottom, included Dr. Eisenhower and representatives from business, labor, and education. The president appointed the committee for both substantive and symbolic reasons: he wanted its members to generate new ideas on inter-American relations, and he also hoped that Latin Americans would interpret his action as a signal that the United States cared about the region.[3] In line with that gesture, Eisenhower revived a proposal he had first broached in 1953 and again asked the State Department to flatter Latin Americans by creating a special, prestigious position of Undersecretary of State for Inter-American Affairs.[4]

Eisenhower's new committee immediately informed the president that symbolic actions alone would not relieve tensions in inter-American relations. In December 1959 Dr. Eisenhower presented his brother with both a summary of the committee's initial deliberations and his own views. Throughout 1959, Dr. Eisenhower had been worried about Fidel Castro and the effect of the Cuban Revolution on Latin America. He had initially thought Castro "egocentric, frighteningly naive, and completely unpredictable."[5] Now, at the end of the year, Dr. Eisenhower saw "a serious revolutionary spirit on the move." Latin Americans resented the prevailing social order, with "a thin layer of prosperity and a vast sea of misery." The Cuban Revolution was popular with the poor, because it "represented to these people a revolt against things as they are." To facilitate peaceful change, Dr. Eisenhower recommended that the United States make a five-year commitment to offer to Latin America $150 million each year in loans repayable in local currencies. This money would come from the Development Loan Fund, with the agency restricting its lending in other areas of the world. Dr. Eisenhower urged the president to act soon, warning that "things are moving awfully fast" and that "if extreme left-wing governments sprang up in a number of the nations, we would find ourselves with problems that would call for vast expenditures."[6]

The president had an opportunity to discuss these issues with committee members in early 1960, when he took them with him on a tour of southern South America. Good-will trips had become a new feature of Eisenhower's diplomacy. He had always dominated the making of foreign policy, but after John Foster Dulles died, and as his own health improved, he became more directly involved in the personal conduct of diplomacy. In the latter half of 1959, for example, the president, displaying boundless energy, hosted Nikita Khrushchev at the presidential retreat, Camp David, and traveled to Europe, the Middle East, and the Indian subcontinent.[7] Eisenhower's first international trip of 1960, which included stops in Argentina, Brazil, Chile, and Uruguay, was intended to demonstrate U.S. support for representative government and for social and economic progress. It was also hoped that key leaders like Arturo Frondizi and Juscelino Kubitschek would denounce Fidel Castro—the trip began a week after the announcement of Cuba's commercial pact with the Soviet Union.[8]

As a public relations gesture, Eisenhower's tour was a resounding success. In sharp contrast to the vice-president's unhappy adventure, the president was greeted by huge, admiring crowds. Eisenhower was a popular world figure, and Latin Americans had not forgotten the general's masterful leadership during World War II.[9] But although he appreciated the affectionate reception, Eisenhower viewed the trip as both a revelation and a sharp disappointment: he was stunned by the ghastly poverty and unspeakable living conditions he encountered in countries that were among the wealthiest and most socially advanced in Latin America. U.S. foreign economic policy had failed; Eisenhower began to grasp that "the private and public capital which had flown bounteously into Latin America had failed to benefit the masses, that the demand for social justice was still rising." Moreover, he was shaken by an open letter he received from the president of the Federation of Students, an anti-Communist group representing 25,000 Chilean university students. Though couched in respectful, dignified tones, the letter accused the United States of being insensitive to the poor and of sustaining the prevailing social order. Eisenhower left South America with a "sense of ominous unrest."[10]

Eisenhower also left the continent without support for an anti-Castro policy. In his meetings with Latin American leaders and in the thirty-seven addresses and toasts he delivered, he pressed his case that Communists had to be excluded from the Western Hemisphere. He emphasized that "for Latin America to progress economically, there must be large-scale private investment along with public investment, and this would be harmed by Castro's behavior."[11] Latin American leaders would not, however, publicly repudiate Castro. They pointed out to Eisenhower that Castro had captured the imagination of the people and that the poor viewed him as a symbol of social change—in fact, a dismayed Eisenhower had read signs among the crowds that said: "We Like Ike; We Like Fidel Too." Furthermore, Latin American officials doubted that communism was a byproduct of propaganda or agitation by alien agents. President Kubitschek predictably stressed that "poverty and frustration of the economically stagnant countries have a far greater capacity for stirring discontent" than Communists. Eisenhower and his party returned to Washington believing that the administration would garner hemispheric support for its Cuban policy only when it formulated "a dramatic, U.S.-backed, democratic development program."[12]

Upon returning from South America, the president authorized the CIA to begin its program to overthrow Castro. The NSC also began a review of NSC 5902/1, the administration's current policy toward Latin America.[13] But Eisenhower and his advisors had little time to deliberate, for by mid-1960 both Latin America and the world seemed to have entered an era of unprecedented turbulence. The president had correctly sensed the meaning of Latin America's dire poverty. The region's future seemed stark, with commodity prices still falling. The new international agreement on coffee had not yet stabilized the price of Latin America's chief export, and Latin American economies were not producing enough new jobs for a population that was growing at a 3 percent annual rate. Outside capital was also unavailable. During the latter half of the 1950s, the amount of money Latin Americans remitted abroad in interest payments and profits almost equaled the amount they attracted from foreigners in loans and new investments. During the postwar period, the lot of Latin Americans had not changed relative to their northern neighbors: per capita income in Latin America was still about one-eighth that of the United States.[14]

Poverty and frustration seemed to be fueling the turmoil that, in 1960, enveloped the area of traditional U.S. strategic interest—the Caribbean littoral. Although administration officials identified Castro's Cuba as the major source of danger in the Caribbean, they also grew alarmed about political movements in such countries as Colombia, Venezuela, the Dominican Republic, and Panama. Rebels who professed leftist political doctrines operated in the mountains of Colombia and Venezuela, challenging the newly elected governments in those countries. Groups of various political persuasions were organizing in the Dominican Republic, vowing to end the thirty-year tyranny of Rafael Trujillo. The administration also faced a mounting political crisis over the Panama Canal Zone. In November 1959, Panamanian students entered the Canal Zone and tried to plant Panamanian flags; in the ensuing melee, more than 120 students were killed or wounded, nine of them being wounded by U.S. troops. President Eisenhower responded by opening skilled positions in the Canal Zone to Panamanians and by permitting the Panamanian flag to fly with the U.S. flag—but he refused to consider the students' fundamental demand, the return of the canal to Panama.[15]

These problems were compounded by a renewed Soviet challenge to U.S. hegemony in the hemisphere: the Soviets had revived their economic offensive of the mid-1950s. In 1959, the value of the Soviet bloc's trade with Latin America, although still a modest 3 percent of Latin America's total trade, matched the 1955 high. Moreover, in late 1959 and early 1960 the Soviet Union sent trade and industrial delegations on tour throughout Latin America; for example, before stopping in Cuba, Vice-Premier Anastas Mikoyan brought a trade fair to Mexico. By mid-1960, in addition to their commercial agreement with Cuba, the Soviets had signed a trade-and-aid agreement with Brazil and were negotiating with Argentina and Chile. Thereafter, Premier Khrushchev made a sensational offer to build a tin smelter in Bolivia.[16] Although they understood that Latin Americans desperately needed new markets and income, administration officials foresaw only trouble if Latin Americans were to strike commercial bargains with the Soviets. As the CIA concluded, trade-and-aid agreements were part of the Soviet plan "to erode and eventually eliminate United States influence in Latin America by promoting anti-American neutralism and ultra-nationalist movements and governments which will increase the vulnerability of America's 'strategic backyard.' "[17]

In 1960, the influence of the United States seemed to be eroding not only in Latin America but throughout the world. The year 1960 was another adverse time for the president and U.S. foreign policy. Eisenhower had rebounded strongly from the disasters of 1958. His fellow citizens applauded his global journeys for peace, and they were heartened by the constructive relationship that he had developed with Soviet Premier Khrushchev during their September 1959 discussions at Camp David. Commentators spoke of the "Eisenhower Resurgence," and his job performance ratings shot up in public opinion polls. The president planned to crown his presidency with a successful summit conference with Khrushchev and a major disarmament treaty. The May 1960 meeting in Paris with Khrushchev collapsed, however, in mutual recrimination over the so-called U-2 incident: just prior to the summit, the Soviets had shot down a U.S. spy plane that had violated Russian air space. The president felt personally defeated, confiding to an aide that "the stupid U-2 mess had ruined all his effort." He wondered whether there was anything "worthwhile left for him to do now until the end of his presidency."[18]

The U-2 incident was only the messiest of a series of humiliations and setbacks suffered by the president and the nation. After returning from Paris, Eisenhower was forced to cancel a trip to Japan when Japanese officials warned him that his presence might provoke violent, anti-American demonstrations. Political violence rocked South Korea and Turkey, staunch U.S. allies. And the United States seemed to be losing the battle for the allegiance of the Third World. During Eisenhower's presidency, thirty Asian and African nations emerged from colonial rule. The leaders of these new nations—for example, Patrice Lumumba of the former Belgian colony of the Congo—were intensely nationalistic and demanded rapid, even radical, socioeconomic change. Revolutions in communications, transportation, and science had imparted to Third World people, in Secretary of State Herter's words, "a new and urgent awareness that, although the misery of man exists as a fact, it need not continue to exist." CIA Director Dulles added that "the spirit of revolution is abroad in the great areas of the world." The United States was facing "a revolt of the have-nots, particularly in Latin America, Asia, and in Africa."[19]

President Eisenhower agreed, telling aides, in mid-1960, that "the world has developed a kind of ferment greater than [I can] remember in recent times." He warned that "the Communists are trying to take control of this." The United States would have to curtail domestic spending "in order to do what we need to do in foreign affairs."[20]

Indeed, President Eisenhower shook off his depression over the Paris summit and roused himself, during the last year of his presidency, to fight communism in the Third World. In regard to Latin America, Eisenhower acted soon after meeting in Washington with Pedro Beltrán, the prime minister of Peru. Placed in office by President Manuel Prado in 1959, in the midst of economic chaos, Beltrán had followed the advice of the United States and stabilized the Peruvian economy through stringent budgetary and currency measures. Now he was turning to the second phase of his economic plan, a program of socioeconomic reform for the poor, who were "increasingly susceptible to the appeal of Communism and 'Castroism.'" Beltrán, described by the State Department as one of the few members of the Peruvian elite with a sense of social responsibility, was proceeding in a moderate, evolutionary way. Instead of challenging Peru's grossly inequitable land-holding patterns, he was colonizing unsettled areas in the Amazon region, east of the Andes mountains. The State Department predicted that Beltrán would probably ask for $100 million over three years to finance his land and housing programs; the president should avoid a specific commitment, but praise Beltrán's "responsible, orderly approach to the problems of housing and land." As the department opined, "in countries like Peru it seems to be a question of either an orderly approach to the problem of land or housing or a revolutionary explosion such as occurred in Bolivia and Cuba."[21]

President Eisenhower left his 9 June 1960 meeting with Prime Minister Beltrán convinced that the United States would have to assist and direct orderly reform in Latin America. Beltrán condemned Castro and communism, but told Eisenhower that people were falling in line behind the "Castro mystique"; warning that "time is of the essence," he called on the United States to assist projects, like housing and land reform, that reached the poor. Eisenhower lamented that his free trade and investment policies of the past seven years had not won over the people of Latin America, but he "declared that we are all together and that no country could remain an island of freedom surrounded by tyranny." The president urged Beltrán to present his views with the "same frankness" to the State Department and especially to Undersecretary Dillon.[22]

On 11 July 1960, a month after his meeting with Beltrán, Eisenhower announced a new program for Latin America, which was subsequently named the Social Progress Trust Fund. The United States would strengthen the social infrastructure of Latin America by providing $500 million to underwrite health, education, housing, and land reform projects. The United States would also grant Chile $100 million to help it recover from a massive earthquake.[23] The new program was the brainchild of Dr. Eisenhower, Undersecretary Dillon, and Prime Minister Beltrán. As Dr. Eisenhower had recommended in December 1959, these social overhead loans would be soft loans, repayable in local currencies. But on Dillon's advice, the program would be administered through the Inter-American Development Bank, not the Development Loan Fund. The program would focus, as Beltrán urged, on the small-scale projects that went directly to people, "so as to influence public opinion." So impressed had the administration been by Beltrán's ideas on reform and anticommunism that it immediately put together a $53-million package to assist his colonization project.[24]

Congress readily acceded to the administration's special request. Legislators accepted the premise that the Third World was a vital cold-war battleground. Democrats on the Senate Foreign Relations Committee, especially Chairman J. William Fulbright, took a special election-year delight in approving what they tagged the administration's "death-bed confession." Fulbright reminded Secretary of State Herter that "these are some of the things this committee has suggested for many years and the administration has objected to." He also recalled that the administration had asked in early 1960 for a modest amount of foreign aid for Latin America, and he sarcastically asked: "Has poverty in Latin America substantially increased in the past few months?" Administration officials defended their performance by pointing out they had been working since 1958 to resolve Latin America's economic problems. But Undersecretary Dillon conceded that the origins of this new program could be found in the Cuban Revolution, noting that "the situation in Cuba is a dramatic picture of what happens when social progress is not keeping up in pace with general economic development." So enthusiastic were Democrats about the new program, they wondered why the administration did not ask for more money and for a long-term commitment of funds. In comments to journalists, President Eisenhower had denied he was proposing a Marshall Plan for Latin America. Dillon assured senators, however, that the United States intended to expand the social progress program.[25]

Eisenhower's July announcement about the Social Progress Trust Fund and its subsequent authorization by Congress marked a turning point in inter-American relations. The United States now had an economic aid program to go along with the regional bank and a more flexible attitude on commodity agreements. The administration also reversed the long-standing U.S. opposition to a Latin American free-trade zone and even promised $10 million to help launch the Central American Common Market. The Eisenhower administration was redeeming the pledges of economic cooperation made by Sumner Welles at the Rio Conference in 1942. In September 1960, the administration brought its new program to an inter-American economic conference held in Bogotá, and for the first time in the postwar period, U.S. diplomats enjoyed convening with Latin Americans. At Bogotá, the United States did not oppose or abstain on any economic resolution. By its own admission, the administration "left with the Latin American community a new conviction that the United States recognized and accepted responsibility for the social and economic development of the area."[26]

Although the Eisenhower administration had broken with its own and the Truman administration's policies on economic aid for Latin America, it had not abandoned its fundamental strategy in the hemisphere: the Social Progress Trust Fund was an anti-Communist measure. Officials described it as "rising to meet the Castro problem" and "action taken in the nick of time." President Eisenhower "thought this type of program was the best answer we could make to the aggressive tactics of international communism."[27] But the Social Progress Trust Fund represented more than a change in tactics, a new readiness to spend public money to defeat communism in the region—the administration had radically changed its view on what fostered communism in Latin America. Through most of the 1950s, the Unites States had been content to rely on dictators to control subversives. But in the aftermath of the Cuban Revolution, the administration concluded that dictators created "Batista-like" conditions, forcing desperate people to embrace radicalism, anti-Americanism, and communism. Officials such as Thomas Mann, Ambassador John Cabot, and Dr. Eisenhower now spoke of the "blindness of the ruling classes in the face of the powerful new forces surging up from below them and clamoring for change." Mann, in particular, bitterly denounced Latin American elites, noting to colleagues that "they always pass the buck to us" and expected the United States "to bail them out."[28]

In light of this analysis, the task for the Eisenhower administration was to devise a way to immunize the poor—the majority of Latin America's population—against revolutionary nationalism. Put another way, the goal of the United States, in Assistant Secretary Rubottom's view, was "to make the leaders, especially the traditional elite groups, fully aware of the critical need to do something to meet the rising expectations of their peoples in order to avoid violent change brought on by over-long suppression of popular pressures." The United States would have to intervene in Latin America or adopt, in Dr. Eisenhower's words, a policy of "collective intervention."[29] But instead of U.S. marines, the administration would deploy the Inter-American Development Bank and the Social Progress Trust Fund. At Bogotá, the U.S. delegation obtained Latin American assent to a resolution that cited the need "to modernize and improve the existing legal and institutional framework to ensure better conditions of land tenure, extend more adequate credit facilities and provide increased incentives in the land tax structure." The Act of Bogotá also noted the need to reexamine "the equity and effectiveness of existing tax schedules." To ensure that these were not just typical, pious inter-American declarations, the administration turned over most of the $500 million to the Inter-American Development Bank. The United States would use the expanded lending power of the bank to entice Latin American nations to reform their archaic social structures: loans would be granted to those governments that imposed progressive income taxes, built public schools, and distributed land to *campesinos*.[30]

With the Act of Bogotá, administration officials believed that they had achieved a conceptual breakthrough in inter-American relations. In Dr. Eisenhower's view, "we had adhered longer than we should have to the Good Neighbor concept of absolute nonintervention." With the Inter-American Development Bank, the United States could intervene in Latin America without having to accept the onus of responsibility for intervention. The bank was a collective group, and Latin Americans had lobbied long and hard for it—but because voting power in the bank was based on capital contributions, the United States would dominate the decision-making process. By expanding and contracting loans, the United States could lead and direct social reform in Latin America. As President Eisenhower saw it, the United States now had a dual-track anti-Communist policy: the Declaration of Caracas of 1954 could be used to rally the hemisphere against Communist imperialism, while the Act of Bogotá would alleviate the social and economic conditions that nourished communism.[31]

However, although Latin American governments were eager for U.S. funds, some leaders objected to the new U.S. policies. Both President Kubitschek of Brazil and President Frondizi of Argentina were skeptical of the Social Progress Trust Fund. Argentina, for example, was an educationally advanced nation and did not need funds for a literacy campaign. Frondizi and Kubitschek wanted the United States to generate economic growth in the hemisphere through massive infusions of capital. Kubitschek still spoke of the United States providing Latin America with $30–40 billion in aid. The two leaders argued that underdevelopment was the key, not Castro; economic growth fueled by gigantic public works projects would create jobs, resolve social inequities, and save the region from communism.[32] Such analyses did not impress Washington. They seemed too indirect and vague. Secretary Herter complained that "the Brazilians had never come up with anything specific, but the nearest thing we can get is that we are to give them untold billions with which to do anything they like."[33] By mid-1960, the Eisenhower administration was prepared to send economic aid to Latin America—but it wanted to fund programs specifically aimed at fighting communism. It had also decided that the United States could best define and direct such programs.

The establishment of the Social Progress Trust Fund was only one of several key decisions made by the Eisenhower administration in 1960 that were aimed at shaping and directing the course of development in Latin America. The administration now favored reform-minded politicians, educators, and military officers. In a remarkable turnabout, the United States embraced, for example, Rómulo Betancourt, the president of Venezuela. During the mid-1950s the administration had disdained and harassed the exiled, self-proclaimed political leftist. In turn, Betancourt had written, while in exile, his monumental *Venezuela: política y petróleo*, a fiery denunciation of U.S. oil companies in Venezuela; he had also condemned the administration for its fawning support of dictator Marcos Pérez Jiménez. But Betancourt was a social democrat in a country with an active radical movement. Although he raised the taxes of oil companies, he did not threaten to expropriate their holdings. And he welcomed the Social Progress Trust Fund.[34] With such actions, he earned Washington's respect and vociferous support. Secretary Herter called the Venezuelan "a leader of the forces of moderation in the current revolutionary struggle in Latin America" and asked President Eisenhower to offer Betancourt "all of the public support we can give him." The president caught the irony in this new feature of U.S. policy; he confided to aides that "it was strange that he used to think of Betancourt as a leftist and now he was beginning to look like a rightist in relation to pro-Castro, pro-Communist attacks against him."[35]

The administration not only preferred social reformers like Pedro Beltrán and Rómulo Betancourt but also attempted to produce them. Beginning about 1960, the CIA tried to accelerate the pace of social reform in Latin America by funding schools for politicians and labor leaders. The agency used private foundations, newspaper guilds, and U.S. labor unions, particularly the American Federation of Labor, as both conduits and covers. For example, it allegedly funneled $1 million through the J. M. Kaplan Fund, a foundation associated with a former president of the Welch Grape Juice Company, to help support the International Labor Research Institute. This institute, which was founded in 1957 and subsequently had schools in Costa Rica, the Dominican Republic, and Mexico, was headed by Norman Thomas, the North American socialist. Its faculty included such "democratic-leftist" politicians as José Figueres and Juan Bosch of the Dominican Republic—again, Latin Americans whom the administration had loathed through most of the 1950s. The institute held ten-week seminars for Latin American politicians. The faculty taught that the region needed democracy and structural reforms, but not communism.[36]

The Department of State supplemented the intelligence agency's work by trying to train the future leaders of Latin America. In their tours of South America, both Vice-President Nixon and President Eisenhower had been confronted by university students. University students had also led anti-American demonstrations in Panama. The president feared that Communists had succeeded in convincing the students that "communism cares for the common man"; his fears were sustained by a CIA study that reported "considerable" Communist influence on student groups in Argentina, Brazil, Cuba, Ecuador, El Salvador, Nicaragua, Panama, Peru, and Venezuela. This was another ominous development, for, in Latin America, student organizations traditionally engaged in national politics. Moreover, Communist countries gave approximately 100 scholarships a year to Latin American students to study in the Soviet bloc, where they would learn "Communist ideology and propaganda activity."[37] The administration responded with a special $2-million appropriation to expand its student-exchange program. Latin American students were brought to North American university campuses for six-week programs so as to create "an increasing number of student leaders politically inclined and well enough informed to champion friendly relations between their countries and the United States." In addition, "a carefully selected group of United States students" were sent to Latin American universities with the mission of "influencing their Latin American student associates." Similar exchange programs of university professors and secondary-school teachers were also instituted.[38]

Although it was important to enlist students and professors in the cold war, the administration still counted on the corps of Latin American military officers to dominate the region's political life. Under the guise of the Western Hemisphere Defense scheme, the administration had transferred, during the 1950s, approximately $400 million of military assistance to Latin America. President Eisenhower and defense analysts discounted an attack on the hemisphere; they also understood that the Latin American armed forces would be useless, if such an attack came. Military aid had been an insurance policy, guaranteeing influence with military officers. But, as they analyzed the Cuban Revolution, administration officials now questioned the wisdom of past policies. Castro's forces, using guerrilla-style tactics, had humiliated Batista's U.S.-equipped army. Defense planners wondered whether other Latin American armed forces would similarly succumb to guerrilla insurgencies. Moreover, they grew increasingly worried that wasteful expenditures on warships, combat jets, and tanks were draining Latin American treasuries of scarce capital—money that could be better spent on projects to alleviate the poverty and frustration that were generating revolutionary ferment in the region.[39] What the United States needed was a Latin American military that would contribute to economic development while it protected the region from subversion.

In 1960, the Eisenhower administration began the process of moving both the Latin American military and U.S. policy away from what one Department of Defense official called an "obsessive concentration" on "external aggression resistant armies." The administration now wanted a Latin American military establishment that was "as small and as inexpensive as possible." President Eisenhower announced the new policy during his trip to South America, calling for a curtailment in arms purchases and an inter-American disarmament treaty. Latin Americans should dedicate their resources to social and economic development.[40] Furthermore, the United States believed that Latin American soldiers should assist their countries' development. Adopting some of the ideas suggested by the Draper Committee of 1959, the administration proposed "civic-action" programs, with soldiers building dams, roads, and other public works projects under the direction of the military corps of engineers. Such efforts would improve the economic infrastructure of Latin American nations and enhance the managerial skills of officers and the technical abilities of enlisted personnel. In August 1960, U.S. military advisors met in the Panama Canal Zone with officers from fifteen Latin American countries and instructed them that their duty was to play a major role in national economic development. By the end of the year, the administration was financing engineering battalions in Bolivia and Honduras and had dispatched a civic-action team to Guatemala.[41]

The Eisenhower administration was not suggesting that Latin American soldiers be transformed into construction workers. Instead, U.S. officials wanted Latin American officers to concentrate on internal security. The new, primary duty of Latin American military units would be, as outlined in an NSC study, to attain "a reasonable military capability to maintain internal security against civil disturbances or insurrection." Internal security, as a Defense Department official put it, had a "transcendent nature"; it was a prerequisite for political and economic development and "a means of insuring against the very real possibility of nullification by the Communists of all U.S. assistance to a given country through takeover from within."[42] But to defeat guerrillas, Latin American armies would have to learn more than new combat tactics. By the end of the Eisenhower presidency, U.S. military planners were using such terms as "counter-insurgency," "modernization," and "nation-building," and they were incorporating these concepts in the courses they taught at military schools in the Canal Zone. In fact, officials such as General Edward Lansdale, who would later design U.S. political/military programs in Southeast Asia, were commenting on inter-American military relations. Latin American soldiers would win the allegiance of rural people and pacify the countryside by combining military and civil functions, assuming the roles of infantrymen, engineers, and social workers. In arguing that the Latin American armed forces must forge an indispensable link with the rural population, U.S. officials were, of course, borrowing from the dictums of such theoreticians of guerrilla warfare as Mao Zedong and Ché Guevara.[43]

The new direction in military policy violated U.S. law. In 1959, congressional Democrats had attached to the mutual security program the stricture that internal security requirements could not normally be the basis for military assistance to Latin America. But legislators were receptive to the administration's plans for "civic-action" teams. They, too, feared that Communist insurgencies would break out throughout Latin America. Moreover, they were heartened by the administration's decision to drop the pretense of hemispheric defense and to define a realistic mission for the Latin American military. Only a few legislators, such as Senator Morse, questioned whether internal security programs would produce a new wave of political repression and military dictatorships in Latin America.[44] The administration was successful, however, in persuading Senator Fulbright, its most influential critic, to give internal security programs a trial run. Secretary Herter had informed the senator of his confidential conversation with President Alberto Lleras Camargo of Colombia: the Colombian had complained that his military staff, which was trained in the United States, thought in terms of classical military organization; what Colombia needed was "an Army equipped and trained for operations designed to clear Colombia of guerrilla elements." Fulbright agreed that he favored "money for internal security over money for old-fashioned cruisers."[45]

With new political, military, economic, and cultural programs, the Eisenhower administration believed that it had, by the end of 1960, set a new course for the Latin American policy of the United States. It had forgone "the easy luxury of being simply anti-Communist" and was responding "dynamically and creatively to our age of revolution." It was no longer satisfied with anti-Communist dictatorships. Beyond wanting governments that were politically stable and internally secure, the administration favored Latin American leaders who provided "rising living standards and a more equitable distribution of national income within the general framework of a free enterprise system and through peaceful evolutionary means rather than violent"—and the Unites States was now prepared to help those leaders reorganize their societies.[46] President Eisenhower and his closest advisors later held that they had risen "to the challenge of the 1960s" and that they could rightfully lay claim to the Alliance for Progress; all President John Kennedy had added to the program was an "appealing title."[47]

The assertion of the Eisenhower administration that it had started the Alliance for Progress was correct. The Kennedy administration built upon such foundations as the Inter-American Development Bank and the Social Progress Trust Fund. It also accepted the premise that economic development had to be accompanied by social reform. It, too, encouraged the "democratic-left" and "middle-class revolutionaries" of Latin America, such as Betancourt and Víctor Haya de la Torre of Peru. Furthermore, in less publicized areas—such as military aid and covert activities—the new government's initiatives were actually extensions of Eisenhower administration policies. President Kennedy was embracing ideas first ventured by the Draper Committee when, in March 1961, he declared that his military aid policy would focus on internal security and civic action. His administration also expanded the CIA training programs for Latin American political reformers and trade-union leaders.[48]

To be sure, the Eisenhower administration was less ambitious than the Kennedy government: it neither pledged to transfer $20 billion to Latin America nor set economic growth targets for the region. In essence, President Kennedy promised to fulfill the goals of President Kubitschek's Operation Pan America. His government also proved more flexible than the Eisenhower administration on negotiating commodity agreements, and it modified the traditional U.S. opposition to state industries. The Kennedy administration loaned money to government enterprises such as the national oil company of Mexico, PEMEX, and the national mining industry of Bolivia.[49] But if Eisenhower had served a third term, it is probable that his Latin American policy would have evolved in a manner similar to that of the Kennedy administration. Undersecretary Dillon had indicated both to Congress and to the inter-American community that the $500 million for the Social Progress Trust Fund was to be seen as a down payment for a future, comprehensive effort; he personally made good on that promise when, as Kennedy's secretary of the treasury, he presented the Alliance program to the inter-American conclave held in August 1961 at Punta del Este, Uruguay. Moreover, with the civic-action team it sent to Guatemala in November 1960, the Eisenhower administration was pointing to the "country-development" teams that officials in the Alliance program would send to Latin American countries to oversee social and economic reform.

The Eisenhower administration had already concluded, of course, that, in view of the irresponsibility of Latin American elites, the United States would have to insist on change in the region.[50]

The Eisenhower administration clearly would have developed a comprehensive reform package like the Alliance for Progress, because by 1960 it accepted the premise that the new, and perhaps decisive, cold-war battleground was the Third World. The old order had disintegrated, and the Soviets, confident that history was on their side, were trying to "mold the new order in their image." The United States could not afford to lose this struggle, for "the world population imbalance is heavily against us and is becoming ever more so." But Latin America, one of the emerging, developing areas, was accessible to the United States. If the United States could harness Latin America's abundant resources, growing economic capabilities, and exploding population to the Western cause, then "our own factors of strength will be materially strengthened." Failure "to align and keep Latin America on our side," however, would call into question the leadership and even the security of the United States. Anticipating the rhetoric of the Kennedy years, the Eisenhower administration declared, as it left office, that the early 1960s would be "years of critical challenge to U.S. policy." The United States must identify with and assist "the legitimate aspirations of the Latin American peoples and states."[51]

It dreaded the consequences of defeat, but the Eisenhower administration, like its successor, was confident that it could win the cold war in Latin America. During the electoral campaign of 1960, Democrats ridiculed the Republican administration, charging that it was tired, unimaginative, and riddled with defeatists—but despite the foreign policy setbacks of 1960, the Eisenhower administration felt certain that it could refashion Latin American societies. During the 1950s, when the administration constantly rebuffed requests for a Marshall Plan for Latin America, it never explicitly denied that a massive, U.S.-directed economic aid plan would transform the region; instead, it pleaded that it had too many other foreign aid burdens to shoulder and advised Latin Americans to adhere to free trade and investment principles. Once the officials perceived a clear and present danger in the region, however, they reacted with enthusiasm and assurance. As veteran State Department officer Thomas Mann later recalled, both the Eisenhower and Kennedy administrations worked under "an illusion of omnipotence": the United States had reconstructed Europe; therefore, "it's going to work in Latin America." In the postwar world, the United States was "on the crest of a wave and nobody, literally nobody on the Hill or anywhere else ever questioned our ability to do anything." Mann, who served as Eisenhower's last assistant secretary of state for Latin America and became the chief administrator for the Alliance for Progress during the Johnson presidency, admitted that, in 1960, he shared that optimism.[52]

But Latin America was not Europe. Western European countries had been devastated by war, but they had financial and technical expertise, institutionalized political parties, skillful politicians, strong national identities, and, except for Germany, a democratic tradition. The United States had helped to rebuild countries whose social fabrics, political traditions, and economic institutions were notably similar to those of North America. On the other hand, the Iberian and Amerindian political heritage—characterized by planned economies, strong central governments, and the organization of society into corporate groups—was virtually nonexistent in the United States. U.S. officials either ignored those differences or seemingly assumed that idealism, energy, and optimism would bridge the vast cultural gap and bring about the "modernization" of Latin America.[53]

As it left office, the Eisenhower administration also left unresolved the question of what the United States would do if socioeconomic elites resisted pressures to modernize. Perhaps the Inter-American Development Bank would not have sufficient leverage to force change. The problem was well illustrated by an exchange in 1960 between Senator Fulbright and Senator Bourke Hickenlooper: Hickenlooper asserted that the Social Progress Trust Fund could succeed only if Latin America's "feudal" social structure was dismantled; Fulbright seconded the need for change, puckishly adding that "the traditional way is to have a revolution."[54] But the initiatives of 1960 and the subsequent Alliance for Progress were born out of a fear of the political and economic consequences of the Cuban Revolution. U.S. officials talked bravely about the "age of revolution" and "inevitable revolutions." Revolutions, however, cannot be easily controlled, nor can their results be confidently predicted; and revolutionary nationalism, even if it had indigenous roots, threatened U.S. trade and investment and smacked of communism. Based on its consistent, overwhelming fear of subversion, the Eisenhower administration, if faced with revolutionary turmoil, would have reconsidered its new-found disdain for Latin American oligarchs and would probably have opted, as did the Kennedy and Johnson administrations, for order and security over democracy and social justice.[55]

During its last year in office, the Eisenhower administration extensively revised the Latin American policy of the United States and initiated a decade-long effort to reform and modernize Latin American societies, in order to make them resistant to Communist subversion. But the administration's new, self-proclaimed policy of intervention went beyond measures designed to transform the social structure of Latin America: in 1960, the Eisenhower administration would also attempt to overthrow a right-wing dictatorship in the Dominican Republic and a radical, revolutionary regime in Cuba. The administration was determined to eliminate Communists from the hemisphere and to eradicate regimes that fostered communism.

CHAPTER 9

THE WAR AGAINST TRUJILLO AND CASTRO

1960–1961

In 1960 the Eisenhower administration happily confessed that it had formulated an interventionist policy for Latin America. Its new political, military, economic, and cultural programs were designed to build sturdy, socially progressive democracies in the region. Moreover, the administration was prepared to put the nation's diplomatic and economic influence behind Latin American leaders who promised to reform their societies. President Dwight Eisenhower and his advisors were less open, however, about another feature of their Latin American policy: during its last year in office, the administration intervened covertly in the Dominican Republic and in Cuba, aiding insurgents who wanted to overthrow Rafael Trujillo and Fidel Castro. So determined was the administration to destroy communism in the hemisphere that it resorted to tactics normally thought permissible only during wartime.

During 1960, the growing hostility between the United States and Cuba captured international attention and became a major domestic political issue in the United States. At the same time, another crisis, which escaped similar public attention, erupted between the United States and Cuba's Caribbean neighbor, the Dominican Republic. By early 1960 the Eisenhower administration had decided that the Dominican dictator, Rafael Trujillo, must relinquish power and leave his country. It was feared that Trujillo was creating "Batista-like" conditions in the Dominican Republic, driving his countrymen into the hands of the Communists. In addition, the administration hoped that, by ousting Trujillo, it would garner Latin American support for its anti-Castro policy.

Rafael Leonidas Trujillo Molina, the absolute military dictator of the Dominican Republic, was a product of the Dominican national guard, the constabulary created by U.S. marines during their occupation of the country between 1916 and 1924. Trujillo, who was recruited by the marines and rose rapidly through the ranks, seized power in 1930 and used his position as commander-in-chief to maintain for three decades one of the most odious regimes in the history of the Americas. He also cultivated relations with Washington: he promoted U.S. trade and investment and retired his nation's substantial international debt; and, with great fanfare, he aligned the Dominican Republic with the United States during World War II and the cold war. In view of Trujillo's ability to keep his country stable and friendly, many North Americans were willing to overlook his gross violations of fundamental human rights. From the Eisenhower administration, for example, Trujillo received hearty praise, "embrasos" from Vice-President Richard Nixon and U.S. ambassadors, and approximately $6 million in military assistance.[1]

But during the late 1950s, a heated debate erupted over U.S. policies toward Trujillo. In 1956 allegations arose that the dictator's henchmen had kidnapped in the United States and murdered Jesús Galíndez, a Spanish citizen and scholar who had written a bitterly anti-Trujillist book. At the time of his abduction, Galíndez was teaching at Columbia University in New York City. Then Charles Murphy, a young aviator from Oregon, disappeared. Murphy had become unwittingly involved in the Galíndez affair, piloting the plane that took Galíndez from New York to the Dominican Republic; he was probably kidnapped and executed by Trujillo's men to guarantee his silence. To cover that crime, Trujillo's agents arrested and murdered in prison Octavio de la Maza, a Dominican pilot and a friend of Murphy's. Dominican officials claimed that de la Maza left a suicide note in which he took responsibility for Murphy's death.[2] These cases gained national attention through the persistent efforts between 1957 and 1959 of Charles Porter, a new congressman from the district in Oregon where Murphy had lived.[3] Porter's campaign against Trujillo was soon joined by his senior colleague, Senator Wayne Morse. In Morse's view, the murders of Galíndez and Murphy were further examples of why the Eisenhower administration should abandon its support of Latin American military dictators.[4]

Rafael Trujillo not only added to the Eisenhower administration's embarrassment about its Latin American policies in the late 1950s but also began to ignore Washington's commands. The dictator, furious at the international uproar over the Galíndez-Murphy affair, seemed to lose his self-control—and after nearly three decades of power, perhaps he felt it no longer necessary to be deferential to his North American patrons. A significant act of defiance came in 1958. When the Eisenhower administration cut off arms shipments to Batista, it also suspended military aid to Trujillo. This action had little practical effect, for Trujillo had taken care to make the Dominican Republic self-sufficient in small arms; the Dominican dictator then, against U.S. wishes, began to ship arms to Batista. Trujillo probably reasoned that the triumph of the guerrilla movement led by Fidel Castro would, by example, encourage his opponents. And in fact, by June 1959, six months after the collapse of the Batista regime, insurgents were using Cuba as a base for armed forays into the Dominican Republic.[5]

Castro's subsequent radicalization of the Cuban Revolution forced the Eisenhower administration to question how much longer it could tolerate Trujillo: it was feared that the Dominican political world might become as polarized as had that of Cuba. In early 1960 Secretary of State Herter warned President Eisenhower that the "situation in Santo Domingo is very bad in that the Trujillo government is acting against the moderates and may soon create a situation like that in Cuba where the opposition is taken over by wild radicals."[6] The administration's fears, however, although truly held, were probably exaggerated. Intelligence officials spoke darkly about Communists infiltrating student and labor groups in the Dominican Republic, but they also estimated that fewer than 100 Dominicans belonged to the Communist party. Opposition to Trujillo was scattered and disorganized. No single, charismatic leader, no Castro, had emerged to challenge the Trujillo tyranny. Indeed, Dominican dissidents and exiles informed U.S. intelligence agents that they did not believe they could oust Trujillo without outside help.[7]

Beyond posing a potential threat to U.S. security, Trujillo was undermining the administration's anti-Castro policy. The administration wanted to build an inter-American democratic front opposed to Castro. But, as the State Department noted, any delay in the end of the Trujillo regime "makes more difficult the achievement of U.S. objectives with respect to Cuba because of the tendency of many Latin Americans to place hatred of Trujillo higher than concern of Castro."[8] Latin American democrats like José Figueres and Rómulo Betancourt despised Trujillo both because he was a ruthless tyrant and because he harbored and funded Latin American counterrevolutionists, leading these democrats to insist, as a price for their support of anti-Castro policies, that the United States oppose all undemocratic regimes, including Trujillo's. President Eisenhower accepted the bargain, telling subordinates in 1960 that "it would seem we should link Trujillo and Castro up and direct our actions against both of them."[9]

Within this new context of inter-American relations, the Eisenhower administration plotted against Trujillo. In mid-April 1960 President Eisenhower approved a State Department paper, which had been discussed before the NSC on 14 January 1960, on policies to be followed "in the event of the flight, assassination, death, or overthrow of Trujillo." The United States would be prepared to dispatch warships to Dominican waters or to land troops on Dominican soil "to prevent a Castro-type government or one sympathetic to Castro." But, in order to avoid military intervention, the United States would attempt to persuade Trujillo to leave and would begin establishing contacts with civilian and military dissidents who could give the island republic "moderate, pro–United States leadership." The U.S. ambassador, Joseph Farland, was ordered to meet immediately with those dissidents, for, as the paper noted, "delay in the end of the Trujillo regime has already tended to make previously pro-American dissident elements—who are increasingly desperate—more responsive to Castro's appeal and more critical of the U.S. for failure actively to help them."[10]

Rafael Trujillo would not cooperate with the U.S. plan. Various emissaries—including Ambassador Farland, Senator George Smathers of Florida, General Edwin Norman Clark, and the former ambassador to Peru and Brazil, William Pawley—journeyed to Ciudad Trujillo (Santo Domingo) to discuss with Trujillo the prospects for his stepping down or permitting a free election. A comfortable exile in perhaps Portugal or Morocco with a "trust fund" was mentioned.[11] But the tough dictator resisted all blandishments. As he told Pawley, "you can come in here with the Marines, and you can come in here with the Army, and you can come in here with the Navy or even the atomic bomb, but I'll never go out of here unless I go on a stretcher."[12]

Trujillo not only refused to abdicate but also became even more of a nuisance and threat to U.S. policies in Latin America. He picked fights with his neighbors, and in April 1960 he aided an unsuccessful attempt by right-wing Venezuelan military officers to overthrow the Betancourt government. Two months later, on 24 June 1960, his agents tried to assassinate President Betancourt by detonating a bomb planted near his passing automobile; Betancourt survived, but he received severe burns on his hands.[13] Trujillo also counterattacked within the United States. He always actively promoted his cause. He had, for example, fifty-four consulates in the United States, more than any other country, and that propaganda mill took out advertisements in newspapers and planted stories with friendly journalists to remind U.S. citizens that Trujillo was a staunch anti-Communist. Further, during the last five years of his rule, he reportedly plied U.S. congressmen with prostitutes and over $5 million in bribes—indeed, Eisenhower, in a private meeting, discussed with Secretary of State Herter the names of two influential legislators who were reported to be "receiving money in one way or another from the Dominican Republic."[14]

Unable to persuade Trujillo to leave, the administration considered violent measures. On 13 May 1960 Eisenhower met with Undersecretary of State C. Douglas Dillon, Assistant Secretary R. Richard Rubottom, and Ambassador Farland. The president opened the session "by saying that he was bombarded by people who are opposed to Castro and Trujillo." He and the State Department officials then reviewed the failures of the Pawley and Smathers missions. Undersecretary Dillon added that he had received a classified report claiming that Trujillo "did not plan to retire 'before the year 2000.'" The discussants agreed that an election, while Trujillo remained on the island, would be meaningless: the dissidents would fear retaliation, and if Trujillo ran for election, he would win because he controlled all news outlets and had popular support. The discussion continued:

> Mr. Rubottom said that Trujillo is involved in all sorts of efforts all over the hemisphere to create disorder. The President commented that Castro is also, and he would like to see them both sawed off. Mr. Dillon commented that the State Department is about ready to propose some additional action against Castro.

The participants concluded their review by both noting the Castro menace and recalling that "under the existing military contingency plan we would send in our forces into the area to keep Castro out." The president also remarked that the problem was "to find a way to give a chance for a new party to form."[15]

It would seem, from his harsh talk of having foreign leaders "sawed off," that President Eisenhower was indicating at the 13 May 1960 meeting that he wanted Rafael Trujillo overthrown. Certainly his subordinates intensified U.S. efforts against Trujillo in the ensuing weeks. On 16 June, Secretary Rubottom gave his "unofficial" approval to a CIA proposal that Henry Dearborn, the deputy chief of mission in the Dominican Republic, become the "communications link" between Dominican dissidents and the CIA. The dissidents were to understand that, although the United States would not take any overt action against Trujillo, it would clandestinely assist the opposition to "develop effective force to accomplish Trujillo overthrow."[16] Then, on 28 June, four days after the attempt on President Betancourt's life, Rubottom met with Colonel J. C. King, chief of the CIA's Western Hemisphere Division. According to King's handwritten notes and subsequent memorandum, Rubottom approved a CIA suggestion to provide the dissidents with "a small number of sniper rifles or other devices for the removal of key Trujillo people from the scenes" and to place the weapons "in hands of the opposition at the earliest possible moment." The CIA thereafter recommended that twelve "sterile" or untraceable rifles with telescopic sights together with 500 rounds of ammunition be delivered to the dissidents.[17]

These rifles, although few in number, would be critical to the Dominicans. When the U.S. marines had occupied the Dominican Republic they disarmed the country and gave the national guard a monopoly over arms and munitions; Trujillo enforced his rule by retaining that policy.[18] And the rifles the CIA proposed to pass to the dissidents would be aimed at Trujillo. As Dearborn advised Rubottom on 14 July 1960, the dissidents were "in no way ready to carry on any type of revolutionary activity in the foreseeable future except the assassination of their principal enemy."[19]

Despite extensive planning, however, the twelve sniper rifles were never furnished to the dissidents. In July, Dearborn informed the CIA that the dissidents now believed that strong action by the OAS could bring Trujillo's downfall without further effort on their part.[20] The OAS met in August 1960 to condemn Trujillo's assassination attempt against Betancourt. The Eisenhower administration, too, perceived the inter-American meeting as a new opportunity to remove Trujillo. Reversing the position he had taken at the foreign ministers' conference in Santiago in August 1959, Secretary Herter called on the OAS to supervise a political transition in the Dominican Republic. At Santiago, Herter had defended the principle of nonintervention, denying that democracy could be imposed on another nation; now he wanted the OAS to be transformed into an "anti-dictatorial alliance," as envisioned by the Larreta Doctrine of 1945 and the contemporary Betancourt Doctrine. The Dominican Republic, Herter argued, would continue its "aggressive and interventionist policy" as long as it was ruled by a dictatorship. The OAS must go beyond punitive measures. Herter proposed that the organization take control of the political machinery of the Dominican Republic, oversee the end of the Trujillo tyranny, establish political parties, and conduct free elections.[21] As he explained to President Eisenhower, his plan had two objectives: a peaceful transition of power would avoid "a revolution which might well produce a communist or Castro-type government in Santo Domingo"; furthermore, "if we prove successful in this, a very useful precedent will have been set for possible later action when the Cuban matter is before us."[22]

Herter's plan shocked Latin Americans and never came to a vote at the OAS. He was frankly suggesting that the OAS renounce the sacred nonintervention principle and assume control of a member state. The key Latin American nations—Argentina, Brazil, and Mexico—were ready to condemn the Dominican Republic for its attack on Venezuela, but they did not want to be seen judging the internal character of the Trujillo regime. In any case, the Dominican Republic rejected the Herter plan. The OAS accordingly voted to recommend to member nations that they break diplomatic relations with the Dominican Republic and impose an arms embargo. The U.S. delegation voted with the Latin American majority. Although disappointed with the collapse of his plan, Herter still thought the OAS action against Trujillo would serve as a precedent for anti-Castro policies.[23] Herter had also successfully convinced the Latin Americans to permit consular representation in the Dominican Republic. Before voting to break relations, Herter had consulted with CIA Director Allen Dulles. Concerned that a rupture in relations "would reduce our ability to affect or control events there," Dulles advised Herter to keep open the three U.S. consulates in the Dominican Republic.[24] Thereafter, CIA agents would operate from these bases.

In accordance with the OAS resolutions, the United States on 26 August 1960 broke diplomatic relations with the Dominican Republic and reaffirmed its arms embargo. It also resorted to economic warfare. Sugar production was a key sector of the Dominican economy, and the Trujillo family controlled major plantations. The president therefore imposed punitive excise taxes on imports of Dominican sugar into the United States. Eisenhower imposed the taxes because he could not convince the agricultural committees to eliminate the Dominican Republic's share of the sugar quota. In July 1960, he had cut the importation of Cuban sugar into the United States; one undesirable effect of this action had been to expand the Dominican Republic's share of the U.S. market. Eisenhower asked legislative leaders to treat the Dominican Republic and Cuba equally, warning that "we cannot expect them [Dominican dissidents] to resist their internal pro-Castro factions unless we decline to favor the Dominican Republic with a large sugar bonus." Eisenhower's failure to sway legislators prompted his concern about bribes and his comment to Secretary Herter that he was "very suspicious about the actions of a number of key people in the agricultural committees of the Congress."[25]

Diplomatic and economic pressure failed to topple Trujillo. The plotting resumed. Between September 1960 and January 1961, officials in the State Department and the CIA constantly discussed covert actions against Trujillo. Logistical and diplomatic problems, however, confounded their work. CIA operatives wondered how they could smuggle weapons to the dissidents; if, for example, sniper rifles were parachuted into the Dominican Republic, their telescopic sights might be damaged. Moreover, the dissidents continually altered their requests, calling at times for antitank weapons, at other times for machine guns, and even once for "a slow-working chemical that could be rubbed on the palm of one's hand and transferred to Trujillo in a handshake, causing delayed lethal results."[26] Officials also worried about who would succeed Trujillo. In October 1960 Undersecretary Dillon informed Eisenhower that "we do not want to take concrete moves against the Dominican Republic just at present, since no successor to Trujillo is ready to take power, and the result might be to bring an individual of the Castro stripe into power there."[27] This concern led the administration to make one last effort to persuade Trujillo to leave office: in the fall of 1960, it apparently sent William Pawley to speak with Trujillo; Pawley, who had journeyed to Havana in November 1958 to see Batista, again failed to convince a dictator to participate in a peaceful transition of power.[28]

Although the administration worried about the outcome of a *golpe de estado*, it also feared the consequences of inaction. Trujillo's opponents were shaken by the administration's congressional defeat over the sugar issue. Writing to Eisenhower, they warned that "Trujillo is subtly causing the Dominican people to believe that he is more powerful than the government of the U.S., because he can 'control' its Congress through certain elements in it who serve his interests"; if the United States continued to buy Dominican sugar, it would be "confirmation of his [Trujillo's] political propaganda which would be fatal for our democratic future."[29] Trujillo also jeopardized the administration's hemispheric policies. Venezuela, for example, was dismayed by Trujillo's victory on the sugar issue. The administration was not adhering to its policy of opposing dictators of the right and left.[30] Accordingly, President Eisenhower and his key advisors again concluded, in late 1960, that they could hope for the support of Latin American democracies for anti-Castro actions only if the United States simultaneously moved against Trujillo. As Whiting Willauer, the State Department officer who coordinated the anti-Cuban program, observed, the United States needed to be " 'on the side of the angels' in the entire problem of dictatorships vs. free governments in the hemisphere."[31]

During its last months in office, the Eisenhower administration renewed its campaign to topple Trujillo. In December 1960 the administration asked OAS members to ban the export of oil, petroleum products, trucks, and spare parts to the Dominican Republic. Ironically, this action displeased some Latin Americans. Six nations, including Argentina and Brazil, abstained on the embargo vote, because the Dominican Republic was not guilty of any new aggression; the United States, they argued, was basing its case for additional sanctions on the internal nature of the Dominican Republic, thereby violating the nonintervention principle.[32] The administration also revived its covert program. On 3 January 1961 President Eisenhower conducted a last, comprehensive review of U.S. policies in the Caribbean. Recalling that his administration had hoped to "move against Trujillo and Castro simultaneously," he ordered his national security advisors to "do as much as we can and quickly about Trujillo."[33] Nine days later, the 5412 Committee (the special group that oversaw covert activities) ruled that the CIA could provide the dissidents with "limited supplies of small arms and other material." Early in 1961, pistols and carbines were passed to the Dominicans. The pistols came through diplomatic pouch to Henry Dearborn, the one U.S. diplomat left behind after the rupture in relations; Dearborn, who was officially consul general and de facto CIA chief of station, gave the Dominicans the carbines that had been left in the U.S. consulate by military guards.[34]

Rafael Trujillo died during the first months of the Kennedy administration. Late in the evening of 30 May 1961, seven Dominicans led by Antonio de la Maza—brother of Octavio, the slain Dominican pilot—ambushed and assassinated Trujillo near San Cristobal, Dominican Republic. The assassins, who also included disgruntled military officers, caught the aged dictator on a lonely stretch of road as he was on his way to visit his twenty-year-old mistress. Using hand-guns and shotguns, they riddled his body with twenty-seven rounds of ammunition. In 1975, a select congressional committee, known as the Church Committee, investigated the U.S. role in the death of Trujillo and found that they could not establish definitively whether the assassins had used the .38 caliber Smith and Wesson pistols passed through diplomatic pouch or whether they carried U.S. carbines, although the committee did have testimony and evidence that the weapons had reached the "action element" of the dissident group.[35]

The Eisenhower administration took extraordinary measures in attempting to drive Rafael Trujillo out of the Dominican Republic. Nevertheless, the primary concern was Fidel Castro, not Trujillo: the steps taken against Trujillo were within the context of the administration's anti-Communist, anti-Castro policies, and the efforts against the Cuban leader and his followers exceeded those taken against Trujillo.

On 17 March 1960 President Eisenhower, as previously noted, authorized a program to replace Castro by covert means. This program included the creation of a unified anti-Castro political opposition, the launching of a propaganda offensive, support for covert activities within Cuba, and the development of a paramilitary force outside of Cuba for future guerrilla actions. The CIA began at once to implement the president's decision, although with the realization that it would take time to coordinate and train the political and military opposition. CIA officials estimated, for example, that it would take six to eight months to reach the initial goal of 300 trained guerrillas. The agency was, however, readily able to beam propaganda to the Cuban people, and on 17 May it began broadcasting anti-Castro messages from Swan Island, a dot of land off the coast of Honduras. Consistent with the administration's desire to appear even-handed, the new radio station attacked first Trujillo and then Castro. President Eisenhower, while wishing that the CIA could expedite its program, approved of the general approach; on 18 August 1960 he received a report on the CIA's progress and then authorized a budget of $13 million for the anti-Castro campaign.[36]

In mounting its covert campaign, the Eisenhower administration was relying on the experience gained in toppling Jacobo Arbenz of Guatemala in 1954. The CIA men who directed the Cuban operation—Allen Dulles, Deputy Director of Planning Richard Bissell, and

Colonel J. C. King—had overseen the anti-Arbenz program. The operatives they used, such as E. Howard Hunt and David Phillips, were also veterans of the Guatemalan campaign. "Radio Swan" was patterned after the "Voice of Liberation," the propaganda the CIA had broadcast from Honduras and Nicaragua to unsettle the Guatemalan population. And the CIA initially intended to build a Cuban military force about the size of Colonel Carlos Castillo Armas's band of insurgents. Indeed, the agency's estimate of six to eight months' preparation for the Cuban rebels was probably based on the experience of taking approximately ten months to assemble the Guatemalan counterrevolutionists.[37] But perhaps the most important lesson learned by the Eisenhower administration from the fall of Arbenz was that it had the ability and responsibility to destroy a Communist government in the Western Hemisphere. After 1954, the administration always included in its classified policy statements the pledge that it would take any action "deemed appropriate" to sever close ties between a Latin American state and the Soviet Union. President Eisenhower was upholding that pledge when he authorized and then funded the covert anti-Castro program.[38]

While the CIA prepared its covert program, the Eisenhower administration attempted to isolate Cuba both economically and diplomatically. In mid-1960 the administration tried to strangle the Cuban economy. In June, U.S.-owned petroleum refineries in Cuba, at the behest of Secretary of the Treasury Robert Anderson, refused to refine the Soviet crude oil that the Cubans had acquired in exchange for their sugar. In July, President Eisenhower ordered a 700,000-ton cut in Cuba's 1960 sugar quota of 3,120,000 tons; because Cuba had already exported 2,300,000 tons of sugar to the United States, Eisenhower's order effectively barred further imports of Cuban sugar. Finally, in October the president imposed a near-total trade embargo on Cuba, limiting exports to food and medicines. United States officials expected that Cuban-American trade, which had amounted to $1.1 billion in 1957, would fall to a value of approximately $100 million. In turn, Castro methodically seized and then expropriated U.S.-owned properties: sugar mills, petroleum refineries, utilities, tire plants, and banks became the property of the Cuban government. By the end of October, U.S. direct investments in Cuba, once valued at more than $900 million, were gone.[39]

The Eisenhower administration averred that its economic sanctions were in response to Cuba's discriminatory treatment of U.S. businesses—but in fact, this new cycle of tension and hostility was initiated by the United States. In the previous year, the administration had been patient in the face of Castro's aggressive behavior, but after March 1960, the United States intentionally provoked the Cubans. Indeed, on the day he cut the sugar quota, President Eisenhower warned his aides "to be alert to the Cuban reaction because when dealing with a 'little Hitler' anything can happen." He accordingly "emphasized the importance of looking forward to subsequent steps which might be needed of an economic, diplomatic, strategic nature."[40] Such strong views prompted CIA Director Dulles to recall that, by mid-1960, "we did have a policy, which was to overthrow Castro in one way or another."[41]

Although the imposition of economic sanctions was part of the strategy to overthrow Castro, U.S. officials surmised that there would be undesirable short-term consequences. Ambassador Philip Bonsal, who actually opposed the sanctions, predicted that reprisals would strengthen Castro domestically and force the Russians to come to the aid of the Cuban Revolution. Assistant Secretary Rubottom added that Castro could not be "intimidated." On the other hand, Secretary of State Herter disliked "pecking away" at Castro; he preferred "something really effective" such as invoking the Trading with the Enemy Act and banning all Cuban trade. Even President Eisenhower confessed that he was "not at all sure that economic sanctions would have any real effect on the Castro regime."[42] But despite these misgivings, the administration pressed on, because it detested Castro and because it wanted to encourage his opponents. It also wanted to preserve U.S. credibility and uphold U.S. will to Latin America and the rest of the world; as National Security Advisor Gordon Gray argued, it was essential "to demonstrate that we would not permit ourselves to be vilified and attacked, and our property expropriated."[43]

These decisions to pursue a campaign of full-scale economic warfare against Cuba suggested that the Eisenhower administration discounted any possibility of a Cuban-American rapprochement. The United States would deal with Castro only if he dismantled the Cuban Revolution and renounced ties with the Soviet Union. To be sure, during 1960 the administration periodically issued public statements raising the possibility of negotiations;[44] but in practice, it rebuffed conciliatory efforts. For example, in mid-1960, when Latin American diplomats offered to mediate between the United States and Cuba, Secretary Herter instructed U.S. representatives in Latin America to discourage such initiatives. As Herter explained, the fundamental problem was not a bilateral issue but rather the "degree to which Soviet and Chicom [Chinese Communist] leadership has designated and used all possible resources to support Cuban regime as its principal instrument to undermine inter-American security and solidarity and degree to which Cuban leadership has eagerly accepted this role."[45]

Rather than having the inter-American community help resolve the Cuban-American confrontation, the Eisenhower administration wanted it to unite behind the United States. In 1954 the administration had obtained Latin American assent to the Declaration of Caracas, and although Latin Americans were unwilling to apply it to the internal affairs of individual countries, the administration had found the declaration useful: it had provided a patina of legitimacy to the covert, unilateral intervention of the United States in Guatemala. In 1960, the administration again wanted diplomatic cover. It also hoped that an anti-Cuban statement would encourage and fortify Castro's Cuban opponents.[46] But, in contrast to 1954, the administration this time moved carefully and cautiously—the Cuban Revolution had struck a responsive chord among Latin American intellectuals and the poor. Moreover, Castro, unlike Arbenz, had become a major international figure. President Eisenhower counseled patience to U.S. legislators, noting that "if the United states did not conduct itself in precisely the right way vis-à-vis Cuba, we could lose all of South America." Furthermore, he feared that if Mexico became "disgruntled" with U.S. tactics, "and if we were to see the Communists come to power there, in all likelihood we would have to go to war about this."[47]

In March 1960 the United States began preparing the case against Cuba that it would take to the OAS. At the same time that he authorized the CIA to begin its covert campaign, Eisenhower directed the State Department to make "every effort" to influence Latin Americans to recognize the Cuban danger and support U.S. actions against Castro.[48] These efforts included, of course, trying to overthrow Trujillo and promising to Latin Americans, through the Social Progress Trust Fund, a substantial economic aid program. Secretary of State Herter presented the U.S. case at the Seventh Meeting of Foreign Ministers of the American Republics, which was held in San José, Costa Rica, in late August, immediately following the Sixth Meeting, which had considered the Dominican Republic's aggression against Venezuela. Herter expected that, at a minimum, the foreign ministers would censure Cuba and call upon it to rid itself of Soviet influence. Perhaps the Latin Americans would even break diplomatic relations and impose sanctions against Cuba, as they had just done with the Dominican Republic. Certainly, Herter thought, the promise of the upcoming economic conference in Bogotá would help convince Latin Americans to follow the U.S. lead.[49]

The Seventh Meeting of Foreign Ministers proved, however, to be a major disappointment to Secretary Herter and President Eisenhower. In making his case, Herter chose not to invoke the Caracas Declaration and charge that Cuba was "dominated or controlled" by Communists; the administration's own national intelligence estimates had failed to establish that charge. Instead, he played on Latin American fears of social upheaval, alleging that Cuba was exporting communism and serving as a surrogate for the Soviet Union. Herter's presentation evoked little enthusiasm from the Latin Americans, save for vigorous responses from the dictatorships in Guatemala, Nicaragua, and Paraguay. The secretary of state found that "the sensitivity on the subject of intervention was unbelievable," with Latin Americans having "two fears—the Cubans and us and were afraid we would take unilateral steps against Cuba."[50] The delegates only agreed, therefore, to pass an innocuous, general resolution that opposed extracontinental intervention in the hemisphere. During the debate, delegates from Brazil, Bolivia, Panama, and Uruguay stressed that they were interested not in condemning Cuba but in having it return to the inter-American fold. Mexican Foreign Minister Manuel Tello went further, favorably comparing the Cuban and Mexican Revolutions and stating categorically that the San José resolution was not aimed at Cuba. Tello had, in Milton Eisenhower's words, "drained the pale blood from the Declaration with his statement in San José."[51] A crestfallen President Eisenhower ordered Herter not to press the "weak-kneed" Latin Americans, noting that "if this is the best that the Secretary can achieve, [I feel I have] no choice but to accept it."[52]

Latin American diplomats were, of course, right to worry that the United States was about to violate the nonintervention principle. What they probably could not have imagined was that officials within the Eisenhower administration were also plotting to discredit and even kill Fidel Castro and his closest advisors. During the period between mid-March and mid-October 1960, the United States was pursuing a multi-track policy against Cuba—organizing and training a political and military opposition, inciting Cubans to rebel, disrupting the Cuban economy, and isolating Cuba diplomatically. These covert and overt actions were supplemented by what a congressional investigating committee would later call plots and schemes that "strain the imagination." CIA technicians worked on devices to undermine Castro's charismatic appeal. In one case, technicians thought they could destroy his masculine image as "The Beard" by dusting his shoes with thallium salts, a strong depilatory that would cause his beard to fall out. The depilatory was to be administered during a trip outside Cuba, when it was anticipated Castro would cooperatively leave his shoes outside the door of his hotel room to be shined.[53] More ominous, but no less bizarre, were proposals to assassinate him. In August 1960 the CIA enlisted underworld figures in the war against Castro; it was hoped that these criminals could either arrange a "gangland-style killing" in which Castro would be gunned down, or manage to deposit poison pills in his coffee. Another scheme was to rig an exotic sea shell with an explosive device and place it in his favorite skin-diving area.[54]

As in the case of arming Trujillo's assassins, it cannot now be determined precisely who knew of and authorized these assassination schemes. In the mid-1970s, Richard Bissell readily admitted to the Church Committee that he had overseen assassination plots. The committee also received compelling evidence that Colonel King had participated in the plots. Indeed, King had proposed, in suggestive language, to CIA Director Dulles that "thorough consideration be given to the elimination of Castro" and that Castro, his brother Raúl, and Ché Guevara "be eliminated in one package." The Church Committee could not, however, say whether Allen Dulles understood that his subordinates were trying to murder Castro. Bissell testified that he had briefed Dulles about the CIA's contacts with underworld figures, but had done so in a "circumlocutious" manner. Bissell explained that he spoke obliquely to Dulles because "there was a reluctance to spread even on an oral record some aspects of this operation"; yet, he was "quite convinced" that Dulles understood the nature of the operation. Although it was unable to render a definitive judgment on the Castro operation, the Church Committee determined that Allen Dulles had authorized another assassination plot in 1960—the plan to kill Patrice Lumumba of the Congo.[55]

The role that President Eisenhower may have played in these machinations also cannot be determined. As with Dulles, the evidence for presidential complicity seems strongest in the Lumumba case, with the Church Committee summarizing that "the chain of events revealed by documents and testimony is strong enough to permit a reasonable inference that the plot to assassinate Lumumba was authorized by President Eisenhower." The CIA's steps against Lumumba directly followed strong expressions of hostility from the president and National Security Advisor Gray. Gray represented the president, "my associate," at the 5412 Committee.[56] It can be similarly speculated that the CIA was motivated by the president's references to Castro as a "madman" and a "little Hitler," by his desire to have Castro and Trujillo "sawed off," and by his order to "do as much as we can and quickly about Trujillo." Decisions to arm Trujillo's opponents, for example, followed shortly after presidential denunciations of Trujillo. Whether the president was then informed of operational plans is uncertain. Bissell testified that he felt certain Dulles would have told Eisenhower enough about an assassination plot to enable him to terminate it but not enough of the details to prevent his plausibly denying knowledge of it;[57] but he had no hard evidence to back this claim. Moreover, close associates, like General Andrew Goodpaster, testified that Eisenhower had never told them about any assassination efforts. The president's son, John Eisenhower, concurred and added that his father "did not discuss important subjects circumlocutiously." Furthermore, Eisenhower constantly worried that, if Castro were removed prematurely, he might be succeeded by another dangerous radical like Ché Guevara.[58]

Whatever the level of authorization and knowledge of the assassination plots against Fidel Castro, they did not work. Indeed, the Eisenhower administration's entire program against Castro was foundering as the U.S. presidential elections approached. The public moves were inconclusive. The Latin Americans had declined to expel Cuba from the inter-American community, and the Cubans were weathering the U.S. economic sanctions. The Russians, as Ambassador Bonsal predicted, had agreed to purchase Cuba's sugar surplus; moreover, the two countries had established formal diplomatic relations in May, and the Russians had begun to ship military equipment to the Cubans. The CIA's covert program had also produced few results. The agency found it impossible to convince Castro's opponents to work together. The opposition was a motley group, consisting of left-wing idealists, middle-class reformers, and *Batistianos*. Allen Dulles claimed that his agents had identified 184 different factions within the exile community. Even if the Cubans were to unite, the Castro regime could not be overthrown through small-scale guerrilla operations. In the summer of 1960, small bands of U.S.-trained guerrillas had been infiltrated into the island—but the rebels, who operated in the Escambray mountains in southern Cuba, were not achieving dramatic victories, and it was difficult to resupply them through airdrops. Castro's militia also seemed increasingly more vigorous and better armed.[59]

These unhappy developments prompted, in the fall of 1960, a reassessment of the Cuban problem both in the White House and in the Central Intelligence Agency. An impatient President Eisenhower prodded the CIA to expedite the covert program, telling Dulles and Bissell: "Boys, if you don't intend to go through with this, let's stop talking about it." The president was particularly upset that the CIA had been unable to organize and unify Castro's opponents, for a covert intervention could be legitimized internationally only if Castro were replaced by reform-oriented leaders who seemed to command widespread, popular support.[60] The president was also exasperated that Cuba had become an issue in the presidential campaign between Vice-President Nixon and John Kennedy. The vice-president, wanting to defend himself from Kennedy's charge that the Republicans had lost Cuba to communism, repeatedly implored the president to strike against Castro. Eisenhower disliked being pressured, and he doubted his decisions could be tied into Nixon's campaign "in any acceptable way." But, after speaking with Nixon, he ordered, on 17 October 1960, the recall of Ambassador Bonsal from Cuba and further reductions in Cuban-American trade. A week later, he began campaigning for Nixon, specifically denouncing Kennedy for his comments on Cuba. Then, on 1 November, the president released a formal statement pledging to defend the U.S. naval base at Guantánamo; he bolstered his statement by dispatching 1400 additional marines to Guantánamo.[61]

Eisenhower may have manipulated the Cuban issue during the last stages of the presidential campaign. But his actions also reflected his administration's hardening attitude and growing alarm about communism in the Western Hemisphere. With Cuba accepting arms from the Soviet Union, the State Department predicted that Cuba would attempt to overthrow Latin American governments. When, in November, political violence rocked both El Salvador and Guatemala, administration officials immediately suspected the Cubans. The United States delayed recognizing the new government in San Salvador and dispatched a naval flotilla to the coast of Guatemala.[62] The administration eventually concluded that the upheavals in Central America were not orchestrated by Castro, but still the president wondered "whether the situation did not have the appearance of beginning to get out of hand." On 29 November 1960, Eisenhower gathered his national security advisors to review the Cuban problem. Noting that he did not want to leave President-elect Kennedy "in the midst of a developing emergency," he asked: "Are we being sufficiently imaginative and bold, subject to not letting our hand appear?" Allen Dulles responded that the CIA now had 500 Cubans training at a secret military base in Guatemala; a problem, however, was that rumors about the camp were circulating in international fora. But Eisenhower was unconcerned, remarking that "even if the operation were known the main thing was not to let the U.S. hand show." Undersecretary of State Dillon also assured Eisenhower that the State Department was being more aggressive; the department planned to meet, in February or March, with Latin American foreign ministers and would again try to persuade them to break relations and to embargo trade with Cuba. Dillon hoped that Latin Americans would now side with the United States, in view of "our recently adopted economic program." Eisenhower urged his aides to coordinate their efforts and added that "we should be prepared to take more chances and be more aggressive."[63]

The CIA took Eisenhower's tough attitude toward Cuba as a signal that it should expedite its new plan for overthrowing Castro. After extended discussions within the CIA task force on Cuba, it was decided on 4 November 1960 to increase the size and redirect the training of the exile force. The agency now envisioned an amphibious assault on the Cuban coast by 600–750 men equipped with weapons of extraordinarily heavy fire power. The assault would be preceded by preliminary air strikes launched from Nicaragua against military targets. Once the exiles had seized a beachhead and established a visible presence in Cuba, it was expected that dissidents would rally to the landing force and presumably trigger a general uprising against Castro. CIA representatives presented this plan to the 5412 Committee on 8 December and were encouraged to continue its development.[64]

The new CIA plan formed, of course, the core of the Bay of Pigs operation, which was launched on 17 April 1961 by the Kennedy administration. Eisenhower and his supporters subsequently disclaimed responsibility for the fiasco, pointing out that they had drawn plans but had not engaged in concrete decision making. But, in fact, the Eisenhower administration had put the United States on a nearly irreversible course to sponsor an exile invasion of Cuba. On 27 November the president-elect was briefed by Dulles on the covert program; two days later, Eisenhower informed aides that he hoped Kennedy would follow the administration's "general line" on Cuba. When Kennedy came to the White House on 6 December to discuss foreign policy issues, he was given an administration position paper that labeled Cuba "the greatest danger to U.S. objectives in Latin America."[65] On 3 January 1961 Eisenhower told his national security advisors that, "when we turn over responsibility on the 20th, our successors should continue to improve and intensify the training and undertake planning when the Cubans themselves are properly organized." And on 19 January, in the final meeting before the inauguration, Eisenhower made it clear to Kennedy that the anti-Cuban project was going well and that it was the new administration's "responsibility" to do "whatever is necessary" to bring it to a successful conclusion. Reviewing the meeting for Kennedy, presidential assistant Clark Clifford observed that he had detected no "reluctance or hesitation" on the part of Eisenhower and that Eisenhower had said that it was U.S. policy to help the exiles "to the utmost" and this effort should be "continued and accelerated."[66] Thus, if Kennedy had canceled the invasion, he would have been rejecting the plans of the nation's most respected military leader, General Eisenhower. He would also have had, as Dulles and Bissell later admitted, a "disposal" problem: it would have been, in the CIA's view, politically embarrassing for the disbanded exile force to be "wandering around the country telling everyone what they have been doing"; the United States would have been perceived as having lost its nerve.[67]

President Eisenhower not only wanted Kennedy to back an invasion of Cuba, but also would probably have authorized one himself if he had stayed in office a few months more. In early January 1961 Eisenhower summarized U.S. policy, noting to aides that there were "only two reasonable courses of action: (1) supporting Cubans to go in March or (2) to abandon the operation." The United States had to act quickly, because Castro was tightening his hold on the island. The revolutionary army of 32,000 men and the 200,000-strong militia were improving their military capabilities, and intelligence analysts calculated that Cuba had received 10,000–12,000 tons of military equipment, including six helicopters, from the Soviet Union. Cuban pilots were also training in Czechoslovakia. Moreover, the United States had to move, because it could not indefinitely keep the exile force in Guatemala—the Cubans would be demoralized if not permitted to invade Cuba soon, and in any case, Guatemalan officials insisted that they leave by 1 March 1961. The problem persisted, however, that no politically viable leader had emerged within the exile community. In the president's view, the United States might simply have to recognize the first men ashore as the governing officials of Cuba.[68]

Although President Eisenhower did not have time to order an invasion of Cuba, he did intensify the pressure against Castro during his last days in office. On 3 January 1961 he broke diplomatic relations with Cuba, and on 5 January he accepted Secretary Herter's recommendation to urge the incoming administration to invoke the Trading with the Enemy Act and suspend trade with Cuba. These sanctions were in response to Castro's new demand that the United States sharply reduce the number of its diplomatic representatives in Cuba. But the administration also hoped to provoke Castro into a political and military blunder. Eisenhower believed that the public would support direct military intervention by U.S. forces only if there were a clear and serious provocation by Cuba. Such a provocation might come over Guantánamo. Indeed, Secretary Herter suggested that "we should stage an 'attack' on Guantánamo." The president did not comment directly on Herter's ploy, but he said that, as to breaking relations, "the quicker we do it the more tempted Castro might be to actually attack Guantánamo." Then, the Cubans "would be kicked out with force."[69]

It is, of course, conceivable that, if President Eisenhower had stayed in office through the first half of 1961, he would have chosen his second option and cancelled the invasion of Cuba, even though he wanted Fidel Castro overthrown. Drawing on his military experience, the president was fond of saying: "Rely on planning, but never trust plans." Eisenhower operated by the axiom that making decisions involved choices, the details of which could not be fully anticipated. During World War II, for example, he had waited until the last minute to signal the invasion of Normandy because he could not predict the weather, although he had planned for meteorological intelligence.[70] It is likely that the former general would have asked probing questions about operational plans for an invasion of Cuba. He would have found out that some State Department officers and military leaders doubted that Castro could be overthrown by a small invading force and believed that the United States would have to give overt, direct military assistance to the exiles.[71] Such actions, Eisenhower might have decided, would have been internationally unacceptable and entailed "the risk of our breaking up the OAS and putting it in Communist hands."[72] And it is possible also that Eisenhower would have concluded that Fidel Castro was not Jacobo Arbenz: the Cuban was decisive and vigorous, and he had a military force that was faithful to him and to the Cuban Revolution.[73]

Yet, in speculating on Eisenhower's probable course of action toward Cuba, it is important to recall his past policies. He sponsored an invasion of Guatemala by a small, lightly equipped band of exiles, and when the forces of Castillo Armas floundered he authorized the use of U.S. planes for bombing runs over Guatemala City. And he bullied international and domestic opponents of his policy. In the president's words, "When you commit the flag you commit it to win." In order to "win," Eisenhower possibly would have provided U.S. air and naval support from the beginning of the Cuban invasion; he certainly would have tried to fortify the embattled Cuban exiles once they encountered a determined response from Castro's men.[74] Moreover, it is instructive to analyze Eisenhower's reaction to the Bay of Pigs. Calling on President Kennedy after the debacle, he counseled against direct military intervention but suggested that the president "do his very best to solidify the OAS against communism, including a readiness to support, at least morally and politically, any necessary action to expel Communist penetration." Privately, however, Eisenhower was less understanding of Kennedy's predicament. Talking with William Pawley, he belittled Kennedy's decision to cancel air support for the Cuban invaders, calling it "a very dreary account of mismanagement, indecision and timidity at the wrong time." The Bay of Pigs, Eisenhower acidly remarked, could be titled a "Profile in Timidity and Indecision."[75]

When President Eisenhower retired from office in January 1961, he left his successor with a new approach toward Latin America. The United States could no longer afford to "neglect" the region, for the cold war had come to Latin America. The Eisenhower administration had instituted new political, military, economic, and cultural policies designed to build Communist-proof societies in Latin America. And in addition to handing over guidelines for the as-yet-unnamed Alliance for Progress, the Eisenhower administration gave the Kennedy government well-developed programs to overthrow governments in the Dominican Republic and Cuba. Because John Kennedy and his advisors shared the Eisenhower administration's intense fear of communism in the hemisphere, they carried on their predecessors' campaigns against Rafael Trujillo and Fidel Castro.

CONCLUSION

A close analysis of U.S. policy toward Latin America during the 1950s sustains many of the new interpretations of the leadership abilities of President Dwight D. Eisenhower. The president was decisive, energetic, and well informed, and he directed the Latin American policy of the United States. Determined, politically influential officials, such as Secretary of State John Foster Dulles and Secretary of the Treasury George Humphrey, deferred to Eisenhower's judgment. On virtually every contentious issue, whether recognition policy, military aid, or development assistance, President Eisenhower's decision became U.S. policy.

The Eisenhower administration also had a coherent, consistent strategy for Latin America: it wanted Latin Americans to support the United States in the cold war, adopt free trade and investment principles, and oppose communism. These goals were outlined in the administration's first position paper on Latin America, NSC 144/1 (1953), and were always listed as the primary objectives of U.S. policy in subsequent statements on the region. Throughout the 1950s, the administration tenaciously pursued its strategy, as revealed in its stance on such disparate issues as the Soviet economic offensive, state oil development, and the trade-union movement in Latin America. To be sure, it had to alter its tactics. In the late 1950s, it gradually concluded that military dictators could no longer be counted on to keep their countries secure, stable, and responsive to U.S. will, and it therefore began to spurn tyrants and to encourage and assist democratic reformers. But although the Eisenhower administration made new friends and reluctantly decided to spend money in the region, it never wavered from its goal of exercising and preserving U.S. leadership in the Western Hemisphere.

President Eisenhower oversaw a well-conceived hemispheric policy. But it does not follow, as "Eisenhower revisionists" would have it, that his stewardship served as an enduring model of presidential restraint. The debate over Eisenhower and his foreign policies has had inherent limitations: it has focused on the means of presidential leadership, not the ends; it has concentrated on strategy, not results. At least as defined by Latin Americans, restraint by the United States would have meant adherence to the nonintervention pledge that formed the basis of the OAS charter. Eisenhower repudiated that principle, however, when he directed a covert intervention to overthrow a popularly elected government in Guatemala. The president acted because he and his advisors suspected that the Arbenz government threatened the national security of the United States—but critics both within the State Department and throughout Latin America accused the administration of perpetrating a "Czechoslovakia in reverse" in Guatemala. In less dramatic fashion, the United States intervened in Latin America by having CIA agents infiltrate and manipulate labor unions, student organizations, and political parties. The administration also took steps in 1960 and in January 1961 to overthrow and perhaps assassinate Fidel Castro and Rafael Trujillo. We cannot be sure whether President Eisenhower was directly involved in these violent activities, but it is ironic that those who most vehemently deny presidential complicity have been those who have also argued that Eisenhower was an active, informed leader. In any case, the assaults on Castro and Trujillo represented, in Eisenhower's words, a policy "approximating gangsterism."

By its own measure, the Eisenhower administration's policy in Latin America was unsuccessful. United States officials defended their cold-war and foreign economic policies by predicting that they would enhance freedom, the respect for human rights, and economic opportunity in Latin America. And in fact, by the end of the 1950s democrats had replaced military dictators throughout the hemisphere—but, other than in Bolivia, the administration could hardly take credit for this democratic trend. Indeed, during much of the decade, U.S. officials were busy hugging and bestowing medals on sordid, often ruthless, tyrants. President Eisenhower publicly recommended democracy for Latin America only after most of the dictators had fallen from power; his destruction of the Arbenz government initiated a ghastly cycle of political repression and violence in Guatemala; and his administration strengthened the Latin American military, an institution responsible for numerous extraconstitutional changes of government in the region.

Nor could the administration legitimately claim that its policies had fostered economic growth and development in the hemisphere. During the 1950s Latin American economies stagnated, with the prices of primary exports, such as coffee, constantly falling. Little progress was made toward economic diversification and industrial development. The Eisenhower administration defended itself by pointing out that the nations that encouraged U.S. trade and investment, such as Cuba and Venezuela, enjoyed the highest per capita incomes in Latin America—but these countries had unbalanced, one-crop economies and grossly inequitable distributions of income and wealth, economic conditions that helped generate political turmoil in both countries in 1958. The administration also failed in Guatemala: the restoration of United Fruit Company's holdings did not create a prosperous or a socially just society. On the other hand, Brazil and Mexico, countries that practiced economic nationalism and rejected U.S. calls for economic austerity, produced impressive, albeit uneven, economic growth during the decade.

Perhaps a more meaningful way to assess the Latin American policy of the Eisenhower administration is to place it within the context of twentieth-century inter-American relations. This analytic approach predictably reveals both continuity and change in the administration's hemispheric policies. The United States emerged from World War II as the world's dominant power with global ambitions and responsibilities. The Truman government believed that regional concerns would have to be subordinated to the more significant task of rebuilding Western Europe and Japan and containing the Soviet Union. The Eisenhower administration accepted its predecessor's contention that winning the cold war took precedence over being a good neighbor: a Marshall Plan for Latin America was unfeasible because the United States needed to rush money to Asia and Europe, the first lines of defense against international communism.

The tactics employed by the Eisenhower administration in Latin America differed in degree, however, from those used by the Truman government. The Truman administration debated about injecting its fear of global Communist expansion into regional affairs; officials were reluctant to push anti-Communist pacts in Latin America, because they understood that reactionary Latin American elites would try to curry favor with the United States by branding all social change as "communism." The Truman administration also declined to intervene militarily in Guatemala. Instead, it resorted to political and economic pressure in an attempt to force the Guatemalan government to expel radicals and honor U.S. investments—the same methods, in effect, that the Roosevelt administration had used against Argentina, Bolivia, and Chile during World War II. Admittedly, by the time of the Korean War officials were beginning to be less concerned about the impact that cold-war policies might have on Latin America. In an important speech in 1950, Assistant Secretary of State Edward Miller implied that the United States might violate the OAS charter and intervene unilaterally to prevent communism in Latin America. Moreover, the Truman administration decided to swallow its misgivings about the effects of military aid and to arm Latin America against communism.

President Eisenhower and his closest advisors did not worry about confusing regional and global issues. During the 1950s, they interpreted inter-American affairs almost solely within the context of the Soviet-American confrontation. Administration officials willingly embraced military dictators who professed to be anti-Communist. In the administration's view, intervention against the Arbenz government was justified because the survival of the "Free World" was at stake; because the intervention was covert, it was hoped that it would be less offensive to Latin Americans than the overt military invasions during the first three decades of the twentieth century. U.S. officials also denied that economic nationalism was a byproduct of the Spanish-American heritage or a response to Latin America's woeful economic state. Economic nationalism weakened respect for private property and individual initiative; it was, therefore, to be condemned, because it injured U.S. businessmen and smacked of communism.

The Eisenhower administration's virulent anticommunism did not prevent it from being innovative in inter-American affairs. In the aftermath of the Nixon tour of South America, political upheavals throughout the hemisphere, and the onset of the Cuban Revolution, administration officials developed a new definition and defense of intervention: the United States had a responsibility to uplift, reform, and "modernize" Latin American societies. It should not hesitate to use institutions and programs like the Inter-American Development Bank, the Social Progress Trust Fund, student exchanges, and civic-action campaigns to force Latin Americans to dismantle their oligarchic social structures. By intervening in Latin America with economic, military, and cultural aid programs, the United States could build nations that were democratic, progressive, and anti-Communist. The view that U.S.-directed reform could serve as an alternative to revolution and communism formed the core of programs such as the Alliance for Progress of the 1960s and the Caribbean Basin Initiative of the 1980s.

Another legacy of the Eisenhower administration was an expanded list of what actions might be "deemed appropriate" to protect U.S. national security and win the cold war in Latin America. Eisenhower's immediate successors could reasonably argue that their actions were in the tradition of Eisenhower's interventions in Guatemala, Cuba, and the Dominican Republic. John Kennedy carried out the invasion of Cuba and continued, through "Operation Mongoose," the campaign to wreck the Cuban economy and eliminate Fidel Castro. Lyndon Johnson, in a manner reminiscent of the plotting against Arbenz, encouraged Brazilian generals to overthrow the leftist government of João Goulart in 1964, and in 1965 he ordered 20,000 marines to invade the Dominican Republic to prevent an alleged Communist conspiracy to seize control of the country. This "Johnson Doctrine" for Latin America was a manifestation of the policy that the Eisenhower administration had secretly adopted. Richard Nixon, perhaps recalling his days as vice-president and Eisenhower's attacks on communism in Latin America, directed, between 1970 and 1973, a campaign to destabilize the government of socialist Salvador Allende of Chile.[1] The Kennedy, Johnson, and Nixon governments also continued programs begun by the Eisenhower administration to use the CIA and U.S. military to train Latin American police and military for urban and rural warfare against suspected Communists. Graduates of these U.S. training programs were later accused of committing murder and torture in Latin America during the late 1960s and throughout the 1970s.[2]

The administration of Dwight D. Eisenhower was particularly zealous in the fight against communism. But, in pursuing this conflict, the administration was also upholding customary U.S. policies. Throughout the twentieth century, the United States has practiced sphere-of-influence politics in the Western Hemisphere: it has tried to maintain peace and order, exclude foreign influences, expand U.S. trade and investment, and shape Latin America's development. The anti-Communist crusade of the Eisenhower administration was rooted in this tradition.

NOTES

ABBREVIATIONS

CFEP	Council on Foreign Economic Policy Records, Eisenhower Library
Church Committee	U.S. Senate Select Committee to Study Governmental Operations with Respect to Intelligence Activities
DDE	Dwight David Eisenhower
Draper Committee	U.S. President's Committee to Study the U.S. Military Assistance Program Records, Eisenhower Library
DSB	*Department of State Bulletin*
DSR	Department of State Records, National Archives
ECLA	U.N. Economic Commission For Latin America
Fairless Committee	U.S. President's Citizen Advisers on the Mutual Security Program Records, Eisenhower Library
FRUS	*Papers Relating to the Foreign Relations of the United States, 1861–1954*
HCFA	U.S. Congress House Committee on Foreign Affairs
NSC	National Security Council
OCB	Operations Coordinating Board
OSANSA	White House Office of the the Special Assistant for National Security Affairs Records, Eisenhower Library
OSS	White House Office of the Staff Secretary Records, Eisenhower Library
SCFR	U.S. Senate Committee on Foreign Relations
Sprague Committee	U.S. President's Committee on International Information Activities Records, Eisenhower Library
WHOF	White House Official File, Eisenhower Library
Whitman	Ann Whitman File, Dwight D. Eisenhower Papers, Eisenhower Library

INTRODUCTION

1 For traditional interpretations of Eisenhower and Dulles, see Childs, *Eisenhower: Captive Hero*; Hoopes, *Devil and John Foster Dulles*; Hughes, *Ordeal of Power*; Shannon, "Eisenhower as President," 390–98. For a review of the historiographic

literature on Eisenhower, see Bernstein, "Foreign Policy in the Eisenhower Administration," 17–20, 29–30, 38; DeSantis, "Eisenhower Revisionism," 190–207; Joes, "Eisenhower Revisionism," 561–71; McAuliffe, "Commentary / Eisenhower, the President," 625–32; Reichard, "Eisenhower as President," 265–81; Schlesinger, "The Ike Age Revisited," 1–11.

2 For the new Eisenhower scholarship, see Ambrose, *Eisenhower: The President*; Divine, *Blowing on the Wind*; Greenstein, *Hidden-Hand Presidency*; Neal, "Why We Were Right to Like Ike," 49–65; Parmet, *Eisenhower and the American Crusades*.

3 Eisenhower quoted in Ambrose, *Eisenhower: The President*, 626.

4 Divine, *Eisenhower and the Cold War*, 152–55; Murray and Blessing, "Presidential Performance Study," 535–55; Ambrose, *Eisenhower: The President*, 627.

5 Eisenhower quoted in Soapes, "A Cold Warrior Seeks Peace," 58.

6 For a review of the state of the literature, see McMahon, "Eisenhower and Third World Nationalism," 453–73.

7 Robert Divine, one of the leading proponents of the new scholarship on Eisenhower, notes that interpretations have been based on secondary-source materials and that there is a need for archival research on Eisenhower's foreign policies (*Eisenhower and the Cold War*, ix).

8 For information on the holdings of the Eisenhower Library, see McAuliffe, "Commentary / Eisenhower, the President," 626; Rabe, "The Johnson (Eisenhower?) Doctrine," 95–100; Immerman, "Diplomatic Dialings," 1–15.

9 Eisenhower, *Mandate for Change*, 503; Eisenhower, *Waging Peace*, 515–39.

10 Milton Eisenhower, *The Wine Is Bitter*, 161–63, 248–51.

11 Betancourt, *Venezuela: Oil and Politics*, 359–67; Figueres, "Problems of Democracy in Latin America," 11–21; Santos, "Latin American Realities," 245–57.

12 Nixon, *Six Crises*, 183–230.

13 Ibid., 355–56; Beck, "Necessary Lies, Hidden Truths," 37–59; Berle, "The Cuban Crisis," 40–55.

14 Hilsman, *To Move a Nation*, 30–33; Schlesinger, *A Thousand Days*, 164, 170–75, 186–201, 226–43; Sorensen, *Kennedy*, 294–309, 533–40.

15 Baily, *United States and the Development of South America*, 79; Connell-Smith, *United States and Latin America*, 187–225; Gil, *Latin American–United States Relations*, 189–221; Hilton, "United States, Brazil, and the Cold War," 599–624; Parkinson, *Latin America, the Cold War, and the World Powers*, 52; Wagner, *United States Policy toward Latin America*, 19. One new study that analyzes inter-American relations for the period 1942–54 is Wood, *Dismantling of the Good Neighbor Policy*; Wood's purpose is to examine how the Good Neighbor policies of the 1930s fared during the war and in the immediate postwar period.

16 Eisenhower, *Mandate for Change*, 507–11, 679.

17 Immerman, *CIA in Guatemala*; Schlesinger and Kinzer, *Bitter Fruit*.

18 Cook, *Dwight David Eisenhower*; Cook, *Declassified Eisenhower*, vi–xxi. See also Wood, *Dismantling of the Good Neighbor Policy*, 189–90.

19 This point is made in two perceptive studies of Eisenhower's foreign economic policy: see Griffith, "Dwight D. Eisenhower and the Corporate Commonwealth," 87–122; Kaufman, *Trade and Aid*, 6–11. Both authors argue that Eisenhower was innovative and informed in his efforts to reform the international capitalist system and to bring the benefits of that system to poor nations, but Eisenhower's ex-

treme anticommunism distorted those efforts. For two earlier studies that try to present a balanced view of Eisenhower, see Charles C. Alexander, *Holding the Line,* and Lyon, *Eisenhower: Portrait of a Hero.*

CHAPTER 1

1 Eisenhower's speech in 9/26–10/13/52 (3) folder, box 2, Speech series, Whitman. See also Eisenhower to H. Ramiriez, Executive Secretary of Chamber of Commerce of Latin America in the United States, 24 October 1952, file 116-J, box 584, WHOF.

2 Sessions, "The Clark Memorandum Myth," 40–58; Curry, *Hoover's Dominican Diplomacy,* 8–9.

3 Connell-Smith, *United States and Latin America,* 158; Smith, "Good Neighbor Policy," 67.

4 Steward, *Trade and Hemisphere,* 270; Wood, *Making of the Good Neighbor,* 203–82.

5 Duggan, *The Americas,* 97–100; Guerrant, *Roosevelt's Good Neighbor Policy,* 195–206.

6 Gil, *Latin American–United States Relations,* 155–56; Gellman, *Good Neighbor Diplomacy,* 227; Guerrant, *Roosevelt's Good Neighbor Policy,* 212; Wood, *Making of the Good Neighbor,* 167.

7 J. Richard Snyder, "William S. Culbertson in Chile," 21. For the thesis that the Good Neighbor policy began in the Hoover administration, see DeConde, *Herbert Hoover's Latin American Policy,* 123–27. Kenneth J. Grieb argues that President Harding established the basis for improved inter-American relations (*Latin American Policy of Warren G. Harding,* 191).

8 Benjamin, *United States and Cuba,* 171–82; Pulley, "United States and the Trujillo Dictatorship," 30–31; Schmidt, *United States Occupation of Haiti,* 165; Blasier, "United States, Germany, and the Bolivian Revolutionaries," 26–54; Francis, *Limits of Hegemony,* 112; Woods, *Roosevelt Foreign-Policy Establishment,* 131–66.

9 Haines, "Under the Eagle's Wing," 373–88 (quotation on p. 387); Ninkovich, *Diplomacy of Ideas,* 36–49; Hilton, "Brazilian Diplomacy and the Washington–Rio de Janeiro 'Axis,' " 201; McCann, "Brazil, the United States, and World War II," 59–76; Smith, "Good Neighbor Policy," 86–87.

10 Steward, *Trade and Hemisphere,* 279–85; Green, *Containment of Latin America,* 37–58; Koppes, "Good Neighbor Policy and the Nationalization of Mexican Oil," 62–81; Rabe, *Road to OPEC,* 87–93.

11 Schmidt, *United States Occupation of Haiti,* 231. See also Gellman, *Roosevelt and Batista,* 233–36; Millett, *Guardians of the Dynasty,* 194–96; Pulley, "United States and the Trujillo Dictatorship," 27.

12 Langley, *Banana Wars,* 221–23.

13 Aranha quoted in McCann, *Brazilian-American Alliance,* 62. See also Benjamin, *United States and Cuba,* 185; Gellman, *Roosevelt and Batista,* 4–5; Haines, "Under the Eagle's Wing," 374; Francis, *Limits of Hegemony,* 241–43; Ninkovich, *Diplomacy of Ideas,* 24–30; Pike, *United States and the Andean Republics,* 241–42; Smith, "Good Neighbor Policy," 65.

14 Pike, *United States and the Andean Republics,* 240; Rabe, *Road to OPEC,* 46, 99;

Bushnell, *Eduardo Santos and the Good Neighbor*, 7, 120; Schmitt, *Mexico and the United States*, 189–91; Schlesinger and Kinzer, *Bitter Fruit*, 26; Leonard, *United States and Central America*, 9, 12–13.

15 Gellman, *Good Neighbor Diplomacy*, 2, 179–80, 209–10.

16 Diary entries, 29 April 1945, 2 May 1945, and 10 May 1945, Stimson diaries.

17 Tillapaugh, "Closed Hemisphere and Open World?" 25–42; Trask, "Impact of the Cold War," 271–84.

18 Braden, *Diplomats and Demagogues*, 316–38, 356–70; Trask, "Spruille Braden versus George Messersmith," 69–95.

19 Braden, "Our Foreign Policy and Its Underlying Principles and Ideals," *DSB* 14 (24 February 1946): 294–97; Atkins and Wilson, *United States and the Trujillo Regime*, 15–19; Rabe, *Road to OPEC*, 100–101.

20 Green, *Containment of Latin America*, 276–83.

21 *FRUS, 1948*, 9:141–52; *DSB* 20 (2 January 1949): 30.

22 Trask, "Spruille Braden versus George Messersmith," 90; Rabe, *Road to OPEC*, 114–15; Rafael Trujillo's meetings with Presidents Truman and Eisenhower, 13 January 1953 and 6 March 1953, *FRUS, 1952–54*, 4:935–37.

23 *FRUS, 1948*, 9:193–206.

24 Blasier, *Giant's Rival*, 16–18, 33.

25 Green, "Cold War Comes to Latin America," 154–59.

26 Rabe, "Elusive Conference," 279–88; Hilton, "United States, Brazil, and the Cold War," 601–3.

27 Duggan, *The Americas*, 123–26; Francis, *Limits of Hegemony*, 37–38. See also Oral History of José Figueres, p. 2. Figueres estimated that Costa Rica, by selling its coffee at the controlled price of 18 cents a pound, contributed at least one-half the value of four coffee crops to the war effort.

28 Rabe, "Elusive Conference," 285–88.

29 On U.S. policy toward state oil companies, see Secretary of State Byrnes to Ambassador to Mexico George Messersmith, 8 November 1945, *FRUS, 1945*, 9:1161; Ambassador to Brazil Herschel Johnson to State Department, 4 January 1952, DSR 832.2553/1–452. On U.S. foreign economic policy, see Heston, "Cuba, the United States, and the Sugar Act," 5; *FRUS, 1952–54*, 4:485–90, 502–16; Rabe, *Road to OPEC*, 106–11.

30 Immerman, *CIA in Guatemala*, 7–13; Johnson quoted in Hilton, "United States, Brazil, and the Cold War," 604.

31 Acheson, "Waging Peace in the Americas," *DSB* 21 (26 September, 1949): 462–66; *FRUS, 1950*, 2:590. Bryce Wood believes that the key to Acheson's speech is that he reaffirmed the nonintervention pledge (*Dismantling of the Good Neighbor Policy*, 139).

32 *FRUS, 1950*, 2:594–96, 673–79; Report of Executive Secretary James Lay to NSC, Annex No. 2, "Estimates for Military and Economic Assistance Programs, 1951–1955," 8 December 1950, *FRUS, 1950*, 1:443; Annex to NSC 144, 6 March 1953, NSC 144 folder, box 4, OSANSA. For background on the Point Four program, see Erb, "Prelude to Point Four," 249–69.

33 Edward Miller to Paul Nitze, Director of Policy Planning Staff, 27 September 1950, *FRUS, 1950*, 2:686–87.

34 Ambassador Stanton Griffis to State Department on Secretary Miller's meeting with President Perón, 1 March 1950, *FRUS, 1950*, 2:696–701; "Policy Statement

on Argentina," 21 March 1950, DSR 611.35/3–2150; memorandum, Acheson meeting with President Truman, 24 April 1950, DSR 611.35/4–2450; Peterson, *Argentina and the United States*, 473–81; *FRUS, 1952–54*, 4:409–18, 423–27.

35 *FRUS, 1950*, 2:625–28; HCFA, *Executive Session Hearings, 1951–56*, 16:404.

36 "Y" (Halle), "On a Certain Impatience with Latin America," 565–79; *FRUS, 1950*, 2:624; Acheson, *Present at the Creation*, 257–58. See also George Kennan's appraisal of Latin America, *FRUS, 1950*, 2:598–623.

37 *DSB* 21 (26 September 1949): 462; *FRUS, 1950*, 2:592–93; HCFA, *Executive Session Hearings, 1951–56*, 16:392–95; Blasier, *Giant's Rival*, 17.

38 "Non-Intervention and Collective Responsibility in the Americas," *DSB* 22 (15 May 1950): 768–70. Under the OAS charter, collective security actions could be taken only with the approval of at least fourteen of the twenty-one American states. See also historian Walter LaFeber's analysis of Miller's speech (*Inevitable Revolutions*, 94–95).

39 Child, *Unequal Alliance*, 15–16; Leffler, "American Conception of National Security," 354–55; Rabe, "Inter-American Military Cooperation," 132–36.

40 Rabe, "Inter-American Military Cooperation," 137–47; Pach, "Containment of U.S. Military Aid," 225–43.

41 NSC 56/2 is in *FRUS, 1950*, 1:626–37; Department of State, Office of Public Affairs, *Military Assistance to Latin America*, 1–6. For NSC 68, "United States Objectives and Programs for National Security," see *FRUS, 1950*, 1:234–92; Wells, "Sounding the Tocsin," 116–58.

42 Draft paper, "Development of U.S. Latin American Policy in Terms of U.S. World Objectives, 1950–1955," 9 November 1950, *FRUS, 1950*, 2:634.

43 *FRUS, 1951*, 2:964–65, 969; Stebbins, *United States in World Affairs, 1951*, 303, 313.

44 Miller to Paul Nitze, Director of Policy Planning Staff, 26 September 1950, *FRUS, 1950*, 1:654–64; Brazilian Foreign Minister Fortuna quoted in Hilton, "United States, Brazil, and the Cold War," 609; for Brazilian loan, see *FRUS, 1952–54*, 4:607–9.

CHAPTER 2

1 NSC 144/1, 18 March 1953, *FRUS, 1952–54*, 4:6–10.

2 Oral History of Robert C. Hill, p. 75; Ambrose, *Eisenhower: Soldier, General of the Army, President-Elect*, 56–58; Eisenhower, *Waging Peace*, 514.

3 Ambrose, *Eisenhower: Soldier, General of the Army, President-Elect*, 75–79; diary entries, 22 January 1942 and 1 November 1946, Ferrell, *Eisenhower Diaries*, 44, 137.

4 Pach, "Containment of U.S. Military Aid," 235, 241–43.

5 Immerman, *CIA in Guatemala*, 124; Pruessen, *John Foster Dulles*, xiii.

6 Ambrose, *Eisenhower: The President*, 25; Divine, *Eisenhower and the Cold War*, 25; Greenstein, *Hidden-Hand Presidency*, 87–91, 124.

7 Nelson, "'Top of the Policy Hill,'" 307–26; Eisenhower, *Waging Peace*, 370.

8 Diary entry, 14 May 1953, Ferrell, *Eisenhower Diaries*, 238.

9 Milton Eisenhower to Dwight Eisenhower, 6 July 1954, Eisenhower, Milton–1954 (2) folder, box 12, Name series, Whitman.

10 SCFR, *Nomination of John Foster Dulles*, 10, 30–31.

11 Pickett, "The Eisenhower Solarium Notes," 1–10; Guhin, *John Foster Dulles*, 2–10, 304–6.

12 Diary entry, 6 January 1953, Ferrell, *Eisenhower Diaries*, 223.

13 Summary of discussion, special meeting of NSC, 31 March 1953, box 4, NSC series, Whitman.

14 Dulles to Allen Dulles, 25 February 1954, 1–2/54 (2) folder, box 2, Telephone Conversations series, John Foster Dulles papers; Cabinet meeting, 26 February 1954, C-12 folder, box 2, Cabinet series (Minnich notes), OSS; testimony of Dulles, 7 January 1954, in SCFR, *Executive Sessions, 1954*, 6:15.

15 Cabot to Dulles, 28 March 1953, DSR 611.20/3–2853.

16 Eisenhower quoted in *DSB* 28 (2 February 1953): 169; Dulles quoted in *DSB* 28 (9 February 1953): 214–15.

17 132nd meeting of NSC, 18 February 1953, box 4, NSC series, Whitman.

18 *FRUS, 1952–54*, 4:1–10.

19 Annex to NSC 144, 6 March 1953, NSC 144 folder, box 4, OSANSA. The Latin American reformers cited are: Lázaro Cárdenas, president of Mexico (1934–40); Juan José Arévalo, president of Guatemala (1945–50); José Figueres, president of Costa Rica (1953–58); Jorge Elíecer Gaitán, leader of the Liberal party in Colombia who was assassinated in 1948; Rómulo Betancourt, leader of the Acción Democrática party of Venezuela; Víctor Raul Haya de la Torre, leader of the "Aprista" movement in Peru; Carlos Ibáñez del Campo, president of Chile (1952–58); Juan Perón, president of Argentina (1946–55); Getulio Vargas, president of Brazil (1950–54); and Ramón Grau San Martín, president of Cuba (1944–48).

20 Annex to NSC 144, 6 March 1953, NSC 144 folder, box 4, OSANSA. It cannot be definitively determined if the conclusions on unilateral intervention are incorporated in NSC 144/1: portions of the relevant paragraph—5-d—are exempted from declassification; see *FRUS, 1952–54*, 4:7. See also Rabe, "The Johnson (Eisenhower?) Doctrine," 97.

21 First progress report on NSC 144/1, 23 July 1953, *FRUS, 1952–54*, 4:12–14; Eisenhower to Dulles, 7 August 1953, 8/53 folder, box 1, Dulles-Herter series, Whitman; Dulles to Eisenhower, 3 September 1953, 1953 (2) folder, box 1, White House Correspondence series, Dulles papers; Cabot to Dulles, 28 March 1953, DSR 611.20/3–2853.

22 Dulles to Eisenhower, 26 February 1953, 1–4/53 folder, box 10, Telephone series, Dulles papers.

23 Progress Report on NSC 5432/1, 19 January 1955, *FRUS, 1952–54*, 4:106–7; State Department officer R. Richard Rubottom to Cabot, 19 March 1953, DSR 611.20/3–1953.

24 Dulles to U.S. Embassies in Latin America, 18 August 1953, DSR 720.001/8–1853; Dulles to U.S. Embassies in Latin America, 19 April 1954, DSR 720.001/4–1954; U.S. Ambassador Francis White, Mexico City, to Dulles, 21 April 1954, DSR 720.001/4–2154.

25 Meany quoted in Cabot's memorandum of conversation with Meany and Romualdi, 12 March 1953, DSR 820.06/3–1253. See also Cabot's memorandum of conversation with Paul Reed of the United Mine Workers, 16 March 1953, DSR 820.06/3–1653; Undersecretary Smith to U.S. Embassy, Santiago, Chile, 23 April 1953, DSR 820.00-TA/4–2353; Dulles to U.S. Embassies in Latin America, 29 June 1953, DSR 820.062/6–2953.

26 Cabot's recommendation to Dulles cited in memorandum of J. T. Fishburn, State Department labor advisor, to Cabot, 23 March 1953, DSR 820.06/3–2353. The 16 March memorandum of Cabot to Dulles, which Fishburn cited, was not found in the appropriate decimal file. It cannot be determined whether Secretary Dulles accepted the recommendation to fund the U.S. trade-union movement, but in the late 1960s allegations arose that, beginning in 1959, the CIA had transferred funds to noncommunist labor movements in Latin America; see *New York Times*, 19 February 1967, 1, 32, and 22 February 1967, 1, 17. See also Morris, *CIA and American Labor*, 78–79, 150–56.

27 Child, *Unequal Alliance*, 115–21; Francis, "Military Aid to Latin America," 391–96.

28 141st meeting of NSC, 28 April 1953, *FRUS, 1952–54*, 4:146–47; entry, 20 July 1954, Eisenhower conversation with Senator Malone, 7/54 (2) folder, box 2, Ann Whitman Diary, Whitman.

29 Eisenhower quoted in *FRUS, 1952–54*, 4:42; Smith quoted in ibid., 79; SCFR, *Hearings on the Mutual Security Act, 1954*, 357.

30 *FRUS, 1952–54*, 4:9; Child, *Unequal Alliance*, 120; Pancake, "Military Assistance as an Element of U.S. Foreign Policy in Latin America," 85–86; Rabe, "Inter-American Military Cooperation," 142; Tomasek, "Defense of the Western Hemisphere," 355–59.

31 Collins quoted in memorandum of meeting between State Department and Joint Chiefs of Staff, 22 May 1954, *FRUS, 1952–54*, 4:150–53; Shaw to State Department, 4 September 1953, ibid., 1473–80; Warren to State Department, 11 May 1953, ibid., 1643–47; George O. Spencer, special assistant for inter-American military assistance, to Assistant Secretary Henry Holland, 4 November 1954, DSR 720.MSP/11–454.

32 Eisenhower to Dulles, 16 June 1953, 5–12/53 folder (3), box 10, Telephone series, Dulles papers.

33 Rock, *Argentina, 1516–1982*, 262–80; Scobie, *Argentina*, 232–38; Solberg, *Oil and Nationalism in Argentina*, 165.

34 Nufer to State Department, 5 February 1953, *FRUS, 1952–54*, 4:427–36, 439–40; Peterson, *Argentina and the United States*, 487–89.

35 Dulles to Eisenhower, 18 June 1953, *FRUS, 1952–54*, 4:440–41; Perón to Eisenhower, 20 July 1953, 7/53 folder, box 1, Dulles-Herter series, Whitman; Milton Eisenhower to Dwight Eisenhower, 11 January 1954, Eisenhower, Milton, S. Amer. Rpt. (1) folder, box 13, Name series, Whitman; Milton Eisenhower to Dwight Eisenhower, 6 July 1954, Argentina (7) folder, box 1, Dulles-Herter series, Whitman; Milton Eisenhower, *The Wine Is Bitter*, 64–66.

36 Eisenhower to Dulles, 6 November 1953, *FRUS, 1952–54*, 4:449–50; memorandum of conversation with Dulles by Durward V. Sandifer, attaché-designate to Argentina, 24 March 1954, ibid., 467–68; National Intelligence Estimate on Argentina, 9 March 1954, ibid., 464.

37 Peterson, *Argentina and the United States*, 489; *FRUS, 1952–54*, 4:469–84.

38 Milton Eisenhower's report, "United States–Latin American Relations: Report to the President," is in *DSB* 29 (23 November 1953): 695–717; Stebbins, *United States in World Affairs, 1953*, 344–45.

39 Dulles to Eisenhower, 19 November 1953, *FRUS, 1952–54*, 4:450–52; Cabot memorandum of conversation with members of the Inter-American Association

for Freedom and Democracy, 30 December 1953, DSR 611.20/12–3053; Bainbridge C. Davis, Office of South American Affairs, to Assistant Secretary Henry Holland on exile of Rómulo Betancourt, 14 July 1954, DSR 731.00/7–1454; Robert J. Alexander, *Rómulo Betancourt*, 361–62; *FRUS, 1952–54*, 4:1669–74.

40 Assistant Secretary Henry Holland to Dulles, 20 December 1954, *FRUS, 1952–54*, 4:1674–75; Rabe, *Road to OPEC*, 127.

41 Oral history of Dreier, p. 10.

42 Oral history of Figueres, pp. 32–35.

43 Cabot to NSC, 9 September 1953, DSR 631.20/9–953.

44 Vacs, *Discreet Partners*, 13–17; Blasier, *Giant's Rival*, 27; National Intelligence Estimate on Argentina, 9 March 1954, *FRUS, 1952–54*, 4:463–64.

45 Although the Truman administration adopted a de facto recognition policy, as late as 1952 it tried to show its displeasure about extraconstitutional changes of government and violations of human rights. See, for example, Assistant Secretary Miller to Ambassador in Cuba Willard Beaulac on meeting Fulgencio Batista, 10 June 1952, *FRUS, 1952–54*, 4:875–76; and Miller to Department of Defense on military aid to the Dominican Republic, 14 March 1952, ibid., 932–33.

CHAPTER 3

1 Grieb, *Guatemalan Caudillo*, 15–25, 32–50; Immerman, *CIA in Guatemala*, 31–37.

2 Immerman, *CIA in Guatemala*, 37–43; Schlesinger and Kinzer, *Bitter Fruit*, 25–35.

3 Immerman, *CIA in Guatemala*, 44–57.

4 Schlesinger and Kinzer, *Bitter Fruit*, 37–47.

5 Ibid., 49–52.

6 Adams, *Crucifixion by Power*, 184–94; Immerman, *CIA in Guatemala*, 61–67.

7 Adams, *Crucifixion by Power*, 394–401; Immerman, *CIA in Guatemala*, 65–67; Schlesinger and Kinzer, *Bitter Fruit*, 53–56.

8 Schlesinger and Kinzer, *Bitter Fruit*, 65–77; Immerman, *CIA in Guatemala*, 68–79. For a defense of United Fruit's activities in Central America, see May and Plaza, *United Fruit Company in Latin America*, 162–69, 183–218.

9 Immerman, *CIA in Guatemala*, 79–82; Schlesinger and Kinzer, *Bitter Fruit*, 75–77.

10 *FRUS, 1952–54*, 4:1056–57.

11 National Intelligence Estimate, "Probable Developments in Guatemala," 11 March 1952, *FRUS, 1952–54*, 4:1031–37; National Intelligence Estimate, "Probable Developments in Guatemala," 19 May 1953, ibid., 1061–71; Schneider, *Communism in Guatemala*, 185–217.

12 Immerman, *CIA in Guatemala*, 82–100; Schlesinger and Kinzer, *Bitter Fruit*, 56–63.

13 Memorandum of conversation between Eisenhower and Toriello, 16 January 1954, *FRUS, 1952–54*, 4:1095–97; diary entry, 26 April 1954, Ferrell, *Diary of James C. Hagerty*, 48; Peurifoy to State Department, 17 December 1953, *FRUS, 1952–54*, 4:1091–93.

14 Undersecretary of State Smith to Eisenhower, 15 January 1954, Guatemala (6) folder, box 24, International series, Whitman.

15 Draft for NSC prepared by Bureau of Inter-American Affairs, 19 August 1953, *FRUS, 1952–54*, 4:1074–86. See also Schneider, *Communism in Guatemala*, 197.

16 HCFA, *Executive Session Hearings, 1951–56*, 16:398.

17 *FRUS, 1952–54*, 4:1027–56; Schoenfeld quoted in memorandum of State Department conversation, "Export Control Policy toward Guatemala," 14 October 1952, ibid., 1046–48.

18 Immerman, *CIA in Guatemala*, 118–22; Schlesinger and Kinzer, *Bitter Fruit*, 102.

19 Deputy Assistant Secretary of State Thomas Mann to Acheson, 3 October 1952, *FRUS, 1952–54*, 4:1041–43; Smith to Bruce, 12 December 1952, ibid., 1055–56; Wood, *Dismantling of the Good Neighbor Policy*, 159.

20 Peurifoy to State Department, 23 December 1953, *FRUS, 1952–54*, 4:1093–95; Staff Study of Bureau of Inter-American Affairs, 19 August 1953, ibid., 1083.

21 *DSB* 30 (26 April 1950): 638–39; Dulles quoted in memorandum of conversation of 189th meeting of NSC, 18 March 1954, *FRUS, 1952–54*, 4:304–6.

22 Cabot to Acting Secretary of State, 10 February 1954, *FRUS, 1952–54*, 4:279–92.

23 Smith to certain diplomatic offices in the American republics, 18 February 1954, ibid., 299–300.

24 Oral history of Figueres, pp. 32–35; oral history of Rafael de la Colina, Mexican ambassador to U.N., p. 22; NSC 16, 22 March 1948, *FRUS, 1948*, 9:193–203.

25 Dulles to diplomatic offices in American republics, 15 January 1954, *FRUS, 1952–54*, 4:267–71; Cabot to Acting Secretary of State, 10 February, 1954, ibid., 279–92.

26 "Report of Actions Taken by the United States Information Agency in the Guatemalan Situation," 27 July 1954, ibid., 1212–17; *DSB* 30 (29 March 1954): 466; Eisenhower, *Mandate for Change*, 507–11.

27 Stebbins, *United States in World Affairs, 1954*, 370–77; Immerman, *CIA in Guatemala*, 143–51; Schlesinger and Kinzer, *Bitter Fruit*, 142–45.

28 Cabinet meetings, 26 February 1954 and 5 March 1954, C-12 folder, box 2, Cabinet series (Minnich notes), OSS; Cabinet meeting, 26 February 1954, box 3, Cabinet series, Whitman; Smith to Dulles, 9 March 1954, *FRUS, 1952–54*, 4:303; Dulles speech at Caracas in *DSB* 30 (15 March 1954): 379–83.

29 Dulles testimony in HCFA, *Selected Executive Session Hearings, 1951–56*, 16:502–15. Dulles was less critical of Mexico in his report to the NSC; see *FRUS, 1952–54*, 4:304–6.

30 Slater, *OAS and United States Foreign Policy*, 118–20.

31 Third Progress Report on NSC 144/1, 25 May 1954, *FRUS, 1952–54*, 4:47; Halle to Director of Policy Planning Staff, 28 May 1954, ibid., 1148. See also analysis of Caracas resolution by John Moors Cabot (Cabot oral history, p. 8).

32 Minutes of meeting held in office of Assistant Secretary of State for Inter-American Affairs Henry Holland, 10 May 1954, *FRUS, 1952–54*, 4:1102–5; notes on meeting of the Guatemalan Group, 16 June 1954, ibid., 1170–72.

33 Dulles and Eisenhower quoted in memorandum of discussion of 199th meeting of NSC, 27 May 1954, ibid., 1134. For Uruguay's position, see memorandum of conversation between Holland and Ambassador José A. Mora, 23 June 1954, ibid., 1170 n. 3.

34 Ibid., 1188.

35 Slater, *OAS and United States Foreign Policy*, 125–26.

36 Eisenhower, *Mandate for Change*, 507; Dulles to Allen Dulles, 7 April 1954, 3–4/54 (1) folder, box 2, Telephone series, Dulles papers; Third Progress Report on

NSC 144/1, 25 May 1954, *FRUS, 1952–54,* 4:45–47.

37 Good accounts can be found in Immerman, *CIA in Guatemala,* 161–86; Schlesinger and Kinzer, *Bitter Fruit,* 159–225; Wise and Ross, *Invisible Government,* 165–83; Wood, *Dismantling of the Good Neighbor Policy,* 152–90.

38 Ambrose, *Ike's Spies,* 7.

39 Pickett, "The Eisenhower Solarium Notes," 1–10; New Basic Concept, 30 July 1953, Project Solarium (10) folder, box 10, Subject series, OSANSA; Cook, *Declassified Eisenhower,* 181–83.

40 Roosevelt, *Countercoup: The Struggle for the Control of Iran.*

41 Immerman, *CIA in Guatemala,* 133–68; Schlesinger and Kinzer, *Bitter Fruit,* 99–117.

42 National Intelligence Estimate, "Probable Developments in Guatemala," 19 May 1953, *FRUS, 1952–54,* 4:1067.

43 Dulles to Secretary of Defense Charles Wilson, 9 April 1953, ibid., 144–46; memorandum of conversation, Department of State–Joint Chiefs of Staff meeting, 22 May 1953, ibid., 150–53; editorial note, ibid., 168–69.

44 Allen Dulles to Eisenhower, 20 June 1954, ibid., 1174–76 (emphasis is in memorandum); Schlesinger and Kinzer, *Bitter Fruit,* 16, 157–90.

45 Peurifoy to State Department, 7 July 1954, *FRUS, 1952–54,* 4:1202–8; Immerman, *CIA in Guatemala,* 161–77; Schlesinger and Kinzer, *Bitter Fruit,* 191–225.

46 Holland to Dulles, "Arms for Guatemala from Europe," 24 May 1954, *FRUS, 1952–54,* 4:1125–26; Peurifoy to State Department, 24 May 1953, ibid., 1127–28; Ambassador to Sweden John Moors Cabot to Robert Woodward, State Department, 10 May 1954, Part I: Latin America, microfilm reel #2, Cabot papers. In April 1954, Cabot had been transferred from the Latin American section of the State Department to Stockholm.

47 Memorandum of conversation between Ambassador João Carlos Muniz of Brazil and Dulles, 11 May 1954, *FRUS, 1952–54,* 4:1106; Ambassador to Honduras Whiting Willauer to State Department, 9 June 1954, ibid., 1164 n. 4; Armstrong quoted in Immerman, *CIA in Guatemala,* 185.

48 Milton Eisenhower to president, 6 July 1954, Eisenhower, Milton–1954 (2) folder, box 12, Name series, Whitman; Dulles to Senator Lyndon Baines Johnson, 28 June 1954, 6/54 (1) folder, box 2, Telephone series, Dulles papers, Mansfield quoted in SCFR, *Executive Sessions, 1954,* 6:344; Fulbright's views in SCFR, *Executive Sessions, 1959,* 11:528.

49 Halle to Robert Bowie, Director of Policy Planning Staff, 28 May 1954, *FRUS, 1952–54,* 4:1139–49; Leddy to Peurifoy, 5 June 1954, ibid., 1156–57.

50 An economic interpretation can be found in Schlesinger and Kinzer, *Bitter Fruit,* 106–7, 203. Castillo Armas quoted in Nixon's account to the NSC of his trip to Guatemala, minutes of 240th meeting of the NSC, 10 March 1955, box 6, NSC series, Whitman.

51 Dulles quoted in *DSB* 30 (21 June 1954): 950–51.

52 Dulles quoted at 202nd meeting of NSC, 17 June 1954, *FRUS, 1952–54,* 4:224–26; see also ibid., 191–96, 262–63. On 2 July 1954, the Department of Justice filed in New Orleans an antitrust suit against United Fruit; this suit, which dragged on until 1958, disrupted United Fruit's business in Guatemala.

53 National Intelligence Estimate, "Probable Developments in Guatemala," 19 May

1953, FRUS, 1952–54, 4:1061. Richard Immerman (in his authoritative study, CIA in Guatemala, 79–82, 182–86) analyzes how strategic and economic concerns became intertwined. See also Cook, Declassified Eisenhower, 231.

54 Eisenhower and Dulles quoted in memorandum of conversation, 199th meeting of NSC, 24 May 1954, FRUS, 1952–54, 4:1132; Immerman, CIA in Guatemala, 235–36 n. 47. Dulles also tried to influence the reporting on Guatemala of the London Times; see Dulles to Frank Wisner of CIA, 12 June 1954, 5–6/54 (2) folder, box 2, Telephone series, Dulles papers.

55 NSC 5419/1, 28 May 1954, FRUS, 1952–54, 4:1135–36.

56 Eisenhower's remark to Goodpaster quoted in Ambrose, Eisenhower: The President, 196; Ambrose interviewed General Goodpaster.

57 Diary entry, 19 June 1954, reprinted in FRUS, 1952–54, 4:1173–74. For Attorney General Herbert Brownell's opinion, see ibid., 1133.

58 Eisenhower quoted in diary entry, 24 June 1954, Ferrell, Diary of James C. Hagerty, 74–75; FRUS, 1952–54, 4:1182–85; Ambrose, Eisenhower: The President, 196–97.

59 Dulles to McCardle, June 1954, 5–6/54 (1) folder, box 2, Telephone series, Dulles papers; Eisenhower quoted in Phillips, Night Watch, 50–51.

60 Schlesinger and Kinzer, Bitter Fruit, 188–89; Slater, OAS and United States Foreign Policy, 128; Assistant Secretary Holland quoted in conversation with Adolf Berle, diary entry, 1 July 1954, Berle papers.

61 Gillin and Silvert, "Ambiguities in Guatemala," 469–82; Adams, Crucifixion by Power, 194–205; Schlesinger and Kinzer, Bitter Fruit, 221–25, 235–36; American Federation of Labor quoted in Romualdi, Presidents and Peons, 240–46; Immerman, CIA in Guatemala, 197–201.

62 Dulles quoted in meeting with Castillo Armas, 22 July 1956, Panama Chronology folder, box 39, International series, Whitman; Briefing Folder on Guatemala, 1 February 1955, box 1, series 361, Nixon papers; minutes of 240th meeting of the NSC, 10 March 1955, box 6, NSC series, Whitman; Eisenhower to Castillo Armas, 1 February 1955, and John Eisenhower to president, 3 July 1957, both in Guatemala (6) folder, box 24, International series, Whitman.

63 Phillips, Night Watch, 53.

64 Dulles to Secretary of Defense Wilson, 27 October 1954, FRUS, 1952–54, 4:1234–36; Dulles to Eisenhower on visit of President-elect Ydígoras, 22 February 1958, Guatemala (5) folder, box 24, International series, Whitman; Eisenhower to Ydígoras, 12 September 1960, Guatemala (2) folder, box 24, International series, Whitman; Schlesinger and Kinzer, Bitter Fruit, 120–22, 237.

CHAPTER 4

1 Diary entry, 2 July 1953, Ferrell, Eisenhower Diaries, 242–45; Griffith, "Dwight D. Eisenhower and the Corporate Commonwealth," 87–122.

2 President Eisenhower to Milton Eisenhower, 1 December 1954, 12/54 (2) folder, box 8, DDE Diaries, Whitman; Kaufman, Trade and Aid, 12–33; Department of State, Agency for International Development, U.S. Overseas Loans and Grants, 6.

3 Hilton, "United States, Brazil, and the Cold War," 613–14.

4 Cabinet meeting, 3 July 1953, C-6 folder, box 1, Cabinet series (Minnich notes), OSS.

5 *FRUS, 1952–54*, 4:2–8.

6 Kaufman, *Trade and Aid*, 29–32. See also U.S. Export-Import Bank, *Semiannual Report, July 1 to December 31, 1953*, 22–23.

7 Milton Eisenhower's report is in *DSB* 29 (23 November 1953): 696–717 (the emphasis is in the report); Milton Eisenhower, *The Wine Is Bitter*, 199.

8 Hilton, "United States, Brazil, and the Cold War," 615.

9 *DSB* 29 (23 November 1985): 715–17.

10 Cabot to Dulles, 28 March 1953, DSR 611.20/3–2853; State Department officer Edward Cale to Cabot, 23 June 1953, DSR 820.00/6–2353; Cabot's speech to Pan American Society, *DSB* 29 (19 October 1953): 513–18; Cabot to Milton Eisenhower, 12 December 1957, part 1: Latin America, microfilm reel #1, Cabot papers.

11 Cabot to Undersecretary Smith, 20 January 1954, *FRUS, 1952–54*, 4:203–5; U.S. Export-Import Bank, *Semiannual Report, January 1 to June 30, 1953*, 22–23.

12 Kaufman, *Trade and Aid*, 30; Ambrose, *Eisenhower: The President*, 23, 441.

13 Dulles to Eisenhower, 3 September 1953, 1953 (2) folder, box 1, White House Memorandums series, Dulles papers; memorandum of conversation between Dulles, Cabot, and others, 2 October 1953, *FRUS, 1952–54*, 4:197–201.

14 Cabot to Dulles, 13 January 1954, *FRUS, 1952–54*, 4:266–67 n. 4; Kaufman, *Trade and Aid*, 30; oral history of Deputy Undersecretary of State for Economic Affairs Herbert V. Prochnow, pp. 12, 45.

15 Dulles's speech at Caracas in *DSB* 30 (15 March 1954): 379–83; memorandum of conversation with Eisenhower by Cabot, 21 January 1954, *FRUS, 1952–54*, 4:206–7; Cabinet meeting, 5 March 1954, C-12 folder, box 2, Cabinet series (Minnich notes), OSS.

16 Cabot oral history, pp. 3, 13; Cabot to NSC, 9 September 1953, DSR 631.20/9–953; Holland to Dulles, 8 July 1954, DSR 611.20/7–854.

17 Cabinet meeting, 5 March 1954, C-12 folder, box 2, Cabinet series (Minnich notes), OSS.

18 Eisenhower quoted in Kaufman, *Trade and Aid*, 39; memorandum of conversation between Eisenhower and Arthur Flemming, Office of Defense Mobilization, 19 July 1954, 7/54 (3) folder, box 2, Whitman Diary, Whitman.

19 Dulles to Holland, 28 June 1954, 6/54 (1) folder, box 2, Telephone series, Dulles papers; Cabot to State Department officer Robert Woodward, 11 March 1954, DSR 731.00/3–1154.

20 *FRUS, 1952–54*, 4:313.

21 Ibid., 67–88.

22 Ibid., 314–44; Stassen quoted in minutes of FOA staff meeting, 21 June 1954, ibid., 321–25.

23 Ibid., 344–52.

24 Ann Whitman to president on call of Dr. Eisenhower, 28 October 1954, 10/54 (1) folder, box 3, Whitman Diary, Whitman; Milton Eisenhower to Dulles, 27 October 1954, 9–10/54 (1) folder, box 3, Telephone series, Dulles papers. Just prior to the Rio Conference, the administration decided to join the International Finance Corporation, an institution for expanding private investment in the Third World. Latin Americans did not consider this a significant concession to their position; see Kaufman, *Trade and Aid*, 46–49.

25 Bohan to Henry Holland, 26 October 1954, OF-79-A-2 (Inter-American Economic

and Social Council), WHOF; Bohan, "Reflections on United States Economic Co-operation with Latin America" (September 1968 draft), box 14, Bohan papers.

26 Holland to Smith, 10 November 1954, *FRUS, 1952–54*, 4:342–44; Holland to Woodward, 19 September, 1954, ibid., 332–35; Holland testimony in SCFR, *Hearings on the Mutual Security Act, 1954*, 341–43, 366; Dulles to Woodward, 27 October 1954, 9–10/54 (1) folder, box 3, Telephone series, Dulles papers.

27 Dulles to Eisenhower, 11/54 (1) folder, box 3, Dulles-Herter series, Whitman; diary entry, 2 December 1954, Ferrell, *Diary of James C. Hagerty*, 122.

28 President Eisenhower to Dr. Eisenhower, 1 December 1954, 12/54 (2) folder, box 8, DDE Diaries, Whitman.

29 Memorandum of conversation between Holland and Muniz, 15 May 1954, DSR 611.20/5–1554; Hilton, "United States, Brazil, and the Cold War," 618.

30 Furtado, *Economic Development of Latin America*, 19–34; Graham, *Great Britain and the Onset of Modernization in Brazil*, 319–24; McCann, "Brazil, the United States, and World War II," 63–64; Ortiz, *El ferrocarril en la economía argentina*; Scalabrini Ortiz, *Política británica*.

31 Furtado, *Economic Development of Latin America*, 35–42; Baer, "The Economics of Prebisch," 203–18; Milton Eisenhower, *The Wine Is Bitter*, 105.

32 Furtado, *Economic Development of Latin America*, 47–48; *DSB* 31 (25 October 1954): 600–606; HCFA, *Hearings on the Mutual Security Act of 1953*, 374.

33 Furtado, *Economic Development of Latin America*, 54–64.

34 ECLA, *Economic Survey of Latin America, 1953*, 3–10, 29–51; Furtado, *Economic Development of Latin America*, 166–74; Baer, "The Economics of Prebisch," 212–16; State Department report on economic matters, April 1954, *FRUS, 1952–54*, 4:306–11.

35 ECLA, *Economic Survey of Latin America, 1954*, 16–21; Dell, *Inter-American Development Bank*, 5–8; Levinson and de Onís, *Alliance That Lost Its Way*, 39–41.

36 Stebbins, *United States in World Affairs, 1954*, 400–403; Dell, *Inter-American Development Bank*, 7–8.

37 Commerce Department, *Survey of Current Business* 36 (August 1956): 19; *DSB* 30 (11 January 1954): 48–53; *DSB* 31 (25 October 1954): 600–606.

38 Eisenhower to Dulles, 17 November 1954, 1954 (1) folder, box 1, White House Memorandums series, Dulles papers.

39 Ibid.; Holland quoted in HCFA, *Selected Executive Session Hearings, 1951–56*, 16:555; Rostow, *Eisenhower, Kennedy, and Foreign Aid*, 198–201; Scobie, *Argentina*, 238–41. For a contemporary critique of Prebisch's ideas, see "The Third World: Back to the Farm," *New York Times*, 28 July 1985, business section, 1, 8.

40 Holland address to the Pan American Society, *DSB* 31 (8 November 1954): 684–90; Holland to Woodward, 19 September 1954, *FRUS, 1952–54*, 4:332–35.

41 Latin American officials quoted in minutes of Inter-American Economic and Social Council, 2 September 1954, Correspondence file: Numeric file II, F-1, box 2, Bohan papers.

42 Secretary of the Treasury Humphrey's statement at Rio Conference, *DSB* 31 (6 December 1954): 863–69; Stebbins, *United States in World Affairs, 1954*, 400–403.

43 Cabinet meeting, 3 December 1954, C-19 folder, box 2, Cabinet series (Minnich notes), OSS.

44 Oral history of Rubottom, p. 29; Bohan to Nelson Rockefeller, 24 February 1955,

Correspondence file, box 1, Bohan papers; Cabot to Dulles, 25 April 1958, part 1: Latin America, microfilm reel #2, Cabot papers.

45 Department of State, Agency for International Development, *Overseas Loans and Grants*, 33–61; Robert J. Alexander, *Bolivian National Revolution*, 268; Blasier, *Hovering Giant*, 144.

46 Klein, *Bolivia*, 223–37.

47 Address of Assistant Secretary Cabot to General Federation of Women's Clubs, *DSB* 29 (26 October 1953): 554–59; President Paz Estenssoro to Eisenhower, *DSB* 29 (2 November 1953): 584–85; memorandum of conversation between Eisenhower and President-Elect Siles, 23 July 1956, Panama Chronology (7/23–24/56) folder, box 39, International series, Whitman.

48 National Intelligence Estimate on Bolivia, 19 March 1954, *FRUS, 1952–54*, 4:547–57; testimony of Acting Assistant Secretary Robert Woodward, 16 July 1953, to HCFA, *Selected Executive Session Hearings, 1951–56*, 16:430–34.

49 Malloy, *Bolivia*, 216–42; Patch, "Bolivia: U.S. Assistance in a Revolutionary Setting," 124–30; *FRUS, 1952–54*, 4:550–51.

50 Commerce Department, *Survey of Current Business* 36 (August 1956): 19; Eisenhower quoted in memorandum of conversation recorded by Assistant Secretary Cabot, 22 June 1953, *FRUS, 1952–54*, 4:532–33; Stebbins, *United States in World Affairs, 1951*, 317; SCFR, *Hearings on the Mutual Security Act, 1955*, 291.

51 SCFR, *Hearings on the Mutual Security Act, 1955*, 291; *FRUS, 1952–54*, 4:553.

52 Cabinet meeting, 3 July 1953, C-6 folder, box 1, Cabinet series (Minnich notes), OSS; Secretary of State to Embassy in Bolivia, 12 March 1953 and 20 March 1953, *FRUS, 1952–54*, 4:522–26; memorandum of conversation between Assistant Secretary Holland and President Paz Estenssoro, 30 September 1954, ibid., 566–67.

53 Milton Eisenhower to president, 11 January 1954, S. Amer. Rpt. (1) folder, box 13, Name series, Whitman; Milton Eisenhower, *The Wine Is Bitter*, 124, 194; President Eisenhower to President Paz, *DSB* 29 (2 November 1953): 584–85; Second Progress Report on NSC 144/1, 20 November 1953, *FRUS, 1952–54*, 4:27.

54 Robert J. Alexander, *Bolivian National Revolution*, 162–70; Blasier, *Hovering Giant*, 137, 141; Klein, *Bolivia*, 240; Wilkie, *Bolivian Revolution*, 33; memorandum of conversation between Vice-President Nixon and officials of Bolivian national oil company, 15 May 1958, box 1, series 397, Nixon papers.

55 Blasier, *Hovering Giant*, 138–40; Klein, *Bolivia*, 236.

56 Eder, *Inflation and Development in Latin America*, 87–88, 143–48, 220; Robert J. Alexander, *Bolivian National Revolution*, 207–10; Blasier, *Hovering Giant*, 138–40.

57 Robert J. Alexander, *Bolivian National Revolution*, 216–20; Malloy, *Bolivia*, 182.

58 Klein, *Bolivia*, 240–42; Patch, "Bolivia: U.S. Assistance in a Revolutionary Setting," 132–75; the official quoted is Assistant Secretary of State R. Richard Rubottom, in ibid., 159.

59 Andrade, *My Missions for Revolutionary Bolivia*, xv.

60 Ambassador Philip Bonsal to State Department on conversation between President Siles and Assistant Secretary Rubottom, 7 May 1958, box 1, series 397, Nixon papers; Blasier, *Hovering Giant*, 141–42; Patch, "Bolivia: U.S. Assistance in a Revolutionary Setting," 155–56; Siles quoted in ibid., 175.

61 Eisenhower quoted in Andrade, *My Missions for Revolutionary Bolivia*, 180.

62 Memorandum of conversation between Siles and Eisenhower, 23 July 1956, Pa-

nama Chronology (7/23–24/56) folder, box 39, International series, Whitman;
memorandum of conversation between Nixon and Siles, 5 May 1958, Bolivia-
Maps folder, box 2, series 401, Nixon papers.

CHAPTER 5

1 Charles C. Alexander, *Holding the Line*, 100.
2 Dulles to Eisenhower, summation of Latin American policy, 29 September 1956,
  OF-116-J-1 (Latin America), WHOF.
3 Dulles news conference, *DSB* 35 (15 October 1956): 575–76; Eisenhower to Dr. Eisenhower and Eisenhower to Dulles, both 27 September 1956, Telephone folder
  (9/56), box 18, DDE Diaries, Whitman.
4 Dulles quoted in Stebbins, *United States in World Affairs, 1956*, 238.
5 Holland to Dulles, 28 September 1956, 7–9/56 (1) folder, box 5, Telephone series,
  Dulles papers.
6 Minutes of 237th meeting of NSC, 17 February 1955, box 6, NSC series, Whitman.
7 Memorandum of conversation between Eisenhower and Ibáñez, 23 July 1956, Panama Chronology (7/23–24/56) folder, box 39, International series, Whitman;
  memorandum of conversation between Eisenhower and Dulles on Colombia, 23
  August 1955, Meetings with President–1955 (2) folder, box 3, White House Memorandums series, Dulles papers; memorandum of conversation between Eisenhower
  and Dr. Gainza Paz, 10 April 1957, Argentina (7) folder, box 2, International series,
  Whitman.
8 *DSB* 32 (31 January 1955): 178–82; *DSB* 34 (27 February 1956): 339–40;
  Ameringer, *Democratic Left in Exile*, 206–16; Barber, *United States in World Affairs, 1955*, 220–21.
9 Diary entry, 25 July 1956, Ferrell, *Eisenhower Diaries*, 328; memorandum of Eisenhower conversations with Stroessner and Somoza, both 23 July 1956, Panama
  Chronology (7/23–24/56) folder, box 39, International series, Whitman; Eisenhower statement on Somoza in *DSB* 35 (15 October 1956): 573; Ameringer, *Democratic Left in Exile*, 217.
10 Woodward related this charge to Adolf Berle; see diary entry, 8 February 1955,
   Berle Diaries.
11 Warren to Rollin Atwood, Director, Office of South American Affairs, 8 December
   1954, *FRUS, 1952–54*, 4:1674–75; for accounts of Gardner's activities, see Bonsal,
   Cuba, Castro, and the United States, 13; Earl E. T. Smith, *Fourth Floor*, 20; and
   Phillips, *Night Watch*, 63–64; Pheiffer quoted in Atkins and Wilson, *United
   States and the Trujillo Regime*, 71; for Bonsal's diplomacy, see again, Bonsal,
   Cuba, Castro, and the United States, 27.
12 Briefing on Cuba, 31 January 1955, box 1, series 361, Nixon papers; Briefing on
   Dominican Republic, 3 February 1955, box 1, series 361, Nixon papers.
13 Nixon's toast to Batista (n.d., but February 1955), box 1, series 362, Nixon papers.
14 Cabinet meeting, 11 March 1955, C-22 folder, box 3, Cabinet series (Minnich
   notes), OSS. See also Nixon's report to the NSC, minutes of 240th meeting of NSC,
   10 March 1955, box 6, NSC series, Whitman.
15 Although the Eisenhower administration was not responsible for dictatorships in
   Latin America, its approval was valued by dictators. Trujillo, for example, released
   to the Dominican public a friendly letter he had received from Eisenhower, dem-

onstrating to opponents that he commanded the respect of the United States; see Berle, "To the South," 37. Ambassador Philip Bonsal, who accompanied Richard Nixon on his tour of Central America, also found that dictators like Batista coveted U.S. support (Bonsal, *Cuba, Castro, and the United States,* 13).

16 Progress report by OCB on NSC 5432/1, 6 April 1956, NSC 5432/1 folder, box 13, OSANSA; Gordon Gray, Assistant Secretary of Defense, to Joseph Dodge, White House (n.d., but probably May 1956), U.S. Policy toward Latin America (3) folder, box 12, Briefing Notes subseries, OSANSA.

17 Minutes of 296th meeting of NSC, 6 September 1956, box 8, NSC series, Whitman; Report of General J. Lawton Collins and Ambassador John C. Hughes, 23 February 1957, Latin American Trip, box 2, Fairless Committee.

The question of whether U.S. military aid encourages militarism in Latin America has been a controversial one in scholarly circles. For various perspectives on the debate, see Feldman, "Argentina, 1945–1971," 321–36; Fossum, "Factors Influencing the Occurrence of Military Coups D'Etat," 228–51; Lieuwen, *Arms and Politics,* 226–44; Powell, "Military Assistance and Militarism," 382–92; Tomasek, "Defense of the Western Hemisphere," 374–401; Wolf, "Political Effects of Military Programs," 871–93; Wynia, "Militarism Revisited," 105–19.

The position of political scientist Lars Schoultz seems persuasive, however. Schoultz argues that military aid can never be a "neutral" instrument of foreign policy, for it "inevitably increases the ability of military forces to coerce"; it is not possible for the United States "to pursue the goal of access and influence without simultaneously increasing the coercive power of the military" (*Human Rights,* 246–47).

18 Minutes of 296th meeting of NSC, 6 September 1956, box 8, NSC series, Whitman.

19 Ibid.; minutes of 297th meeting of NSC, 20 September 1956, box 8, NSC series, Whitman.

20 NSC 5613/1, 25 September 1956, NSC 5613 (2) folder, box 18, OSANSA; Progress Report on U.S. Policy toward Latin America, 1 October 1957, and Director of Mutual Security Program to OCB, 30 August 1957, both in U.S. Policy toward Latin America (3) folder, box 12, Briefing Notes subseries, OSANSA.

21 Testimony of Assistant Secretary Holland on training of anti-Communist forces, in SCFR, *Executive Sessions, 1956,* 8:241; section on training of police forces in progress report by OCB on NSC 5613/1, 11 September 1957, NSC 5613/1 (1) folder, box 18, Policy Papers subseries, OSANSA; Hinckle and Turner, *The Fish Is Red,* 56–57.

22 Kaufman, *Trade and Aid,* 58–73; progress report by OCB on NSC 5432/1, 6 April 1956, NSC 5432/1 folder, box 13, OSANSA.

23 Report by Economic Intelligence Committee of CIA, "Sino-Soviet Bloc Postwar Economic Activities in Underdeveloped Areas," 8 August 1956, Mullin, H. J., folder, box 8, Fairless Committee; Allen, *Soviet Influence in Latin America,* 8–9; Barber, *United States in World Affairs, 1955,* 223–24.

24 NSC 5613/1, 25 September 1956, NSC 5613 (2) folder, box 18, OSANSA; memorandum of Eisenhower conversation with President Juscelino Kubitschek of Brazil, 22 July 1956, Panama Chronology (7/22/56) folder, box 39, International series, Whitman; memorandum of Eisenhower conversation with Dr. José Loreto Arismendi, Foreign Minister of Venezuela, 23 November 1956, Venezuela (2) folder, box 50, International series, Whitman.

25 Kane, "Reassessing the Bureaucratic Dimensions of Foreign-Policy Making," 46–65; Assistant Secretary Holland's testimony on Sugar Act, *DSB* 33 (18 July 1955): 120–23; Kaufman, *Trade and Aid*, 118–19; memorandum of conversation between Eisenhower and Peruvian Prime Minister Manuel Cisneros, 14 October 1957, and President Manuel Prado of Peru to Eisenhower, 25 October 1958, both in Peru (2) folder, box 40, International series, Whitman.

26 NSC 5613/1, 25 September 1956, NSC 5613 (2) folder, box 18, OSANSA.

27 Minutes of 296th meeting of NSC, 6 September 1956, box 8, NSC series, Whitman; Rabe, "The Johnson (Eisenhower?) Doctrine," 98–99.

28 Progress report of OCB on NSC 5613/1, 11 September 1957, NSC 5613/1 (1) folder, box 18, Policy Papers subseries, OSANSA; Allen, *Soviet Influence in Latin America*, 8–9, 34–45; Vacs, *Discreet Partners*, 17–18; Blasier, *Giant's Rival*, 17.

29 John Foster Dulles quoted in Stebbins, *United States in World Affairs, 1957*, 259–60; progress report by OCB on NSC 5613/1, 11 September 1957, NSC 5613/1 (1) folder, box 18, Policy Papers subseries, OSANSA; Allen Dulles quoted in SCFR, *Executive Sessions, 1958*, 10:111.

30 NSC 5613/1, 25 September 1956, NSC 5613 (2) folder, box 18, OSANSA; for Holland's diplomacy, see *DSB* 32 (11 April 1955): 598–604; *DSB* 34 (18 June 1956): 106–13; Briggs, *Farewell to Foggy Bottom*, 183.

31 SCFR, *Hearings on the Mutual Security Act, 1958*, 411.

32 Holland to Undersecretary of State through Secretary of State, 29 March 1955, Export-Import Bank folder, box 1, series 361, Nixon papers.

33 Dulles to Eisenhower, 14 June 1955, and Undersecretary of State Herbert Hoover, Jr., to Eisenhower, 7 February 1955, both in Mexico, Misc. (2) folder, box 35, International series, Whitman; minutes of 240th meeting of NSC, 10 March 1955, box 6, NSC series, Whitman; Dulles to Eisenhower, 19 March 1957, 3/57 folder, box 6, Dulles-Herter series, Whitman.

34 Minutes of 237th meeting of NSC, 17 February 1955, box 6, NSC series, Whitman; Peterson, *Argentina and the United States*, 509–12; Solberg, *Oil and Nationalism in Argentina*, 165–68.

35 Eisenhower to Dulles on conversation with Kubitschek, 5 January 1956, and Eisenhower to Hoover, 13 January 1956, both in Telephone Calls (1/56) folder, box 12, DDE Diaries, Whitman; Eisenhower to Hoover, 24 March 1956, Telephone Calls (3/56) folder, box 13, DDE Diaries, Whitman. Eisenhower actually sent a U.S. oilman, W. Alton Jones, to Brazil; nothing significant came of the mission, however, for Brazilian nationalist feelings were intense on the question of oil development.

36 Cabot to Dulles, 25 April 1958, part 1: Latin America, microfilm reel #2, Cabot papers.

37 For investment figures, see Commerce Department, *Survey of Current Business* 40 (September 1960): 20; Holland and Dulles quoted in Rabe, *Road to OPEC*, 130.

38 Rabe, *Road to OPEC*, 130–31.

39 ECLA, *Economic Survey of Latin America, 1958*, 71; Hartlyn, "Military Governments and the Transition to Civilian Rule," 269; Barber, *United States in World Affairs, 1955*, 237.

40 Herbert Prochnow, Deputy Undersecretary of State for Economic Affairs, to Joseph Dodge, Council on Foreign Economic Policy, 9 April 1956, CFEP 537–International Coffee Agreement (1) folder, box 7, CFEP; Clarence Randall, Council on Foreign

Economic Policy, to Thomas Mann, State Department, 16 December 1957, CFEP 531 (2) folder, box 6, CFEP.

41 Dulles to Eisenhower, 5 August 1957, 8/57 (2) folder, box 7, Dulles-Herter series, Whitman.

42 Stebbins, *United States in World Affairs, 1957*, 279–85.

43 Kaufman, *Trade and Aid*, 95–112; Rostow, *Eisenhower, Kennedy, and Foreign Aid*, 198–201.

44 Memorandum of conversation between Eisenhower and Dr. Gainza Paz, Editor of *La Prensa*, 10 April 1957, Argentina (7) folder, box 2, International series, Whitman; memorandum of conversation between Eisenhower and Ambassador Dr. Don Barros Hurtado of Argentina, 23 June 1958, Argentina (6) folder, box 1, International series, Whitman; testimony of Assistant Secretary of State R. Richard Rubottom, SCFR, *Hearings on the Mutual Security Act, 1957*, 333–34.

45 Oral history of Figueres, pp. 32–35; Tomasek, "Defense of the Western Hemisphere," 390–92. For other contemporary critiques of U.S. policy, see Beltrán, "Foreign Loans and Politics in Latin America," 297–304; Figueres, "Problems of Democracy in Latin America," 11–21; Flores, "Mexico Forges Ahead," 491–503; Galíndez, "Anti-American Sentiment in Latin America," 24–32; Santos, "Latin American Realities," 245–57.

46 Eisenhower to Dulles on meeting with Kubitschek, 5 January 1956, Telephone Calls (1/56) folder, box 12, DDE Diaries, Whitman; Kubitschek statement to press, *DSB* 34 (16 January 1956): 87–88.

47 Eisenhower and Dulles quoted in Hilton, "United States, Brazil, and the Cold War," 618–20; diary entry, 25 July 1956, Ferrell, *Eisenhower Diaries*, 328; see also speech to Brazilian public by Vice-President Nixon, *DSB* 34 (27 February 1956): 335–38.

48 Hickenlooper quoted in SCFR, *Executive Sessions, 1954*, 6:80; memorandum of conversation between Capehart and Eisenhower, 7 March 1955, 3/55 (7) folder, box 4, Whitman Diary, Whitman.

49 SCFR, *Executive Sessions, 1956*, 8:246–48; SCFR, *Hearings on the Mutual Security Act, 1958*, 24, 62, 159; Francis, "Military Aid to Latin America," 396–402.

50 SCFR, *Hearings on the Mutual Security Act, 1955*, 316.

51 Kaufman, *Trade and Aid*, 163–64; SCFR, *Executive Sessions, 1956*, 8:455–62; SCFR, *Executive Sessions, 1957*, 9:650–54.

CHAPTER 6

1 Dulles to Holland, 22 February 1957, 1–2/57 (1) folder, box 6, Telephone series, Dulles papers; Cabot to Robert Woodward, 10 June 1957, part 1, microfilm reel #1, Cabot papers; SCFR, *Nomination of Roy R. Rubottom*.

2 Rubottom to Dulles, 26 December 1957, 12/57 folder, box 7, Dulles-Herter series, Whitman.

3 Dulles to Eisenhower, 28 December 1957, and Eisenhower to Dulles, 31 December 1957, both in 12/57 folder, box 7, Dulles-Herter series, Whitman.

4 Nixon to aides (n.d., but 1958), South American Trip (Misc.) folder, series 390, box 2, Nixon papers.

5 Nixon, *Six Crises*, 183–86.

6 Ibid., 183–230; oral history of Rubottom, pp. 39–42; Rabe, *Road to OPEC*, 134–35.

7 Cabinet meeting, 16 May 1958, C-45 folder, box 5, Cabinet series (Minnich notes), OSS; Nixon, *Six Crises*, 223; Stebbins, *United States in World Affairs, 1958*, 354–55.

8 Memorandum for Secretary of State from CIA Director Dulles, 28 May 1958, Conversations with Dulles, A. W. (Intelligence Material) folder, box 8, Dulles papers; Allen Dulles to John Foster Dulles, 19 June 1958, Telephone Conversations, 6–7/58 (5) folder, box 8, Telephone series, Dulles papers; Annex B, "CIA Intelligence Annex: Sino-Soviet Bloc Activity in Latin America," 15 April 1958, in OCB progress report on NSC 5613/1, 3 June 1958, NSC 5613 (1) folder, box 18, Policy Papers subseries, OSANSA; Annex C, "CIA Intelligence Annex: Sino-Soviet Bloc Activities in Latin America," 12 November 1958, in OCB progress report on NSC 5613/1, 2 December 1958, NSC 5613/1 (1) folder, box 18, Policy Papers subseries, OSANSA.

9 SCFR, *Executive Sessions, 1958*, 10:220–83; HCFA, *Review of the Relations of the United States and Other American Republics*; HCFA, Subcommittee on Inter-American Affairs, *Report on United States Relations with Latin America*; SCFR, Senator Wayne Morse, *Report on Study Trip to South America*; SCFR, *Latin America: Venezuela, Brazil, Peru, Bolivia, and Panama. A Report of Senator George D. Aiken*; Milton Eisenhower, "Report to the President," *DSB* 40 (19 January 1959): 89–105; memorandum of meeting with president by Gordon Gray, Special Assistant for National Security Affairs, on USIA study, 17 October 1958, Meetings with the President–1958 (2) folder, box 3, Presidential subseries, Special Assistants series, OSANSA.

10 Report of Business Advisory Council in letter, John Moore of W. R. Grace Company to Nixon, 21 July 1958, in RN Recommendations–Latin America folder, box 10, series 401, Nixon papers; Guggenheim to Eisenhower, 26 May 1958, and Fleming to Eisenhower, 19 November 1958, both in OF-116-J-Latin America, WHOF.

11 Charles C. Alexander, *Holding the Line*, 242; Ambrose, *Eisenhower: The President*, 436–86.

12 Diary entry, 13 May 1958, 5/58 (1) folder, box 10, Whitman Diary, Whitman; Eisenhower, *Waging Peace*, 519.

13 Cabinet meeting, 16 May 1958, C-45 folder, box 5, Cabinet series (Minnich notes), OSS; S. Everett Gleason to Robert Cutler, "Report on Nixon Oral Briefing to NSC," 26 May 1958, U.S. Policy toward Latin America (3) folder, box 12, Briefings subseries, OSANSA; Nixon, *Six Crises*, 191–92.

14 Memorandum of conversation between Dulles and president, 18 May 1958, Meetings with President, 1–6/58 (2) folder, box 6, White House Memorandums series, Dulles papers; Dulles to Nixon, 19 May 1958, 4–5/58 folder, Telephone series, box 8, Dulles papers; Cabinet meeting, 16 May 1958, C-45 folder, box 5, Cabinet series (Minnich notes), OSS.

15 HCFA, Subcommittee on Inter-American Affairs, *Report on United States Relations with Latin America*, 3.

16 Paragraph 22-b of NSC 5902/1, 16 February 1959, NSC 5902/1 (1) folder, box 26, Policy Papers subseries, OSANSA.

17 Szulc, *Twilight of the Tyrants*, 3–8; Hartlyn, "Military Governments and the Transition to Civilian Rule," 245–81; Rabe, *Road to OPEC*, 132–33; Ameringer, *Democratic Left in Exile*, 20–21.

18 Eisenhower's statement of 14 August 1958 in box 893, OF-227-Venezuela, WHOF;

Atkins and Wilson, *United States and the Trujillo Regime*, 14–15; see also memorandum of conversation between Eisenhower and Frondizi, 2 January 1959, and Christian Herter to Eisenhower on Aramburu visit, 3 November 1959, both in Argentina (1) folder, box 1, International series, OSS; Eisenhower to Rómulo Betancourt, 20 December 1958, OF-227-Venezuela, box 893, WHOF; Dulles to Eisenhower on President-elect Jorge Alessandri of Chile, 29 October 1958, Chile (5) folder, box 7, International series, Whitman; briefing memorandum for Eisenhower on visit of Colombian President Alberto Lleras Camargo, 31 March 1960, Colombia (2) folder, box 7, International series, Whitman; Ewell, *Indictment of a Dictator*, 59–79; Nixon to Dulles on Estrada, 19 May 1958, 4–5/58 (1) folder, box 8, Telephone series, Dulles papers.

19 Betancourt quoted in Rabe, *Road to OPEC*, 146–47; oral history of Rubottom, p. 77.

20 Herter quoted in Slater, *OAS and United States Foreign Policy*, 94–96; Ameringer, *Democratic Left in Exile*, 284–87; Atkins and Wilson, *United States and the Trujillo Regime*, 105.

21 The senators' letter is in U.S. President's Committee to Study the United States Military Assistance Program, *Composite Report*, 185–87.

22 Ibid., vii–viii, 195–97; Schoultz, *Human Rights*, 211.

23 Dulles to Eisenhower, 13 September 1958, ICA (3) folder, box 15, Alphabetical subseries, Subject series, OSS; memorandum of conversation with Fulbright, 2 February 1959, E through I (1) folder, box 1, General Correspondence series, Dulles papers.

24 U.S. President's Committee to Study the United States Military Assistance Program, *Composite Report*, 145–69. In the mid-1960s, the Johnson administration conducted an extensive study of military assistance for Latin America. In reviewing the program since its inception in 1951, officials could find no empirical evidence to support the Draper Committee's contention that military aid promoted democracy or economic progress; see, for examples, study by Office of Assistant Secretary of Defense, International Security Affairs, "U.S. Policies toward Latin American Military Forces," 25 February 1965, vol. 3 (1–6/65); and memorandum, Sayre to McGeorge Bundy, 8 October 1964, vol. 2 (9–12/64), both in box 2, National Security Council (Latin America–Country) Files, Johnson Library.

25 Admiral Robert B. Carney to Draper, 13 February 1959, Sixth Committee Meeting folder, box 2, and Dulles (Herter) to Draper, 17 February 1959, Letter to John Foster Dulles folder, box 9, both in Draper Committee.

26 SCFR, *Hearings on the Mutual Security Act, 1959*, 543–60; SCFR, *Hearings on the Mutual Security Act, 1960*, 345–70; SCFR, *Executive Sessions, 1959*, 11:519–37, 606–26; oral history of Rubottom, p. 59.

27 Nixon, *Six Crises*, 208–9; Achilles to State Department, 16 May 1958, South American Trip folder, box 1, series 397, Nixon papers; paragraph 29 of Annex B, "General Considerations," of NSC 5902/1, 16 February 1959, NSC 5902/1 (1) folder, box 26, Policy Papers subseries, OSANSA.

28 Kennedy, Long, and Fulbright quoted in SCFR, *Executive Sessions, 1959*, 11:519–37, 606–26.

29 Stinson and Cochrane, "Movement for Regional Arms Control in Latin America," 3; Dulles to Eisenhower on meeting with Costa Rican officials, 26 March 1958, Costa Rica (2) folder, box 8, International series, Whitman.

30 Comments by Senators Church, Fulbright, and Morse on discussions with Latin American ambassadors, in SCFR, *Executive Sessions, 1959,* 11:521, 536; memorandum of conversation between Eisenhower and President Jorge Alessandri of Chile, 29 February 1960, Chile (1) folder, box 10, International Trips and Meetings series, OSS; memorandum of conversation between Herter, Dulles, and Chilean Foreign and Defense Ministers, DDE to SA (2–3/60) folder, box 10, International Trips and Meetings series, OSS; Stinson and Cochrane, "Movement for Regional Arms Control in Latin America," 4–5.

31 Memorandum of Nixon conversations with Arturo Frondizi, 6 May 1958; Lleras Camargo, 11 May 1958; Ponce Enríquez, 9 May 1958; and Luis Batlle Berres of Uruguay, 29 April 1958, all in box 1, series 397, Nixon papers; memorandum of conversation with Siles Zuazo, 5 May 1958, Bolivia-Maps folder, box 2, series 401, Nixon papers.

32 Kubitschek to Eisenhower, 28 May 1958, Brazil (8) folder, box 4, International series, Whitman; *DSB* 38 (30 June 1958): 1090–91.

33 Eisenhower to Kubitschek, 5 June 1958, Brazil (8) folder, box 4, International Series, Whitman; Dulles to Eisenhower on Rubottom meeting with Kubitschek, 20 June 1958, Brazil (7) folder, box 4, International series, Whitman.

34 See, for examples, President Frondizi to Eisenhower, 9 August 1960, Argentina (1) folder, box 1; President Alessandri to Eisenhower, 30 January 1959, Chile (7) folder, box 7; President Lleras Camargo to Eisenhower, 24 September 1958, Colombia (4) folder, box 7; President Mario Echandi of Costa Rica to Eisenhower, 28 September 1959, Costa Rica (1) folder, box 8, all in International series, Whitman.

35 Oral history of C. Douglas Dillon, pp. 26–30, Columbia University; oral history of Rubottom, p. 32; oral history of Thomas Mann, pp. 20–23, 37; Cabot to Milton Eisenhower, 23 October 1957 and 12 December 1957, both in part 1: Latin America, microfilm reel #1, Cabot papers; Milton Eisenhower, *The Wine Is Bitter,* 161–63, 205–9.

36 Oral history of Dillon, pp. 35–36, Columbia University; oral history of Dillon, pp. 35–41, Dulles Oral History Collection; Dillon to Senator J. William Fulbright, 2 April 1958, folder 4, box 125, Fulbright papers; oral history of Milton Eisenhower, p. 95, Columbia University; Hyman, "Mr. Dillon and the Fight for Foreign Aid," 10–15.

37 Randall to Mann, 16 December 1957, CFEP 531 (2) folder, box 6, Policy Papers series, CFEP; testimony of Mann, 3 March 1959, in SCFR, *Executive Sessions, 1959,* 11:190–220; Kaufman, *Trade and Aid,* 77–80.

38 Memorandum to Council on Foreign Economic Policy from Randall, 28 June 1958, CFEP 531 (1) folder, box 6; Donald Carmichael, OCB, to Matthew Marks, OCB, 15 July 1959, CFEP 531 (2) folder, box 6; Edward Galbreath, of Council on Foreign Economic Policy Staff, to Randall, 21 October 1958, CFEP 531 (2) folder, box 6; and Mann briefing to Council on Foreign Economic Policy, 23 October 1958, CFEP 560 (1) folder, box 13, all in Policy Papers series, CFEP; Mann to Cabot, 26 January 1959, part 1: Latin America, microfilm reel #2, Cabot papers; Eisenhower, *Waging Peace,* 517; Stebbins, *United States in World Affairs, 1959,* 368.

39 Dell, *Inter-American Development Bank,* 12–15; Kaufman, *Trade and Aid,* 164–66.

40 Memorandum by Don Paarlberg of staff meeting with president on development bank, 5 March 1959, Staff Notes, 3/1–3/15/59 (2) folder, box 39, DDE Diaries,

Whitman; Dell, *Inter-American Development Bank*, 15.

41 NSC 5902/1 and Annex B, "General Considerations," 16 February 1959, NSC 5902/1 (1) folder, box 26, Policy Papers subseries, OSANSA.

42 Kaufman, *Trade and Aid*, 166; Stebbins, *United States in World Affairs, 1958*, 367–69; Stebbins, *United States in World Affairs, 1959*, 366–67.

43 SCFR, *Hearings on the Mutual Security Act, 1959*, 217; SCFR, *Hearings on the Mutual Security Act, 1960*, 348, 375.

44 Unsigned memorandum for president, "Problems in US-Brazil Relations," May 1959, Brazil (5) folder, box 4, International series, Whitman; Stebbins, *United States in World Affairs, 1959*, 361–62.

45 President quoted in Ambrose, *Eisenhower: The President*, 486; president to Dr. Eisenhower, 26 November 1958, Report to President folder, box 7, Milton Eisenhower papers; Dr. Eisenhower's statement to NSC contained in memorandum from Gordon Gray to Philip J. Halla, 9 February 1959, U.S. Policy toward Latin America (2) folder, box 12, Briefing Notes subseries, OSANSA; president quoted in Cabinet meeting, 27 February 1959, C-49 folder, box 5, Cabinet series (Minnich notes), OSS.

46 Dulles to Eisenhower, 7 August 1958, Meetings with the President, 7–12/58 (9) folder, box 7, White House Memorandums series, Dulles papers; Kubitschek quoted in Hilton, "United States, Brazil, and the Cold War," 622.

47 Dulles testimony, 2 July 1954, in SCFR, *Executive Sessions, 1954*, 6:466; Dulles testimony, 19 May 1958, in SCFR, *Executive Sessions, 1958*, 10:232–37; Dulles to Eisenhower, 3 August 1958, Meetings with the President, 7–12/58 (9) folder, box 7, White House Memorandums series, Dulles papers.

48 Annex C, "Sino-Soviet Bloc Activities in Latin America," 12 November 1958, in OCB report on NSC 5613/1, 2 December 1958, NSC 5613/1 (1) folder, box 18, Policy Papers subseries, OSANSA; "Communist Strategy in Latin America," in Annex B, "General Considerations," NSC 5902/1, 16 February 1959, NSC 5902/1 (1) folder, box 26, Policy Papers subseries, OSANSA; Allen, *Soviet Influence in Latin America*, 6.

CHAPTER 7

1 Lockwood, *Castro's Cuba*, 154–65; Ruiz, *Cuba: The Making of a Revolution*, 133; Blasier, *Giant's Rival*, 99–102. The estimate of the strength of the Cuban Communist party is taken from a CIA study; see 5 November 1959 testimony of General Charles P. Cabell, Deputy Director of the CIA, in Senate Judiciary Committee, *Communist Threat to the United States through the Caribbean*, 161.

2 Ruiz, *Cuba: The Making of a Revolution*, 143–51; Thomas, *Cuba: The Pursuit of Freedom*, 1093–1189.

3 Commerce Department, *Survey of Current Business* 40 (September 1960): 20; Ruiz, *Cuba: The Making of a Revolution*, 4–17; Bonsal, *Cuba, Castro, and the United States*, 42–45; Domínguez, *Cuba: Order and Revolution*, 67–68. Domínguez estimates the value of U.S. direct investments at $1 billion in 1958.

4 Bonsal, *Cuba, Castro, and the United States*, 13, 47; Phillips, *Night Watch*, 63. Gardner defended his diplomacy in his 27 August 1960 testimony to Senate Judiciary Committee, *Communist Threat to the United States through the Caribbean*, 663–80.

5 Eisenhower to Ambassador Arthur Gardner, 11 January 1957, Cuba (2) folder, box 8, International series, Whitman; Earl E. T. Smith, *Fourth Floor*, 20–24; memorandum of telephone conversation between Eisenhower and Dulles, 7 August 1957, Telephone (8/57) folder, box 26, DDE Diaries, Whitman.

6 Earl E. T. Smith, *Fourth Floor*, 155–60.

7 Oral history of William Pawley, pp. 11–13; memorandum of conversation between Eisenhower and Herter on William Pawley, 15 February 1960, Staff Notes–2/60 (1) folder, box 47, DDE Diaries, Whitman; Earl E. T. Smith, *Fourth Floor*, 165–71; Blasier, "Elimination of United States Influence," 46–48.

8 Herter quoted in Ambrose, *Eisenhower: The President*, 505; Rubottom quoted in SCFR, *Executive Sessions, 1958*, 10:787.

9 Dulles quoted in Ambrose, *Eisenhower: The President*, 505; testimony of Dulles, 26 January 1959, in SCFR, *Executive Sessions, 1959*, 11:124–26; testimony of General Cabell of CIA, 5 November 1959, in Senate Judiciary Committee, *Communist Threat to the United States through the Caribbean*, 162–63; National Intelligence Estimate on Cuba of 29 December 1959 cited in memorandum, Herter to Eisenhower, 17 March 1960, 3/60 (2) folder, box 10, Dulles-Herter series, Whitman.

10 Eisenhower, *Waging Peace*, 521; Ambrose, *Eisenhower: The President*, 505.

11 Diary entry, 5 January 1959, of Eisenhower conversation with Herter on Earl Smith, 1/59 (2) folder, box 10, Whitman Diary, Whitman; Herter quoted in Noble, *Christian A. Herter*, 178. The State Department issued a public statement defending Smith and U.S. policy during the Batista years; see *DSB* 40 (2 February 1959): 162–63.

12 Bonsal, *Cuba, Castro, and the United States*, 26–27.

13 Acheson to Herbert Matthews, 19 March 1959, General Correspondence–1959 folder, box 1, Matthews papers; Welch, "Herbert L. Matthews and the Cuban Revolution," 1–5.

14 Eisenhower, *Waging Peace*, 522–23; testimony of Dulles, 26 January 1959, in SCFR, *Executive Sessions, 1959*, 11:124–26; Rubottom's testimony, 9 March 1959, in ibid., 207.

15 Herter to Eisenhower, with notation by Eisenhower, 23 April 1959, Cuba (1) folder, box 8, International series, Whitman.

16 Nixon, *Six Crises*, 352; Eisenhower, *Waging Peace*, 523.

17 A memorandum of Nixon's conversation with Castro can be found in Safford, "Nixon-Castro Meeting of 19 April 1959," 425–31. Nixon had previously released only portions of the account of his meeting with Castro; Safford found a complete summary in the papers of Senator Mike Mansfield.

18 The conspiracy thesis can be found in James, *Cuba: The First Soviet Satellite in the Americas*, and Weyl, *Red Star over Cuba*. The betrayal thesis can be found in Draper, *Castro's Revolution: Myths and Realities*, 3–57.

19 A good example of this thesis can be found in Williams, *United States, Cuba, and Castro*, 27–42, 81–87. An excellent survey of the historiographic literature on the United States and the Cuban Revolution can be found in Welch, *Response to Revolution*, 9–26.

20 Memorandum on Batista exile to Europe in State Department officer John Calhoun to Andrew Goodpaster, 19 August 1959, Cuba-1959 (1) folder, box 4, International series, OSS; memorandum of conversation by John Eisenhower on meeting between president, Herter, and State Department officer Livingston Mer-

chant on Cuban counterrevolutionists, 27 October 1959, Staff Notes–10/59 (1) folder, box 45, DDE Diaries, Whitman; "U.S. Expresses Concern to Cuba over State of Relations," *DSB* 41 (16 November 1959): 715–18.

21 Secretary of State Dulles to Eisenhower, 7 January 1959, Cuba-1959 (1) folder, box 4, International series, OSS.

22 Bonsal, *Cuba, Castro, and the United States*, 39–40; Bonsal to Herbert Matthews, 14 August 1959, General Correspondence–1959 folder, box 1, Matthews papers; oral history of Thomas Mann, p. 76; Blasier, "Elimination of United States Influence," 52; Noble, *Christian A. Herter*, 181.

23 Domínguez, *Cuba: Order and Revolution*, 143–47; Ruiz, *Cuba: The Making of a Revolution*, 4–5, 169; Blasier, "Elimination of United States Influence," 52.

24 Herter to Eisenhower, "Current Basic United States Policy toward Cuba," 5 November 1959, Cuba-1959 (1) folder, box 4, International series, OSS; Eisenhower indicated his approval of the document by initialing it. See also Noble, *Christian A. Herter*, 188–89.

25 Memorandum of conversation with Eisenhower by Gray, 29 December 1959, Meetings with President, 6–12/59 (1) folder, box 4, Presidential subseries, Special Assistants series, OSANSA.

26 King and Dulles quoted in Church Committee, *Alleged Assassination Plots*, 92–93. The 5412 Committee consisted of the undersecretary of state, the deputy secretary of defense, the national security advisor, and the director of the CIA.

27 Memorandum of conversation between Eisenhower and Herter, 23 January 1960, and memorandum of conversation between Eisenhower, Herter, Bonsal, and Rubottom, 25 January 1960, both in Staff Notes–1/60 (1), box 47, DDE Diaries, Whitman.

28 *DSB* 42 (15 February 1960): 237–39; Bonsal, *Cuba, Castro, and the United States*, 110, 121–23. Bonsal favored the conciliatory statement, but conceded that little would come of it. For the Latin American reaction to the U.S. statement, see Herter to Eisenhower, 2 February 1960, 2/60 folder, box 10, Dulles-Herter series, Whitman. Latin Americans praised the moderate tone of the statement and criticized Castro for his bombastic attacks on the United States, but they also warned that reprisals against Cuba "would provoke anti-American sentiment in the Americas."

29 SCFR, *Executive Sessions, 1960,* 12:85–92, 116–60.

30 Ibid., 116–60; oral history of Hill, pp. 100–101; oral history of Mann, pp. 74–75.

31 Memorandum of conversation between Eisenhower and Smathers, 18 February 1960, Staff Notes–2/60 (1) folder, box 47, DDE Diaries, Whitman; Smathers quoted in SCFR, *Executive Sessions, 1960,* 12:157.

32 *Operation Zapata*, 3–4. See also Record of Action No. 2191 of 436th Meeting of the NSC, 10 March 1960, Records of Action by NSC, 1960 (1) folder, box 3, NSC series, Whitman.

33 Eisenhower, *Waging Peace*, 533; Wyden, *Bay of Pigs*, 24–25; Ambrose, *Eisenhower: The President*, 640.

34 Herter to Eisenhower, "Status of Possible OAS Action on Cuba," 17 March 1960, 3/60 (2) folder, box 10, Dulles-Herter series, Whitman.

35 Bonsal, *Cuba, Castro, and the United States*, 131–32.

36 For an analysis of Latin American trade with the Soviet bloc, see "Sino-Soviet Bloc Activity in Latin America—CIA Intelligence Précis," 14 March 1960, in An-

nex A, ocb Report on Latin America (NSC 5902/1), 6 April 1960, NSC 5902/1 Latin America (1) folder, box 26, Policy Papers subseries, OSANSA; Blasier, *Giant's Rival*, 33–37.

37 Matthews to Arthur Sulzberger on meeting with State Department officials, 5 July 1960, box 27, Matthews papers; Mann quoted in SCFR, *Executive Sessions, 1960,* 12:119; Hill quoted in ibid., 151; Willauer's notes for conference with Herter (n.d., but 1959), Letters M–Z Official-Classified (4) folder, box 20, Christian Herter papers, Eisenhower Library; memorandum of conversation between Eisenhower and Herter, 17 March 1960, Staff Notes 3/60 (2) folder, box 48, DDE Diaries, Whitman.

38 Bonsal, *Cuba, Castro, and the United States,* 135. By 1 May 1960, Castro was publicly charging that the United States was organizing an invasion force; see Blasier, "Elimination of United States Influence," 69.

39 Bonsal, *Cuba, Castro, and the United States,* 110.

40 Blasier, *Giant's Rival,* 102–5; Ruiz, *Cuba: The Making of a Revolution,* 116; Welch, *Response to Revolution,* 18.

41 Castro quoted in Safford, "Nixon-Castro Meeting of 19 April 1959," 428.

42 Domínguez, *Cuba: Order and Revolution,* 143–49; Lockwood, *Castro's Cuba,* 154–65; Szulc, "Fidel Castro's Years as a Secret Communist," 47–48, 70–74, 121; Welch, *Response to Revolution,* 14–21.

43 Memorandum of telephone conversation between Herter and Eisenhower, 27 October 1959, Pres. Telephone Calls, 1959 (1) folder, box 10, Telephone series, Herter papers; Blasier, "Elimination of United States Influence," 59.

44 Suárez, *Cuba: Castroism and Communism,* 137–42; Domínguez, *Cuba: Order and Revolution,* 149.

45 Welch, *Response to Revolution,* 21–26.

CHAPTER 8

1 Milton Eisenhower, *The Wine Is Bitter,* 230; oral history of Milton Eisenhower, p. 101, Columbia University; Dwight Eisenhower, *Waging Peace,* 533.

2 SCFR, *Hearings on the Mutual Security Act, 1960,* 345–48; Acting Secretary of State Dillon to Eisenhower, 17 May 1960, 5/50 (2) folder, box 10, Dulles-Herter series, Whitman.

3 Memorandum of conversation between Eisenhower and National Advisory Committee on Inter-American Affairs, 3 December 1959, Staff Notes (12/59) folder, box 49, DDE Diaries, Whitman. Additional material on the committee can be found in OF-116-J-12 (National Advisory Committee on Inter-American Affairs), WHOF.

4 As it did in 1953, the State Department objected to Eisenhower's proposal for an Undersecretary of State for Latin America; department officers pointed out that other areas of the world would feel slighted. See Herter to Eisenhower, 5 May 1960, 5/60 (3) folder, box 10, Dulles-Herter series, Whitman.

5 Milton Eisenhower to Nixon, 12 May 1959, Milton Eisenhower folder, box 238, series 320, Nixon papers.

6 Milton Eisenhower to president (n.d., but probably December 1959), Eisenhower, Milton–1958 (2) folder, box 13, Name series, Whitman.

7 Ambrose, *Eisenhower: The President,* 532–53.

8 Herter to Eisenhower on proposed trip to Latin America, 29 December 1959, 12/59 (1) folder, box 10, Dulles-Herter series, Whitman; memorandum of conversation

between Eisenhower and Herter, 8 February 1960, Staff Notes–2/60 (1) folder, box 47, DDE Diaries, Whitman.

9 Herter to Eisenhower on Latin American reaction to trip, 12 March 1960, 3/60 (2) folder, box 10, Dulles-Herter series, Whitman; oral history of Vernon Walters, pp. 77–78.

10 Eisenhower, *Waging Peace*, 528–33; Milton Eisenhower, *The Wine Is Bitter*, 242–48.

11 Memorandum for record by General Andrew Goodpaster of conversation between Eisenhower and President Kubitschek, 23 February 1960, Brazil (2) folder, box 2, International series, OSS; Eisenhower quoted in his conversation with Herter, 30 August 1960, 8–9/60 (2) folder, box 4, State Department subseries, Subject series, OSS.

12 Kubitschek to Eisenhower, 19 July 1960, Brazil (2) folder, box 4, International series, Whitman; Herter to Eisenhower on "Status of Possible OAS Action on Cuba," 17 March 1960, 3/60 (2) folder, box 10, Dulles-Herter series, Whitman.

13 Minutes of Secretary Rubottom's report on president's trip to South America, 29 March 1960, OCB Minutes–1960 (2) folder, box 4, Administrative subseries, OCB series, OSANSA; Bromley Smith, Executive Director of the NSC Planning Board, to Karl Harr, Special Assistant to the President, 19 April 1960, U.S. Policy toward Latin America (1) folder, box 12, Briefing Notes subseries, NSC series, OSANSA.

14 Furtado, *Economic Development of Latin America*, 43–49; NSC 6009, "Capabilities of Latin America as a Supply Base in the Event of a Nuclear Attack on the United States," 27 May 1960, National Security Council Records, National Archives; U.S. Export-Import Bank, *Semiannual Report, January 1 to June 30*, 1960, 141.

15 LaFeber, *Panama Canal*, 124–31. See also NSC 6026, "U.S. Policy on the Panama Canal and a Future Inter-Oceanic Canal in Central America," 29 December 1960, National Security Council Records, National Archives.

16 Blasier, *Giant's Rival*, 33–37; Blasier, *Hovering Giant*, 141–42; Vacs, *Discreet Partners*, 17–18.

17 Annex A, "Sino-Soviet Activity in Latin America," CIA Intelligence Précis, 14 March 1960, in OCB Report on Latin America, 6 April 1960, NSC 5902/1 (1) folder, box 26, Policy Papers subseries, OSANSA.

18 Charles C. Alexander, *Holding the Line*, 243–51; Eisenhower quoted in Ambrose, *Eisenhower: The President*, 580.

19 Herter to Eisenhower, 6 January 1961, 1/61 folder, box 11, Dulles-Herter series, Whitman; Dulles to Sprague Committee, 21 November 1960, Staff Working Papers (4), box 19, Sprague Committee.

20 Memorandum of conversation between Eisenhower, Herter, and Dillon, 10 August 1960, 8–9/60 (1) folder, box 4, State Department subseries, Subject series, OSS.

21 Briefing paper on Prime Minister Beltrán (n.d., but June 1960), Peru (2) folder, box 12, International series, OSS.

22 Memorandum of conversation between Eisenhower and Beltrán with portions exempted from declassification, 9 June 1960, Staff Notes 6/60 (2) folder, box 50, DDE Diaries, Whitman. See also Zoumaras, "Containing Castro: Promoting Homeownership in Peru," 161–81.

23 Eisenhower's announcement in *DSB* 43 (1 August 1960): 166–68; Eisenhower to A. H. Sulzberger of *New York Times*, 8 July 1960, Dictation (7/60) folder, box 51,

DDE Diaries, Whitman; Eisenhower, *Waging Peace*, 536; Kaufman, *Trade and Aid*, 199–200.

24 Dillon to Eisenhower, 17 May 1960, 5/60 (2) folder, box 10, Dulles-Herter series, Whitman; Herter to Eisenhower on Peru, 26 July 1960, Peru (1) folder, box 40, International series, Whitman.

25 SCFR, *Hearings on American Republics Cooperation Act*, 3–49; SCFR, *Executive Sessions, 1960*, 12:682–91; Eisenhower comment in *DSB* 43 (1 August 1960): 168.

26 Dillon, in Bogotá, to State Department, 11 September 1960, 8–9/60 (2) folder, box 4, State Department subseries, Subject series, OSS; testimony of Secretary Herter, 6 January 1961, in SCFR, *Executive Sessions, 1961*, 13:10–11; quoted material in Statement of U.S. Policy toward Latin America (draft), 15 November 1960, U.S. Policy toward Latin America (1) folder, box 12, Briefing Notes subseries, NSC series, OSANSA.

27 Notes on report of Thomas Mann on Bogotá Conference, 12 October 1960, CFEP Briefings 4–10/60 (1) folder, box 1, Office series, CFEP; Ambassador to Brazil John Cabot to Thomas Cabot, 20 September 1960, part 1: Latin America, microfilm reel #4, Cabot papers; memorandum of Eisenhower's conversation with Ambassador to Chile Walter Mueller, 2 September 1960, Chile (1) folder, box 7, International series, Whitman.

28 Milton Eisenhower, *The Wine Is Bitter*, 161–63; Cabot to Senator Leverett Saltonstall, 17 August 1959, part 1: Latin America, microfilm reel #3, Cabot papers; Mann quoted in Herbert Matthews's letter to Sulzberger, 5 July 1960, box 27, Matthews papers; Statement of U.S. Policy toward Latin America (draft), 15 November 1960, U.S. Policy toward Latin America (1) folder, box 12, Briefing Notes subseries, NSC series, OSANSA.

29 Rubottom to Sprague Committee, 2 June 1960, #12 Latin America (4) folder, box 3, Sprague Committee; Milton Eisenhower, *The Wine Is Bitter*, 230.

30 Dreier, *Organization of American States*, 106–7; Dell, *Inter-American Development Bank*, 25–26, 31; oral history of Thomas Mann, p. 23.

31 Milton Eisenhower, *The Wine Is Bitter*, 251; Dwight Eisenhower, *Waging Peace*, 533.

32 Memorandum of conversation between Eisenhower and Dillon on letter from President Frondizi, 19 August 1960, Staff Notes 8/60 (2) folder, box 51, DDE Diaries, Whitman; Eisenhower to President Frondizi, 7 September 1960, Argentina (3) folder, box 1, International series, OSS; State Department analysis, "Argentine Politico-Economic Situation," 11 September 1960, Argentina (1) folder, box 1, International series, Whitman; President Frondizi's conversation with Arthur Schlesinger, Jr., in Schlesinger, *A Thousand Days*, 177–78; President Kubitschek to Eisenhower, 19 July 1960, Brazil (2) folder, box 4, International series, Whitman; Hilton, "United States, Brazil, and the Cold War," 622–23.

33 Herter to Nelson Rockefeller, 3 August 1960, 7–8/60 (1) folder, box 13, Telephone series, Herter papers. The Eisenhower administration did arrange, in late 1960, a $100-million credit for highway and housing construction in Argentina: see Herter to Eisenhower, 2 September 1960, Argentina (1) folder, box 1, International series; Peterson, *Argentina and the United States*, 519.

34 Betancourt's book has been translated into English: Betancourt, *Venezuela: Oil and Politics*. See also Robert J. Alexander, *Rómulo Betancourt*, 553.

35 Herter to Eisenhower, 15 April 1960, and Herter to Eisenhower, 31 October 1960,

both in Venezuela (1) folder, box 50, International series, Whitman; Eisenhower quoted in memorandum of conversation between Eisenhower and national security advisors, 29 November 1960, 1960 Meetings with President, vol. 2 (2) folder, box 5, Presidential subseries, Special Assistants series, OSANSA.

36 Agee, *Inside the Company,* 75–78, 135–36; Morris, *CIA and American Labor,* 78–79, 151–56; *New York Times,* 19 February 1967, 1, 32; ibid., 22 February 1967, 17. The authorization for this program may have come from paragraph no. 30 of NSC 5902/1; this paragraph was exempted from declassification but appears in Statement of U.S. Policy toward Latin America (draft), 15 November 1960, U.S. Policy toward Latin America (1) folder, box 12, Briefing Notes subseries, NSC series, OSANSA. The paragraph reads: "Seek—if necessary—by direct communication at acceptable expense to U.S. relations with the existing government—to influence moderate elements of anti-Communist leftist and/or nationalist political and labor movements and other reform groups to identify their aspirations for reform with cooperation with the U.S. and, as appropriate, utilize their potential as a means of limiting Communist influence."

37 Annex D, CIA Report, "Communist Influence on Student Groups in Latin America," 15 December 1959, Latin America folder, box 3, OCB series, OSANSA.

38 Annex C, Report on Latin American Student Program, 6 January 1960, Latin America folder, box 3, OCB series, OSANSA; testimony of Kenneth Holland, President of International Education, OCB Minutes–1960 (1) folder, box 4, Administrative subseries, OCB series, OSANSA; Agee, *Inside the Company,* 114.

39 Department of Defense, Office of Special Operations, to OCB, 14 September 1960, #28 Military (4) folder, box 8, Sprague Committee.

40 Ibid.; paragraph no. 72 in Statement of U.S. Policy toward Latin America (draft), 15 November 1960, U.S. Policy toward Latin America (1) folder, box 12, Briefing Notes subseries, NSC series, OSANSA; Stinson and Cochrane, "Movement for Regional Arms Control in Latin America," 14; Eisenhower, *Waging Peace,* 532.

41 Annexes C, D, and E in U.S. President's Committee to Study the United States Military Assistance Program, *Supplement to the Composite Report: Annexes;* paper, "U.S. Military Personnel in Latin America" (n.d., but 1960), #12 Latin America (1) folder, box 3, Sprague Committee; Van Cleve, "Political Use of Military Aid," 20–22; Barber and Ronning, *Internal Security and Military Power,* 84.

42 Paragraph no. 72 (a.) in Statement of U.S. Policy toward Latin America (draft), 15 November 1960, U.S. Policy toward Latin America (1) folder, box 12, Briefing Notes subseries, NSC series, OSANSA; Department of Defense, Office of Special Operations, to OCB, 14 September 1960, #28 Military (4) folder, box 8, Sprague Committee.

43 Lansdale to Waldemar Nielson, Executive Director of Sprague Committee, 8 July 1960, #28 Military (8) folder, box 8, Sprague Committee; Barber and Ronning, *Internal Security and Military Power,* 58–76, 147–49; Schoultz, *Human Rights,* 217–21.

44 SCFR, *Executive Sessions, 1961,* 13:579–80. By the early 1960s, military officers in seven Latin American countries had overthrown popularly elected governments; counterinsurgency units, trained by the United States, participated in these *golpes* (see Lieuwen, *Generals vs. Presidents,* 124–29).

45 Memorandum of conversation between Herter and Fulbright, 7 April 1960, 3–6/60 (3) folder, box 12, Telephone series, Herter papers. See also State Department

briefing memorandum for president on visit of President Lleras Camargo to United States, 31 March 1960, Colombia (2) folder, box 7, International series, Whitman.

46 "General Considerations" section of Statement of U.S. Policy toward Latin America (draft), 15 November 1960, U.S. Policy toward Latin America (1) folder, box 12, Briefing Notes subseries, NSC series, OSANSA.

47 Eisenhower, *Waging Peace*, 539; Charles C. Alexander, *Holding the Line*, 262; Kaufman, *Trade and Aid*, 209.

48 Milton Eisenhower, *The Wine Is Bitter*, 323; Barber and Ronning, *Internal Security and Military Power*, 73; Morris, *CIA and American Labor*, 78–79.

49 Wagner, *United States Policy toward Latin America*, 41.

50 Historian Walter LaFeber suggests that Eisenhower would not have formulated a comprehensive economic aid program for Latin America (*Inevitable Revolutions*, 136–44). LaFeber bases his analysis on the actions and views expressed by Eisenhower and his advisors, such as Thomas Mann, in 1958–59; he does not, however, carry his analysis through 1960, the year of change in Eisenhower's approach to Latin America.

51 Herter to Eisenhower, 6 January 1961, 1/61 folder, box 11, Dulles-Herter series, Whitman; in this letter, Herter submitted his resignation, summarized Eisenhower's foreign policy, and outlined the challenges ahead. See also Statement of U.S. Policy toward Latin America (draft), 15 November 1960, U.S. Policy toward Latin America (1) folder, box 12, Briefing Notes subseries, NSC series, OSANSA.

52 Oral history of Mann, pp. 2–30. See also Zoumaras, "Containing Castro," 181.

53 Packenham, *Liberal America and the Third World*, 34–35, 111–60; Kaufman, *Trade and Aid*, 98, 115. For the political ideas of Latin American intellectuals and reformers, see Ameringer, *Democratic Left in Exile*, 20–21.

54 Fulbright and Hickenlooper quoted in SCFR, *Executive Sessions, 1960*, 12:697–98; memorandum of conversation between President Eisenhower and Hickenlooper in memorandum for Ann Whitman from Ed McCabe, 13 September 1960, folder 5, OF-116-J (Latin America), WHOF.

55 President Kennedy's frequently cited remark about U.S. policy toward the Dominican Republic, in the aftermath of the assassination of Rafael Trujillo, is particularly revealing. Kennedy said: "There are three possibilities in descending order of preference: a decent democratic regime, a continuation of the Trujillo regime, or a Castro regime. We ought to aim at the first, but we really can't renounce the second until we are sure that we can avoid the third" (Schlesinger, *A Thousand Days*, 641). For the policy of the Johnson administration and the so-called Mann Doctrine, see Baily, *United States and the Development of South America*, 105–9.

CHAPTER 9

1 Langley, *Banana Wars*, 141–54; Atkins and Wilson, *United States and the Trujillo Regime*, 36–52; Briefing Folder on Dominican Republic, 3 February 1955, box 1, series 361, Nixon papers.

2 Ameringer, *Democratic Left in Exile*, 167–74; Atkins and Wilson, *United States and the Trujillo Regime*, 69–74; Diederich, *Trujillo: The Death of the Goat*, 14–19; Wiarda, *Dictatorship and Development*, 147–70.

3 Charles Porter to Secretary of State Dulles, 13 March 1957, Dominican Republic,

1957–59 folder, box 15, Porter papers; *Congressional Record* 103 (28 February 1957): 2815–23; ibid., 103 (15 July 1957): 11754–57; Porter, "Butcher of the Caribbean," 50–66. For a widely read *Life* article on the Galíndez-Murphy case, see "Story of a Dark International Conspiracy," 24–31.

4 Charles Porter to Morse, 29 March 1957, Latin America, 1957 folder, box 75, series A, Morse papers; SCFR, *Nomination of Roy R. Rubottom*, 1–28; SCFR, *Executive Sessions, 1959*, 11:519–37, 606–26.

5 Atkins and Wilson, *United States and the Trujillo Regime*, 90–94.

6 Memorandum of conversation between Eisenhower and Herter, 15 February 1960, Staff Notes, 2/60 (1) folder, box 47, DDE Diaries, Whitman.

7 Current Intelligence Weekly Summary, 31 March 1960, and Intelligence Bulletin, 2 April 1960, both in Cuban Situations, 1959–60 (1) folder, box 6, Briefing Notes subseries, NSC series, OSANSA; memorandum of conversation between Eisenhower, Herter, and Dillon, 10 June 1960, 6/60 (2) folder, box 50, DDE Diaries, Whitman; CIA estimates of Communist party membership in the Dominican Republic in Senate Judiciary Committee, *Communist Threat to the United States through the Caribbean*, 165.

8 State Department paper, "Proposed Plan," on Dominican Republic, 14 April 1960, Intelligence Matters (14) folder, box 15, Administrative subseries, Subject series, OSS.

9 Memorandum of conversation between Eisenhower, Herter, and Dillon, 5 July 1960, 6–7/60 (3) folder, box 4, State Department subseries, Subject series, OSS.

10 Memorandum for president, "Possible Action to Prevent Castroist Takeover of Dominican Republic," with enclosure, "Proposed Plan," 14 April 1960, Intelligence Matters (13 & 14) folder, box 15, Administrative subseries, Subject series, OSS; Church Committee, *Alleged Assassination Plots*, 192.

11 Senator Smathers to Trujillo, 7 April 1960, 5/60 (3) folder, box 10, Dulles-Herter series, Whitman; General Clark to Eisenhower, "U.S. Plan for Trujillo's Retirement," 14 April 1960, 4/60 (1) folder, box 49, DDE Diaries, Whitman; memorandum of conversation between Eisenhower, Herter, and Clark, 25 April 1960, Intelligence Matters (14) folder, box 15, Administrative subseries, Subject series, OSS; Herter to Andrew Goodpaster on Clark plan, 22 April 1960, 3–6/60 (2) folder, box 12, Telephone series, Herter papers; Dillon to Eisenhower, 12 May 1960, and memorandum of conversation between Dillon, Smathers, and Pawley, 16 May 1960, both in Dominican Republic folder, box 4, International series, OSS.

12 Oral history of Pawley, pp. 33–34.

13 Rabe, *Road to OPEC*, 141–42.

14 Ameringer, *Democratic Left in Exile*, 266–67; Atkins and Wilson, *United States and the Trujillo Regime*, 76–77; Espaillant, *Trujillo: The Last Caesar*, 75; memorandum of conversation between Eisenhower and Herter, 30 August 1960, State Department 8–9/60 (2) folder, box 4, State Department subseries, Subject series, OSS. The legislators identified by Eisenhower and Herter were Representative Harold Cooley, Democrat of North Carolina, and Senator Allen Ellender, Democrat of Louisiana; Cooley was chair of the House Agricultural Committee, the body that allocated a sugar import quota to the Dominican Republic.

15 Memorandum of conference with the president, 13 May 1960, State Department 3–5/60 (6) folder, box 4, State Department subseries, Subject series, OSS; General Goodpaster transcribed the conversation on 16 May 1960.

16 Church Committee, *Alleged Assassination Plots*, 192–93.

17 Ibid., 193–94. In affidavits submitted to the Church Committee, both Rubottom and King stated that they did not recall discussing any proposal for supplying sniper rifles (see footnote no. 1 in ibid., 193). But, as indicated in the text of the report, the Church Committee reviewed both King's handwritten notes and his subsequent memorandum about the June meeting.

18 Atkins and Wilson, *United States and the Trujillo Regime*, 30–36; Calder, *Impact of Intervention*, 115–82; Wiarda, *Dictatorship and Development*, 42–60. Arturo Espaillant, a former chief of Trujillo's military intelligence service, argued that weapons could be obtained in the Dominican Republic from military bases; he noted that weapons from the CIA for dissidents were for "psychological" support (*Trujillo: The Last Caesar*, 11).

19 Church Committee, *Alleged Assassination Plots*, 195.

20 Ibid., 194.

21 Slater, *OAS and United States Foreign Policy*, 190–91; Dreier, *Organization of American States*, 99–100; Atkins and Wilson, *United States and the Trujillo Regime*, 116–19.

22 Herter to Eisenhower, 18 August 1960, 8/60 (2) folder, box 11, Dulles-Herter series, Whitman. In a 19 August 1960 reply to Herter, Eisenhower heartily approved of Herter's tactics.

23 Dreier, *Organization of American States*, 99–100; Slater, *OAS and United States Foreign Policy*, 192; Herter to Eisenhower, 22 August 1960, 8/60 (2) folder, box 11, Dulles-Herter series, Whitman.

24 Telephone calls between Herter and Dulles, 19 August 1960, 7/1–8/31/60 folder, box 13, Telephone series, Herter papers.

25 Memorandum of conversation with legislative leaders, 23 August 1960, Legislative Leaders, 1960 (4) folder, box 3, Legislative Leaders series, Whitman; memorandum of conversation between Eisenhower and Herter, 30 August 1960, State Department 8–9/60 (2) folder, box 4, State Department subseries, Subject series, OSS; Eisenhower, *Waging Peace*, 535.

26 Church Committee, *Alleged Assassination Plots*, 194–215.

27 Memorandum of conversation between Dillon and Eisenhower, 13 October 1960, Staff Notes, 10/60 (1) folder, box 53, DDE Diaries, Whitman; Eisenhower, *Waging Peace*, 535.

28 Memorandum of telephone conversation between Herter and Dulles, 8 September 1960, 9/60–1/61 (3) folder, box 13, Telephone series, Herter papers; memorandum of conversation between Eisenhower, Dillon, and Assistant Secretary Thomas Mann, 17 October 1960, Staff Notes, 10/60 (1) folder, box 53, DDE Diaries, Whitman; memorandum of conversation between Herter and Mann, 26 October 1960, 9/60–1/61 (2) folder, box 13, Telephone series, Herter papers. In these memorandums of conversation, the name of the emissary is exempted from declassification, but from the context of the conversations, it seems reasonable to conclude that Pawley was sent to Ciudad Trujillo.

29 State Department to Eisenhower, with messages from Dominican dissidents and from Henry Dearborn, Consul General in Dominican Republic, 9 September 1960, Dominican Republic folder, box 4, International series, OSS.

30 Memorandum of conversation between Eisenhower and Marcos Falcón Briceño, Foreign Minister of Venezuela, 3 November 1960, Venezuela (1) folder, box 50, In-

ternational series, Whitman; Herter to Eisenhower, 8 December 1960, 12/60 (2) folder, box 11, Dulles-Herter series, Whitman.

31 Willauer to Undersecretary of State for Political Affairs Livingston Merchant, "The Interconnection of the Cuban and Dominican Problems Politically," 18 January 1961, 1960 Meetings with President, vol. 2 (2) folder, box 5, Presidential subseries, Special Assistants series, OSANSA.

32 Herter to Eisenhower, 8 December 1960, 12/60 (2) folder, box 11, Dulles-Herter series, Whitman; Slater, *OAS and United States Foreign Policy*, 194. The U.S. proposal carried by a vote of 14–1–6; the Dominican Republic opposed the motion, and Argentina, Brazil, Guatemala, Haiti, Paraguay, and Uruguay abstained.

33 Memorandum of conversation between Eisenhower, Gordon Gray, and others, 3 January 1961, 1960 Meetings with President, vol. 2 (2) folder, box 5, Presidential subseries, Special Assistants series, OSANSA; Gray transcribed the conversation on 9 January 1961.

34 Church Committee, *Alleged Assassination Plots*, 196–200. Documentary evidence is lacking to prove that members of the 5412 Committee, except for Allen Dulles, understood that the Dominicans wanted weapons for assassination purposes. In considering the matter, the 5412 Committee discussed Assistant Secretary of State Thomas Mann's recommendation to supply the dissidents with "small explosive arms" for sabotage potential. But Mann did not believe such a minor measure would topple the Trujillo government. Mann, who succeeded Rubottom as assistant secretary of state for Latin American Affairs, later denied any knowledge of assassination plots against Trujillo: see oral history of Mann, p. 85. See also Diederich, *Trujillo: The Death of the Goat*, 40–56, 82–96.

35 Gall, "How Trujillo Died," 19–20; Diederich, *Trujillo: The Death of the Goat*, 97–120; Church Committee, *Alleged Assassination Plots*, 200, 213. The one surviving member of the "action element," Antonio Imbert, denied that the assassins had been armed by the CIA (*New York Times*, 23 June 1975, 17). Historian Howard Wiarda, in his discussion of the literature on the death of Trujillo, notes that for nationalistic reasons Dominicans have wanted to play down any assistance from the United States (*Dictatorship and Development*, 172–73). For a discussion of the role of the Kennedy administration in the Trujillo assassination, see Church Committee, *Alleged Assassination Plots*, 209–15, 262–63.

36 *Operation Zapata*, 3–5; Eisenhower, *Waging Peace*, 534; Phillips, *Night Watch*, 90–91.

37 Immerman, *CIA in Guatemala*, 187–97.

38 Rabe, "The Johnson (Eisenhower?) Doctrine," 95–100.

39 Welch, *Response to Revolution*, 48–63; memorandum of conversation between Eisenhower, Dillon, and others, 13 October 1960, Staff Notes, 10/60 (1) folder, box 53, DDE Diaries, Whitman.

40 Eisenhower quoted on 6 July 1960 in Ferrell, *Eisenhower Diaries*, 379; memorandum of conversation between Eisenhower and State Department officials, 6 July 1960, Staff Notes, 7/60 folder, box 51, DDE Diaries, Whitman.

41 Dulles quoted in *Operation Zapata*, 58–59.

42 Bonsal, *Cuba, Castro, and the United States*, 148–55; Rubottom quoted in memorandum of conversation with Herbert Matthews in Matthews's report to editors of *New York Times*, 17 August 1960, Memorandums folder, box 2, Matthews papers; Herter quoted in memorandum of conversation with Gordon Gray, 1 July 1960, 7–

8/60 folder, box 13, Telephone series, Herter papers; Eisenhower quoted in memorandum of conversation by Gray, 12 July 1960, Meetings with President, vol. 2 (2) folder, box 5, Presidential subseries, Special Assistants series, OSANSA.

43 Gray quoted in memorandum of conversation by Gray, 12 July 1960, Meetings with President, vol. 2 (2) folder, box 5, Presidential subseries, Special Assistants series, OSANSA.

44 See, for example, Eisenhower's 24 August 1960 news conference statement in General Services Administration, *Public Papers of the Presidents: Dwight D. Eisenhower, 1960–1961*, 268.

45 Herter to U.S. Embassies in Latin America, 28 July 1960, Cuba (4) folder, box 4, International series, OSS.

46 Herter to Eisenhower on Cuba and OAS, 23 April 1960, 4/60 (1) folder, box 10, Dulles-Herter series, Whitman; Herter to Eisenhower on Cuba and OAS, 30 June 1960, 6/60 folder, box 10, Dulles-Herter series, Whitman.

47 Eisenhower quoted in Kaufman, *Trade and Aid*, 205; memorandum of conversation between Eisenhower and Dillon on Mexico, 15 October 1960, Staff Notes, 10/60 (1), box 53, DDE Diaries, Whitman.

48 Record of Action No. 2191, 10 March 1960, 436th Meeting of NSC, Records of Action by NSC, 1960 (1) folder, box 3, NSC series, Whitman.

49 Herter to Eisenhower on Cuba and OAS, 30 June 1960, 6/60 folder, box 10, Dulles-Herter series, Whitman; Herter conversation with Nelson Rockefeller on San José Conference, 3 August 1960, 7–8/60 (1) folder, box 13, Telephone series, Herter papers.

50 Slater, *OAS and United States Foreign Policy*, 143–49; Herter to Dillon, 20 August 1960, and Herter to Undersecretary Livingston Merchant, 27 August 1960, both in 7–8/60 (1) folder, box 13, Telephone series, Herter papers.

51 Milton Eisenhower, *The Wine Is Bitter*, 262–64.

52 Memorandum of telephone conversation between Eisenhower and Herter, 25 August 1960, 8/60 (2) folder, box 11, Dulles-Herter series, Whitman; memorandum for record by General Goodpaster of conversation between Eisenhower and Herter on San José, 29 August 1960, Cuba (5) folder, box 4, International series, OSS.

53 Church Committee, *Alleged Assassination Plots*, 71–72.

54 Ibid., 72–82; Ambrose, *Ike's Spies*, 293–306.

55 Church Committee, *Alleged Assassination Plots*, 91–99.

56 Ibid., 51–52; Oral History (1976) of Richard Bissell, pp. 19–23; Kalb, *The Congo Cables*, 46–196. For Eisenhower's relationship with the 5412 Committee, see Ambrose, *Eisenhower: The President*, 506–7.

57 Church Committee, *Alleged Assassination Plots*, 109–11.

58 Ibid., 111–14. The uncertainty that surrounds the issue of Eisenhower's knowledge of assassination plots is revealed in the conflicting interpretations offered by Stephen Ambrose, Eisenhower's preeminent biographer. In his 1981 study, Ambrose wrote that "it is highly unlikely, almost unbelievable," that Allen Dulles would have approved assassination plots "unless he was certain he was acting in accord with the President's wishes" (*Ike's Spies*, 306). But he modified that observation in his 1984 study: noting that he had seen no documentary evidence directly linking Eisenhower with assassination attempts, Ambrose asserted that the president "could have given such orders verbally and privately to Dulles, but if he did he acted out of character" (*Eisenhower: The President*, 557).

59 *Operation Zapata*, 5–6; the views of Dulles on the Cuban exile community are in memorandum of conversation between Eisenhower and his national security advisors, 29 November 1960, 1960 Meetings with the President, vol. 2 (2) folder, box 5, Presidential subseries, Special Assistants series, OSANSA.

60 Eisenhower quoted in Wyden, *Bay of Pigs*, 31, 68.

61 Beck, "Necessary Lies, Hidden Truths," 37–59; Herter to Eisenhower on recall of Ambassador Bonsal, 16 October 1960, 10/60 (1) folder, box 11, Dulles-Herter series, Whitman; memorandum on conversation between Eisenhower, Dillon, and Mann, 17 October 1960, Staff Notes, 10/60 (1) folder, box 53, DDE Diaries, Whitman.

62 Memorandum of conversation between Eisenhower and Dillon on El Salvador, 11 November 1960, Staff Notes, 12/60 folder, box 55, DDE Diaries, Whitman; Herter to Eisenhower on Guatemala, 16 November 1960, 11/60 folder, box 11, Dulles-Herter series, Whitman. In part, the military uprising in Guatemala was a protest against the training of Cuban exiles in Guatemala.

63 Memorandum of conversation between Eisenhower and his national security advisors, 29 November 1960, 1960 Meetings with the President, vol. 2 (2) folder, box 5, Presidential subseries, Special Assistants series, OSANSA.

64 *Operation Zapata*, 6–7, 58–59.

65 Memorandums of conversation between Eisenhower and his national security advisors, 29 November 1960 and 3 January 1961, both in 1960 Meetings with the President, vol. 2 (2) folder, box 5, Presidential subseries, Special Assistants series, OSANSA; memorandum, "Cuba and Latin America," in account of 6 December 1960 meeting between Eisenhower and Kennedy, 12/60 folder, box 11, Whitman Diary, Whitman.

66 Eisenhower quoted in Wyden, *Bay of Pigs*, 88; Ambrose, *Eisenhower: The President*, 614–16.

67 Dulles quoted in Schlesinger, *A Thousand Days*, 242; Bissell cited in Ambrose, *Ike's Spies*, 315.

68 Memorandum of conversation between Eisenhower and national security advisors, 3 January 1961, 1960 Meetings with the President, vol. 2 (2) folder, box 5, Presidential subseries, Special Assistants series, OSANSA; "Report of Military Buildup in Cuba" (n.d., but probably December 1960), Cuba (6) folder, box 4, International series, OSS.

69 Eisenhower and Herter quoted in memorandum of conversation between Eisenhower and national security advisors, 3 January 1961, 1960 Meetings with the President, vol. 2 (2) folder, box 5, Presidential subseries, Special Assistants series, OSANSA; Eisenhower also quoted in telephone conversation with Herter, 3 January 1961, Presidential Telephone Calls, 7/60–1/61 folder, box 10, Telephone series, Herter papers; Herter to Eisenhower on Trading with the Enemy Act, 5 January 1961, 1/61 folder, box 11, Dulles-Herter series, Whitman.

70 Eisenhower quoted in Greenstein, *Hidden-Hand Presidency*, 133. See also Saunders, "Military Force in the Foreign Policy of the Eisenhower Presidency," 111–16.

71 During the last days of the Eisenhower administration, questions were being raised about the soundness of the invasion plan: see, for example, Whiting Willauer to Livingston Merchant, 18 January 1961, 1960 Meetings with the President, vol. 2 (2) folder, box 5, Presidential subseries, Special Assistants series, OSANSA;

Willauer reported that representatives of the CIA, State Department, and Department of Defense had reviewed the invasion plan and concluded that it "might not succeed."

72 Eisenhower quoted in memorandum of discussion with Undersecretary Merchant, 29 December 1960, Staff Notes, 12/60 folder, box 55, DDE Diaries, Whitman.

73 Immerman, *CIA in Guatemala*, 196. In reviewing the *Bay of Pigs* disaster, CIA officials admitted that Castro's forces had fought with unexpected dedication and skill; see *Operation Zapata*, 98.

74 In a recent study, Lucien S. Vandenbroucke, who reviewed the private papers of Allen Dulles, argues that Dulles realized that the invasion plan had serious flaws but believed that once the operation began President Kennedy would provide overt U.S. support to the exiles; Dulles made this assumption because Eisenhower had provided U.S. planes during the Guatemalan operation in 1954, and he expected Kennedy to act as he assumed Eisenhower would have acted (Vandenbroucke, "'Confessions' of Allen Dulles," 365–75). For Richard Bissell's response to this thesis, see "Response to Lucien S. Vandenbroucke," 377–80; Bissell did not categorically reject Vandenbroucke's argument. See also Powers, *Man Who Kept the Secrets*, 117.

75 Diary entries, 22 April 1961 and 5 June 1961, in Ferrell, *Eisenhower Diaries*, 386–87, 390; Ambrose, *Eisenhower: The President*, 637–40.

CONCLUSION

1 For information on Operation Mongoose, see Church Committee, *Alleged Assassination Plots*, 134–89. For information on other U.S. interventions, see Parker, *Brazil and the Quiet Intervention*; Rabe, "The Johnson (Eisenhower?) Doctrine," 95–100; Church Committee, *Covert Action in Chile*.

2 Schoultz, *Human Rights*, 230–66.

BIBLIOGRAPHY

PRIMARY SOURCES

Private Papers

Berle, Adolf A., Jr. Franklin D. Roosevelt Library, Hyde Park, New York.
Bohan, Merwin L. Harry S Truman Library, Independence, Missouri.
Cabot, John Moors. University Publications of America, Frederick, Maryland.
Dulles, John Foster. Dwight D. Eisenhower Library, Abilene, Kansas.
Eisenhower, Dwight D. Ann Whitman File. Dwight D. Eisenhower Library, Abilene, Kansas.
Eisenhower, Milton S. Dwight D. Eisenhower Library, Abilene, Kansas.
Fulbright, James William. University of Arkansas Library, Fayetteville, Arkansas.
Herter, Christian A. Dwight D. Eisenhower Library, Abilene, Kansas.
Matthews, Herbert L. Butler Library, Columbia University, New York, New York.
Morse, Wayne L. University of Oregon Library, Eugene, Oregon.
Nixon, Richard M. Federal Archives Center, Laguna Niguel, California.
Porter, Charles O. University of Oregon Library, Eugene, Oregon.
Stimson, Henry L. Sterling Library, Yale University, New Haven, Connecticut.
Waugh, Samuel L. Dwight D. Eisenhower Library, Abilene, Kansas.

Unpublished Government Documents and Records

U.S. Council on Foreign Economic Policy. Dwight D. Eisenhower Library, Abilene, Kansas.
U.S. Department of State. Record Group 59. National Archives, Washington, D.C.
U.S. National Security Council. Record Group 273. National Archives, Washington, D.C.
U.S. National Security File. Lyndon Baines Johnson Library, Austin, Texas.
U.S. President's Citizen Advisers on the Mutual Security Program (Fairless Committee). Dwight D. Eisenhower Library, Abilene, Kansas.
U.S. President's Commission on Foreign Economic Policy. Dwight D. Eisenhower Library, Abilene, Kansas.
U.S. President's Committee on International Information Activities (Sprague Committee). Dwight D. Eisenhower Library, Abilene, Kansas.

U.S. President's Committee to Study the U.S. Military Assistance Program (Draper Committee). Dwight D. Eisenhower Library, Abilene, Kansas.

White House Central Files. Dwight D. Eisenhower Library, Abilene, Kansas.

White House Office of the Special Assistant for National Security Affairs. Dwight D. Eisenhower Library, Abilene, Kansas.

White House Office of the Staff Secretary. Dwight D. Eisenhower Library, Abilene, Kansas.

White House Official Files. Dwight D. Eisenhower Library, Abilene, Kansas.

Oral Histories

Bissell, Richard M., Jr. Dwight D. Eisenhower Library, Abilene, Kansas.

Briggs, Ellis O. Dwight D. Eisenhower Library, Abilene, Kansas.

Cabot, John Moors. John Foster Dulles Oral History Collection. Firestone Library, Princeton University, Princeton, New Jersey.

Colina, Rafael de la. John Foster Dulles Oral History Collection. Firestone Library, Princeton University, Princeton, New Jersey.

Dillon, C. Douglas. Columbia University Oral History Collection, New York, New York.

———. John Foster Dulles Oral History Collection. Firestone Library, Princeton University, Princeton, New Jersey.

Dreier, John C. John Foster Dulles Oral History Collection. Firestone Library, Princeton University, Princeton, New Jersey.

Eisenhower, Milton. Columbia University Oral History Collection, New York, New York.

———. Dwight D. Eisenhower Library, Abilene, Kansas.

Figueres, José. Harry S Truman Library, Independence, Missouri.

Hill, Robert C. Dwight D. Eisenhower Library, Abilene, Kansas.

Mann, Thomas C. Dwight D. Eisenhower Library, Abilene, Kansas.

Pawley, William. Herbert Hoover Library, West Branch, Iowa.

Prochnow, Herbert V. John Foster Dulles Oral History Collection. Firestone Library, Princeton University, Princeton, New Jersey.

Rubottom, Roy Richard. John Foster Dulles Oral History Collection. Firestone Library, Princeton University, Princeton, New Jersey.

Walters, Vernon. Dwight D. Eisenhower Library, Abilene, Kansas.

Published Government Documents and Records

Operation Zapata: The "Ultrasensitive" Report and Testimony of the Board of Inquiry on the Bay of Pigs. Introduction by Luis Aguilar. Frederick, Md.: University Publications of America, 1981.

U.N. Economic Commission for Latin America. Economic Survey of Latin America, 1953–1958. New York: U.N. Publishers, 1955–59.

U.S. Congress. Congressional Record 103 (28 February 1957): 2815–23.

———. Congressional Record 103 (15 July 1957): 11754–57.

U.S. Congress. House. Committee on Foreign Affairs. Hearings on the Mutual Security Acts, 1953–1954. 83rd Cong., 1st and 2nd sess. Washington: Government Printing Office, 1953–54.

_____. _A Review of the Relations of the United States and Other American Republics._ 85th Cong., 2nd sess. Washington: Government Printing Office, 1958.

_____. _Selected Executive Session Hearings of the Committee, 1951–1956._ Vol. 16: _Middle East, Africa, and Inter-American Affairs._ Washington: Government Printing Office, 1980.

_____. Subcommittee on Inter-American Affairs. _Report on United States Relations with Latin America._ House Report No. 354. 86th Cong., 1st sess. Washington: Government Printing Office, 1959.

U.S. Congress. Senate. Committee on Foreign Relations. _Executive Sessions of the Senate Foreign Relations Committee (Historical Series), 1953–1961._ Washington: Government Printing Office, 1977–84.

_____. _Hearings on American Republics Cooperation Act._ 86th Cong., 2nd sess. Washington: Government Printing Office, 1960.

_____. _Hearings on the Mutual Security Acts, 1953–1960._ 83rd Cong., 1st sess., to 86th Cong., 2nd sess. Washington: Government Printing Office, 1953–60.

_____. _Latin America: Venezuela, Brazil, Peru, Bolivia, and Panama. A Report of Senator George Aiken._ 86th Cong., 2nd sess. Washington: Government Printing Office, 1960.

_____. _Nomination of John Foster Dulles, Secretary of State–Designate._ 83rd Cong., 1st sess. Washington: Government Printing Office, 1953.

_____. _Nomination of Roy R. Rubottom, Jr._ 85th Cong., 1st sess. Washington: Government Printing Office, 1957.

_____. _Senator Wayne Morse. Report on Study Trip to South America._ 86th Cong., 1st sess. Washington: Government Printing Office, 1960.

U.S. Congress. Senate. Committee on the Judiciary. _The Communist Threat to the United States through the Caribbean. Hearings before the Subcommmittee to Investigate the Administration of the Internal Security Act and Other Internal Security Laws._ 86th Cong., 2nd sess., to 87th Cong., 2nd sess. Washington: Government Printing Office, 1961–62.

U.S. Congress. Senate. Select Committee to Study Governmental Operations with Respect to Intelligence Activities. _Alleged Assassination Plots Involving Foreign Leaders._ Senate Report No. 465. 94th Cong., 1st sess. Washington: Government Printing Office, 1975.

_____. _Covert Action in Chile, 1963–1973, Staff Report._ 94th Cong., 1st sess. Washington: Government Printing Office, 1975.

U.S. Department of Commerce. _Survey of Current Business, 1953–1961._ Washington: Government Printing Office, 1953–61.

U.S. Department of State. _Department of State Bulletin, 1946–1961._ Washington: Government Printing Office, 1946–61.

_____. _Papers Relating to the Foreign Relations of the United States, 1861–1954._ Washington: Government Printing Office, 1861–1983.

_____. Agency for International Development. _U.S. Overseas Loans and Grants, 1945–1975._ Washington: Government Printing Office, 1976.

_____. Office of Public Affairs. _Military Assistance to Latin America._ Washington: Government Printing Office, 1953.

U.S. Export-Import Bank. _Semiannual Report to Congress: 1 January 1953 to 31 December 1960._ Washington: Government Printing Office, 1953–61.

U.S. General Services Administration. _Public Papers of the Presidents: Dwight D. Ei-_

senhower, *1953–1961*. 8 vols. Washington: Government Printing Office, 1958–61.
U.S. President's Citizen Advisers on the Mutual Security Program. *Report to the President*. Washington: Government Printing Office, 1957.
U.S. President's Committee to Study the United States Military Assistance Program. *Composite Report*. Washington: Government Printing Office, 1959.
————. *Supplement to the Composite Report: Annexes*. Washington: Government Printing Office, 1959.

Autobiographies, Memoirs, Published Papers

Acheson, Dean. *Present at the Creation*. New York: W. W. Norton, 1969.
Agee, Philip. *Inside the Company: CIA Diary*. New York: Stonehill Publishing, 1975.
Andrade, Víctor. *My Missions for Revolutionary Bolivia, 1944–1962*. Edited and with an introduction by Cole Blasier. Pittsburgh: University of Pittsburgh Press, 1976.
Arévalo, Juan José. *The Shark and the Sardines*. New York: Lyle Stuart, 1961.
Betancourt, Rómulo. *Venezuela: Oil and Politics*. Boston: Houghton Mifflin, 1979.
Bonsal, Philip. *Cuba, Castro, and the United States*. Pittsburgh: University of Pittsburgh Press, 1971.
Braden, Spruille. *Diplomats and Demagogues: The Memoirs of Spruille Braden*. New Rochelle, N.Y.: Arlington House, 1971.
Briggs, Ellis O. *Farewell to Foggy Bottom: The Recollections of a Career Diplomat*. New York: David McKay, 1964.
Dulles, Allen. *The Craft of Intelligence*. New York: Harper & Row, 1963.
Eisenhower, Dwight D. *Mandate for Change, 1953–1956*. Garden City, N.Y.: Doubleday, 1963.
————. *Waging Peace, 1956–1961*. Garden City, N.Y.: Doubleday, 1965.
Eisenhower, Milton S. *The Wine Is Bitter*. Garden City, N.Y.: Doubleday, 1963.
Ferrell, Robert, ed. *The Diary of James C. Hagerty*. Bloomington: Indiana University Press, 1983.
————. *The Eisenhower Diaries*. New York: W. W. Norton, 1981.
Griffith, Robert, ed. *Ike's Letters to a Friend, 1941–1958*. Lawrence: University Press of Kansas, 1984.
Hilsman, Roger. *To Move a Nation: The Politics of Foreign Policy in the Administration of John F. Kennedy*. Garden City, N.Y.: Doubleday, 1967.
Kennan, George F. *Memoirs, 1925–1950*. New York: Bantam, 1969.
Nixon, Richard M. *Six Crises*. Garden City, N.Y.: Doubleday, 1962.
Phillips, David Atlee. *The Night Watch*. New York: Atheneum, 1977.
Romualdi, Serafino. *Presidents and Peons: Recollections of a Labor Ambassador in Latin America*. New York: Funk and Wagnalls, 1967.
Roosevelt, Kermit. *Countercoup: The Struggle for the Control of Iran*. New York: McGraw-Hill, 1979.
Schlesinger, Arthur M., Jr. *A Thousand Days: John F. Kennedy in the White House*. Boston: Houghton Mifflin, 1965.
Smith, Earl E. T. *The Fourth Floor: An Account of the Castro Communist Revolution*. New York: Random House, 1962.
Smith, Joseph Burkholder. *Portrait of a Cold Warrior*. New York: G. P. Putnam's Sons, 1976.
Sorensen, Theodore C. *Kennedy*. New York: Harper & Row, 1965.

Newspaper

New York Times

SECONDARY SOURCES

Books

Adams, Richard Newbold. *Crucifixion by Power: Essays on Guatemalan National Social Structure, 1944–1966*. Austin: University of Texas Press, 1970.

Alexander, Charles C. *Holding the Line: The Eisenhower Era, 1952–1961*. Bloomington: Indiana University Press, 1975.

Alexander, Robert J. *The Bolivian National Revolution*. New Brunswick, N.J.: Rutgers University Press, 1958.

_____. *Rómulo Betancourt and the Transformation of Venezuela*. New Brunswick, N.J.: Transaction Books, 1982.

Allen, Robert Loring. *Soviet Influence in Latin America: The Role of Economic Relations*. Washington: Public Affairs Press, 1959.

Ambrose, Stephen E. *Eisenhower: Soldier, General of the Army, President-Elect, 1890–1952*. New York: Simon and Schuster, 1983.

_____. *Eisenhower: The President*. New York: Simon and Schuster, 1984.

Ambrose, Stephen E., with Richard H. Immerman. *Ike's Spies: Eisenhower and the Espionage Establishment*. Garden City, N.Y.: Doubleday, 1981.

Ameringer, Charles D. *The Democratic Left in Exile: The Antidictatorial Struggle in the Caribbean, 1945–1959*. Coral Gables: University of Miami Press, 1974.

Atkins, G. Pope, and Larman C. Wilson. *The United States and the Trujillo Regime*. New Brunswick, N.J.: Rutgers University Press, 1972.

Baily, Samuel. *The United States and the Development of South America, 1945–1975*. New York: New Viewpoints, 1976.

Barber, Hollis W. *The United States in World Affairs, 1955*. New York: Harper & Bros., 1956.

Barber, Willard F., and C. Neale Ronning. *Internal Security and Military Power: Counterinsurgency and Civic Action in Latin America*. Columbus: Ohio State University Press, 1966.

Bemis, Samuel Flagg. *The Latin American Policy of the United States*. New York: Harcourt, Brace, 1943.

Benjamin, Jules R. *The United States and Cuba: Hegemony and Dependent Development, 1880–1934*. Pittsburgh: University of Pittsburgh Press, 1977.

Blasier, Cole. *The Giant's Rival: The USSR and Latin America*. Pittsburgh: University of Pittsburgh Press, 1983.

_____. *The Hovering Giant: U.S. Responses to Revolutionary Change in Latin America*. Pittsburgh: University of Pittsburgh Press, 1976.

Bushnell, David. *Eduardo Santos and the Good Neighbor, 1938–1942*. Gainesville: University of Florida Press, 1967.

Calder, Bruce J. *The Impact of Intervention: The Dominican Republic during the U.S. Occupation, 1916–1924*. Austin: University of Texas Press, 1984.

Child, John. *Unequal Alliance: The Inter-American Military System, 1938–1978*. Boulder, Colo.: Westview Press, 1980.

Childs, Marquis. *Eisenhower, Captive Hero: A Critical Study of the General and the President.* New York: Harcourt, Brace, Jovanovich, 1958.

Connell-Smith, Gordon. *The United States and Latin America.* New York: John Wiley, 1974.

Cook, Blanche Wiesen. *The Declassified Eisenhower: A Divided Legacy.* Garden City, N.Y.: Doubleday, 1981.

————. *Dwight David Eisenhower: Antimilitarist in the White House.* St. Charles, Mo.: Forum Press, 1974.

Curry, E. R. *Hoover's Dominican Diplomacy and the Origins of the Good Neighbor Policy.* New York: Garland Publishing, 1979.

DeConde, Alexander. *Herbert Hoover's Latin American Policy.* Stanford: Stanford University Press, 1951.

Dell, Sidney. *The Inter-American Development Bank: A Study in Development Financing.* New York: Praeger, 1972.

Diederich, Bernard. *Trujillo: The Death of the Goat.* Boston: Little, Brown & Co., 1978.

Divine, Robert A. *Blowing on the Wind: The Nuclear Test Ban Debate, 1954–1960.* New York: Oxford University Press, 1978.

————. *Eisenhower and the Cold War.* New York: Oxford University Press, 1981.

Domínguez, Jorge. *Cuba: Order and Revolution.* Cambridge: Belknap Press of Harvard University, 1978.

Draper, Theodore. *Castro's Revolution: Myths and Realities.* New York: Praeger, 1962.

Dreier, John C. *The Organization of American States and the Hemispheric Crisis.* New York: Harper & Row, 1962.

Duggan, Laurence. *The Americas: The Search for Hemispheric Security.* New York: Henry Holt, 1949.

Eder, George Jackson. *Inflation and Development in Latin America: A Case History of Inflation and Stabilization in Bolivia.* Ann Arbor: University of Michigan Press, 1968.

Espaillant, Arturo R. *Trujillo: The Last Caesar.* Chicago: Henry Regency Co., 1963.

Ewell, Judith. *The Indictment of a Dictator: The Extradition and Trial of Marcos Pérez Jiménez.* College Station: Texas A&M Press, 1981.

Francis, Michael J. *The Limits of Hegemony: United States Relations with Argentina and Chile during World War II.* Notre Dame: University of Notre Dame Press, 1977.

Furtado, Celso. *Economic Development of Latin America.* London: Cambridge University Press, 1970.

Gellman, Irwin F. *Good Neighbor Diplomacy: United States Policies in Latin America, 1933–1945.* Baltimore: Johns Hopkins University Press, 1979.

————. *Roosevelt and Batista: Good Neighbor Diplomacy in Cuba, 1933–1945.* Albuquerque: University of New Mexico Press, 1973.

Gerson, Louis L. *John Foster Dulles.* New York: Cooper Square, 1967.

Gil, Federico G. *Latin American–United States Relations.* New York: Harcourt, Brace, Jovanovich, 1971.

Graham, Richard. *Great Britain and the Onset of Modernization in Brazil.* London: Cambridge University Press, 1968.

Green, David. *The Containment of Latin America.* Chicago: Quadrangle, 1971.

Greenstein, Fred I. *The Hidden-Hand Presidency: Eisenhower as Leader*. New York: Basic Books, 1982.

Grieb, Kenneth J. *Guatemalan Caudillo: The Regime of Jorge Ubico*. Athens: Ohio University Press, 1979.

_____. *The Latin American Policy of Warren G. Harding*. Fort Worth: Texas Christian University Press, 1976.

Guerrant, Edward O. *Roosevelt's Good Neighbor Policy*. Albuquerque: University of New Mexico Press, 1950.

Guhin, Michael. *John Foster Dulles: A Statesman and His Times*. New York: Columbia University Press, 1972.

Haglund, David G. *Latin America and the Transformation of U.S. Strategic Thought, 1936–1940*. Albuquerque: University of New Mexico Press, 1984.

Hilton, Stanley E. *Hitler's Secret War in South America, 1939–1945*. Baton Rouge: Louisiana State University Press, 1981.

Hinckle, Warren, and William W. Turner. *The Fish Is Red: The Story of the Secret War Against Castro*. New York: Harper & Row, 1981.

Hoopes, Townsend. *The Devil and John Foster Dulles*. Boston: Little, Brown, 1973.

Hughes, John Emmet. *The Ordeal of Power: A Political Memoir of the Eisenhower Years*. New York: Atheneum, 1963.

Immerman, Richard H. *The CIA in Guatemala: The Foreign Policy of Intervention*. Austin: University of Texas Press, 1982.

James, Daniel. *Cuba: The First Soviet Satellite in the Americas*. New York: Avon Books, 1961.

Johnson, Loch K. *A Season of Inquiry: The Senate Intelligence Investigation*. Lexington: The University Press of Kentucky, 1985.

Kalb, Madeleine G. *The Congo Cables: The Cold War in Africa—From Eisenhower to Kennedy*. New York: Macmillan, 1982.

Kaufman, Burton I. *Trade and Aid: Eisenhower's Foreign Economic Policy, 1953–1961*. Baltimore: Johns Hopkins University Press, 1982.

Klein, Herbert S. *Bolivia: The Evolution of a Multi-Ethnic Society*. New York: Oxford University Press, 1982.

LaFeber, Walter. *Inevitable Revolutions: The United States in Central America*. New York: W. W. Norton, 1983.

_____. *The Panama Canal: The Crisis in Historical Perspective*. Expanded edition. New York: Oxford University Press, 1979.

Langley, Lester D. *The Banana Wars: An Inner History of American Empire, 1900–1934*. Lexington: University Press of Kentucky, 1983.

Leonard, Thomas M. *The United States and Central America, 1944–1949: Perceptions of Political Dynamics*. University, Ala.: University of Alabama Press, 1984.

Levinson, Jerome, and Juan de Onís. *The Alliance That Lost Its Way: A Critical Report on the Alliance for Progress*. Chicago: Quadrangle, 1970.

Lieuwen, Edwin. *Arms and Politics in Latin America*. New York: Praeger, 1960.

_____. *Generals vs. Presidents: Neo-Militarism in Latin America*. New York: Frederick A. Prager, 1964.

Liss, Sheldon B. *The Canal: Aspects of United States–Panamanian Relations*. Notre Dame: University of Notre Dame Press, 1967.

Lockwood, Lee. *Castro's Cuba, Cuba's Fidel*. New York: Vintage Edition of Random House, 1969.

Lyon, Peter. *Eisenhower: Portrait of a Hero.* Boston: Little, Brown, 1974.

McCann, Frank D., Jr. *The Brazilian-American Alliance, 1937–1945.* Princeton: Princeton University Press, 1973.

Malloy, James M. *Bolivia: The Uncompleted Revolution.* Pittsburgh: University of Pittsburgh Press, 1970.

May, Stacy, and Galo Plaza. *The United Fruit Company in Latin America.* Washington: National Planning Association, 1958.

Millett, Richard. *Guardians of the Dynasty: A History of the U.S. Created Guardia Nacional de Nicaragua and the Somoza Family.* Maryknoll, N.Y.: Orbis Books, 1977.

Morris, George. *CIA and American Labor: The Subversion of the AFL-CIO's Foreign Policy.* New York: International Publishers, 1967.

Ninkovich, Frank A. *The Diplomacy of Ideas: U.S. Foreign Policy and Cultural Relations, 1938–1950.* Cambridge: Cambridge University Press, 1981.

Noble, George B. *Christian A. Herter.* New York: Cooper Square, 1970.

Ortiz, Ricardo. *El ferrocarril en la economía argentina.* Buenos Aires: Editorial Catedra Lisandro de la Torre, 1958.

Packenham, Robert A. *Liberal America and the Third World: Political Development Ideas in Foreign Aid and Social Science.* Princeton: Princeton University Press, 1973.

Parker, Phyllis R. *Brazil and the Quiet Intervention, 1964.* Austin: University of Texas Press, 1979.

Parkinson, F. *Latin America, the Cold War, and the World Powers, 1945–1973.* Beverly Hills: Sage Publishers, 1974.

Parmet, Herbert S. *Eisenhower and the American Crusades.* New York: Macmillan, 1972.

Peterson, Harold F. *Argentina and the United States, 1810–1960.* New York: State University of New York Press, 1964.

Pike, Frederick B. *The United States and the Andean Republics: Peru, Bolivia, and Ecuador.* Cambridge: Harvard University Press, 1977.

Powers, Thomas. *The Man Who Kept the Secrets: Richard Helms and the CIA.* New York: Alfred D. Knopf, 1979.

Pruessen, Ronald W. *John Foster Dulles: The Road to Power.* New York: The Free Press, 1982.

Rabe, Stephen G. *The Road to OPEC: United States Relations with Venezuela, 1919–1976.* Austin: University of Texas Press, 1982.

Rock, David. *Argentina, 1516–1982: From Spanish Colonization to the Falklands War.* Berkeley: University of California Press, 1985.

Rostow, W. W. *Eisenhower, Kennedy, and Foreign Aid.* Austin: University of Texas Press, 1985.

Ruiz, Ramón Eduardo. *Cuba: The Making of a Revolution.* New York: W. W. Norton, 1970.

Scalabrini Ortiz, Raúl. *Política británica en el río de la Plata.* Buenos Aires: Editorial Reconquista, 1965.

Schlesinger, Stephen, and Stephen Kinzer. *Bitter Fruit: The Untold Story of the American Coup in Guatemala.* Garden City, N.Y.: Anchor Books, 1983.

Schmidt, Hans. *The United States Occupation of Haiti, 1915–1934.* New Brunswick, N.J.: Rutgers University Press, 1971.

Schmitt, Karl M. *Mexico and the United States: Conflict and Coexistence.* New York: John Wiley, 1973.

Schneider, Ronald M. *Communism in Guatemala, 1944–1954.* New York: Praeger, 1958.

Schoultz, Lars. *Human Rights and United States Policy toward Latin America.* Princeton: Princeton University Press, 1981.

Scobie, James R. *Argentina: A City and a Nation.* 2nd ed. New York: Oxford University Press, 1971.

Slater, Jerome. *The OAS and United States Foreign Policy.* Columbus: Ohio State University Press, 1967.

Solberg, Carl E. *Oil and Nationalism in Argentina.* Stanford: Stanford University Press, 1979.

Stebbins, Richard P. *The United States in World Affairs, 1950–1954, 1956–1960.* New York: Harper & Bros., 1951–55, 1957–61.

Steward, Dick. *Trade and Hemisphere: The Good Neighbor Policy and Reciprocal Trade.* Columbia: University of Missouri Press, 1975.

Suárez, Andrés. *Cuba: Castroism and Communism, 1959–1961.* Cambridge: Massachusetts Institute of Technology Press, 1967.

Szulc, Tad. *Twilight of the Tyrants.* New York: Henry Holt, 1959.

Thomas, Hugh. *Cuba: The Pursuit of Freedom.* New York: Harper & Row, 1971.

Vacs, Aldo César. *Discreet Partners: Argentina and the USSR since 1917.* Pittsburgh: University of Pittsburgh Press, 1984.

Wagner, R. Harrison. *United States Policy toward Latin America.* Stanford: Stanford University Press, 1970.

Welch, Richard E., Jr. *Response to Revolution: The United States and the Cuban Revolution, 1959–1961.* Chapel Hill: University of North Carolina Press, 1985.

Weyl, Nathaniel. *Red Star over Cuba: The Russian Assault on the Western Hemisphere.* New York: Devin-Adair, 1962.

Wiarda, Howard J. *Dictatorship and Development: The Methods of Control in Trujillo's Dominican Republic.* Gainesville: University of Florida Press, 1968.

Wilkie, James W. *The Bolivian Revolution and United States Aid since 1952.* Los Angeles: Latin American Center of University of California, Los Angeles, 1969.

Williams, William Appleman. *The United States, Cuba, and Castro: An Essay on the Dynamics of Revolution and the Dissolution of Empire.* New York: Monthly Review Press, 1962.

Wise, David, and Thomas B. Ross. *The Invisible Government.* New York: Random House, 1964.

Wood, Bryce. *The Dismantling of the Good Neighbor Policy.* Austin: University of Texas Press, 1985.

————. *The Making of the Good Neighbor Policy.* New York: Columbia University Press, 1961.

Woods, Randall Bennett. *The Roosevelt Foreign-Policy Establishment and the 'Good Neighbor': The United States and Argentina, 1941–1945.* Lawrence: Regents Press of Kansas, 1979.

Wyden, Peter. *Bay of Pigs: The Untold Story.* New York: Simon and Schuster, 1979.

Articles and Dissertations

Baer, Werner. "The Economics of Prebisch and ECLA." In *Latin America: Problems of Economic Development*, edited by Charles T. Nisbet, pp. 203–18. New York: Free Press, 1969.

Beck, Kent M. "Necessary Lies, Hidden Truths: Cuba in the 1960 Campaign." *Diplomatic History* 8 (Winter 1984): 37–59.

Beltrán, Pedro G. "Foreign Loans and Politics in Latin America." *Foreign Affairs* 34 (January 1956): 297–304.

Berle, Adolf A., Jr. "The Cuban Crisis." *Foreign Affairs* 39 (October 1960): 40–55.

―――. "To the South: A Continent of Problems." *New York Times Magazine*, 15 July 1956.

Bernstein, Barton. "Foreign Policy in the Eisenhower Administration." *Foreign Service Journal* 50 (May 1973): 17–20, 29–30, 38.

Bissell, Richard M., Jr. "Response to Lucien S. Vandenbroucke, The 'Confessions' of Allen Dulles: New Evidence on the Bay of Pigs." *Diplomatic History* 8 (Fall 1984): 377–80.

Blasier, Cole. "The Elimination of United States Influence." In *Revolutionary Change in Cuba*, edited by Carmelo Mesa-Lago, pp. 43–80. Pittsburgh: University of Pittsburgh Press, 1971.

―――. "The United States, Germany, and the Bolivian Revolutionaries." *Hispanic American Historical Review* 52 (February 1972): 26–54.

Desantis, Vincent P. "Eisenhower Revisionism." *Review of Politics* 38 (April 1978): 190–207.

Erb, Claude C. "Prelude to Point Four: The Institute of Inter-American Affairs." *Diplomatic History* 9 (Summer 1985): 249–69.

Feldman, David L. "Argentina, 1945–1971: Military Assistance, Military Spending, and the Political Activity of the Armed Forces." *Journal of Inter-American Studies & World Affairs* 24 (August 1982): 321–36.

Figueres, José. "The Problems of Democracy in Latin America." *Journal of International Affairs* 9 (May 1955): 11–21.

Flores, Antonio Carillo. "Mexico Forges Ahead." *Foreign Affairs* 36 (April 1958): 491–503.

Fossum, Egil. "Factors Influencing the Occurrence of Military Coups D'Etat in Latin America." *Journal of Peace Research* 3, no. 3 (1967): 228–51.

Francis, Michael J. "Military Aid to Latin America in the U.S. Congress." *Journal of Inter-American Studies* 6 (July 1964): 389–404.

Galíndez, Jesús de. "Anti-American Sentiment in Latin America." *Journal of International Affairs* 9 (May 1955): 24–32.

Gall, Norman. "How Trujillo Died." *New Republic* 148 (13 April 1960): 19–20.

Gillin, John, and K. H. Silvert. "Ambiguities in Guatemala." *Foreign Affairs* 34 (April 1956): 469–82.

Green, David. "The Cold War Comes to Latin America." In *Politics and Policies of the Eisenhower Administration*, edited by Barton Bernstein, pp. 149–95. Chicago: Quadrangle, 1970.

Griffith, Robert. "Dwight D. Eisenhower and the Corporate Commonwealth." *American Historical Review* 87 (February 1982): 87–122.

Haines, Gerald K. "Under the Eagle's Wing: The Franklin Roosevelt Administration Forges an American Hemisphere." *Diplomatic History* 1 (Fall 1977): 373–88.

Hartlyn, Jonathan. "Military Governments and the Transition to Civilian Rule: The Colombian Experience of 1957–1958." *Journal of Inter-American Studies & World Affairs* 16 (May 1984): 245–81.

Heston, Thomas J. "Cuba, the United States, and the Sugar Act of 1948: The Failure of Economic Coercion." *Diplomatic History* 6 (Winter 1982): 1–21.

Hilton, Stanley. "Brazilian Diplomacy and the Washington–Rio de Janeiro 'Axis' during the World War II Era." *Hispanic American Historical Review* 49 (May 1979): 201–31.

_____. "The United States, Brazil, and the Cold War, 1945–1960: End of the Special Relationship." *Journal of American History* 68 (December 1981): 599–624.

Hyman, Sidney. "Mr. Dillon and the Fight for Foreign Aid." *The Reporter* 18 (20 March 1958): 10–15.

Immerman, Richard H. "Diplomatic Dialings: John Foster Dulles Telephone Transcripts." *Newsletter of the Society for Historians of American Foreign Relations* 14 (March 1983): 1–15.

Joes, Anthony James. "Eisenhower Revisionism: The Tide Comes In." *Presidential Studies Quarterly* 15 (Summer 1985): 561–71.

Kane, N. Stephen. "Reassessing the Bureaucratic Dimensions of Foreign-Policy Making: A Case Study of the Cuban Sugar Quota Decision of 1954–1956." *Social Science Quarterly* 54 (March 1983): 46–65.

Kaplan, Stephen S. "U.S. Arms Transfers to Latin America, 1945–1974." *International Studies Quarterly* 19 (December 1975): 399–431.

Koppes, Clayton. "The Good Neighbor Policy and the Nationalization of Mexican Oil: A Reinterpretation." *Journal of American History* 69 (June 1982): 62–81.

Leffler, Melvyn P. "The American Conception of National Security and the Beginnings of the Cold War." *American Historical Review* 89 (April 1984): 346–81.

McAuliffe, Mary S. "Commentary / Eisenhower, the President." *Journal of American History* 68 (December 1981): 625–32.

McCann, Frank D. "Brazil, the United States, and World War II: A Commentary." *Diplomatic History* 3 (Winter 1979): 59–76.

McMahon, Robert J. "Eisenhower and Third World Nationalism: A Critique of the Revisionists." *Political Science Quarterly* 101, no. 3 (1986): 453–73.

Murray, Robert K., and Tim H. Blessing. "The Presidential Performance Study: A Progress Report." *Journal of American History* 70 (December 1983): 535–55.

Neal, Steve. "Why We Were Right to Like Ike." *American Heritage* 37 (December 1985): 49–65.

Nelson, Anna Kasten. "The 'Top of the Policy Hill': President Eisenhower and the National Security Council." *Diplomatic History* 7 (Fall 1983): 307–26.

Pach, Chester J., Jr. "The Containment of U.S. Military Aid to Latin America, 1944–1949." *Diplomatic History* 6 (Summer 1982): 225–43.

Pancake, Frank R. "Military Assistance as an Element of U.S. Foreign Policy in Latin America, 1950–1968." Ph.D. Dissertation, University of Virginia, 1969.

Patch, Richard W. "Bolivia: U.S. Assistance in a Revolutionary Setting." In *Social Change in Latin America Today*, edited by Council on Foreign Relations, pp. 108–76. New York: Harper & Bros., 1960.

Pickett, William B. "The Eisenhower Solarium Notes." *Newsletter of the Society for Historians of American Relations* 16 (June 1985): 1–10.

Porter, Charles O. (as told to Geoffrey Bocca). "The Butcher of the Caribbean." *Coronet* 42 (July 1957): 50–66.

Powell, John Duncan. "Military Assistance and Militarism in Latin America." *Western Political Quarterly* 18 (June 1965): 382–92.

Pulley, Raymond H. "The United States and the Trujillo Dictatorship, 1933–1940: The High Price of Caribbean Stability." *Caribbean Studies* 5 (October 1965): 22–31.

Rabe, Stephen G. "Eisenhower and Latin America: Arms and Dictators." *Peace and Change* 11 (Spring 1985): 49–61.

———. "Eisenhower and the Overthrow of Rafael Trujillo." *Conflict Quarterly* 6 (Winter 1986): 34–44.

———. "The Elusive Conference: United States Economic Relations with Latin America, 1945–1952." *Diplomatic History* 2 (Summer 1978): 279–94.

———. "Inter-American Military Cooperation, 1944–1951." *World Affairs* 137 (Fall 1974): 132–49.

———. "The Johnson (Eisenhower?) Doctrine for Latin America." *Diplomatic History* 9 (Winter 1985): 95–100.

Reichard, Gary W. "Eisenhower as President: The Changing View." *South Atlantic Quarterly* 77 (Summer 1978): 265–81.

Safford, Jeffrey J. "The Nixon-Castro Meeting of 19 April 1959." *Diplomatic History* 4 (Fall 1980): 425–31.

Santos, Eduardo. "Latin American Realities." *Foreign Affairs* 34 (January 1956): 245–57.

Saunders, Richard M. "Military Force in the Foreign Policy of the Eisenhower Presidency." *Political Science Quarterly* 100 (Spring 1985): 97–116.

Schlesinger, Arthur M., Jr. "The Ike Age Revisited." *Reviews in American History* 9 (March 1983): 1–11.

Sessions, Gene A. "The Clark Memorandum Myth." *The Americas* 34 (July 1977): 40–58.

Shannon, William V. "Eisenhower as President: A Critical Appraisal of the Record." *Commentary* 26 (November 1958): 390–98.

Smith, Robert Freeman. "The Good Neighbor Policy: The Liberal Paradox in United States Relations with Latin America." In *Watershed of Empire: Essays on New Deal Foreign Policy*, edited by Leonard P. Liggio and James J. Martin, pp. 65-94. Colorado Springs: Ralph Myles, 1976.

Snyder, J. Richard. "William S. Culbertson in Chile: Opening the Door to a Good Neighbor." *Inter-American Economic Affairs* 26 (Summer 1972): 25–46.

Soapes, Thomas F. "A Cold Warrior Seeks Peace: Eisenhower's Strategy for Nuclear Disarmament." *Diplomatic History* 4 (Winter 1980): 57–71.

Stinson, Hugh B., and James D. Cochrane. "The Movement for Regional Arms Control in Latin America." *Journal of Inter-American Studies* 13 (January 1971): 1–17.

"The Story of a Dark International Conspiracy." *Life* 42 (25 February 1957): 24–31.

Szulc, Tad. "Fidel Castro's Years as a Secret Communist." *New York Times Magazine*, 19 October 1986.

Tillapaugh, J. "Closed Hemisphere and Open World? The Dispute over Regional Security at the U.N. Conference, 1945." *Diplomatic History* 2 (Winter 1978): 25–42.

Tomasek, Robert D. "Defense of the Western Hemisphere: A Need for Reexamination of United States Policy." *Midwest Journal of Political Science* 3 (November 1959): 374–401.

Trask, Roger R. "George F. Kennan's Report on Latin America (1950)." *Diplomatic History* 2 (Summer 1978): 307–11.

_____. "The Impact of the Cold War on United States–Latin American Relations, 1945–1949." *Diplomatic History* 1 (Summer 1977): 271–84.

_____. "Spruille Braden versus George Messersmith: World War II, the Cold War, and Argentine Policy, 1945–1947." *Journal of Inter-American Studies & World Affairs* 26 (February 1984): 69–95.

Van Cleve, John V. "The Political Use of Military Aid: The United States and the Latin American Military, 1945–1965." Ph.D. Dissertation, University of California, Irvine, 1976.

Vandenbroucke, Lucien S. "The 'Confessions' of Allen Dulles: New Evidence on the Bay of Pigs." *Diplomatic History* 8 (Fall 1984): 365–75.

Welch, Richard E., Jr. "Herbert L. Matthews and the Cuban Revolution." *Historian* 47 (November 1984): 1–18.

Wells, Samuel F., Jr. "Sounding the Tocsin: NSC 68 and the Soviet Threat." *International Security* 4 (Fall 1979): 116–58.

Wolf, Charles. "The Political Effects of Military Programs: Some Indications from Latin America." *Orbis* 8 (Winter 1965): 871–93.

Wynia, Gary W. "Militarism Revisited." *Journal of Inter-American Studies & World Affairs* 25 (February 1983): 105–19.

"Y" (Louis Halle). "On a Certain Impatience with Latin America." *Foreign Affairs* 28 (July 1950): 565–79.

Zoumaras, Thomas. "Containing Castro: Promoting Homeownership in Peru, 1956–1961." *Diplomatic History* 10 (Spring 1986): 161–81.

INDEX

the American Republics (1960), 165

Smathers, George, 98, 129, 156

Smith, Earl E. T., 120–22, 124

Smith, Walter Bedell, 31, 35, 48, 50–51, 55

Smith and Wesson pistols, 162

Social Progress Trust Fund, 145, 149, 151, 165, 177; origins of, 141–44

Somoza, Anastasio, 11–12, 36, 48, 86–87

Soviet Union, 12, 15, 18–19, 26, 82, 103, 136, 139, 150; and trade with Latin America, 21, 38, 40, 84, 90–92, 138; and Guatemala, 43, 47, 53, 57, 59–60; political influence of, 102, 114–16, 146; and Cuban Revolution, 118–19, 125, 128–30, 132–33, 163–64, 166, 168–69, 171

Sprague, Mansfield, 98

Stassen, Harold, 71–72

Stettinius, Edward, 13

Stevenson, Adlai E., 29, 85

Stimson, Henry L., 13

Strauss, Lewis L., 59

Stroessner, Alfredo, 86, 96

Suez Canal, 84

Sugar Act of 1956, 90

Sullivan and Cromwell (law firm), 27

Sulzberger, Arthur, 59

Swan Island, 162

Taft, Robert, 68

Tello, Manuel, 166

Tenth Inter-American Conference, 49. *See also* Caracas Conference

Texaco, 103

Texas City, Tex., 79, 81

Thailand, 72

Thomas, Norman, 145

El Tiempo, 86

Tin, 17, 79, 81–82, 138

Toledano, Lombardo, 34

Toriello, Guillermo, 47, 51

Trade: during 1930s, 7–8, 10; during World War II, 8–9, 16–17; during Truman administration, 17–19; of Soviet Union, 40, 90–92, 138; during Eisen-hower administration, 73–77, 95–96, 111–12; with Cuba, 119–20, 130, 163

Trading with the Enemy Act, 164, 172

Trujillo, Rafael, 11, 14–15, 24, 96, 101, 105, 138; Eisenhower administration support of, 87–88, 104, 193 (n. 15); and Cuba, 117, 165, 167–68, 173; overthrow of, 153–62, 175

Truman, Harry S, 6, 12–15, 19, 22, 64; and Guatemala, 48–49

Twentieth Communist Party Congress, 90

26th of July Movement, 117–18, 121, 126

U-2 incident, 139

Ubico, Jorge, 43, 61–62

"ULTRA," 54

United Fruit Company, 27, 188 (n. 52); in Guatemala, 45–48, 51, 57–59, 176

United Kingdom. *See* Great Britain

United Nations, 12–13, 15, 20, 125, 127

United Nations Charter, 53

United Nations Conference on Interna-tional Organization, 12–13

United Nations Security Council, 53, 60

United States Information Agency, 33, 51, 103

University of Havana, 117

University of Tucumán, 43

Uruguay, 14, 21, 40, 61, 92, 136, 166; and Guatemala, 52–54

Vargas, Getulio, 32

Venezuela, 14, 15, 17, 52, 54, 138; and oil, 8, 70, 76; Eisenhower administra-tion praise of, 39, 94, 176; and Guate-mala, 52–54; Nixon tour of, 101–6; and new U.S. reform policies, 144–45; and Dominican Republic, 159, 161, 165

Venezuela: política y petróleo, 144

Vietnam, 1

Villarroel, Gualberto, 10

La Violencia, 74

"Voice of Liberation," 163

Printed in the United States
26583LVS00005B/211-264